Gender, Performance, and Authorship at the Abbey Theatre

Gender, Performance, and Authorship at the Abbey Theatre

ELIZABETH BREWER REDWINE

OXFORD
UNIVERSITY PRESS

OXFORD
UNIVERSITY PRESS

Great Clarendon Street, Oxford, OX2 6DP,
United Kingdom

Oxford University Press is a department of the University of Oxford.
It furthers the University's objective of excellence in research, scholarship,
and education by publishing worldwide. Oxford is a registered trade mark of
Oxford University Press in the UK and in certain other countries

First Edition published in 2021

Impression: 1

Published in the United States of America by Oxford University Press
198 Madison Avenue, New York, NY 10016, United States of America

British Library Cataloguing in Publication Data
Data available

Library of Congress Control Number: 2020949496

ISBN 978–0–19–289634–6

DOI: 10.1093/oso/9780192896346.001.0001

Printed and bound by
CPI Group (UK) Ltd, Croydon, CR0 4YY

To my grandmothers,

*Mari Brainerd Harman (1922–2017) and Elizabeth Lee Brewer (1906–1957),
and to Jill McLean Taylor (1944–2010), with love*

Acknowledgments

Geraldine Higgins and Ronald Schuchard and the Emory University English Department supported this research from the beginning and, with Robert Shaw Smith and Keith Schuchard, have been models of how to live, write, and read in a community. Deepika Bahri and James Flannery helped me see Yeats in new and fruitful ways during my time in graduate school. My writing group with Abby Bender and Natasha Tessone in the early Brooklyn days ushered many of these ideas into print, and I will always be grateful for those afternoons reading each other's work at Natasha's kitchen table.

I thank from the bottom of my heart my family, my husband Jonathan, whose encouragement and help have made my writing possible, and my children Nathaniel Betts, Cal Archer, Lila Harman, and James Edward, who have been patient listeners, riding with me the ups and downs of submission, revision, and publication. "Mom, have you heard from Oxford?" has been a common refrain in our house. My wonderful extended family, Ned and Jane Brewer, Teddy Brewer, Sarah Brewer, Jill Brewer, Adam Nyborg, Brett Harman, Jane Rockwell, Deborah Shinn, Stephen Melsh, George and Winnie Redwine, Jed and Elvia Redwine, David and Kristin Harman, Anne Brewer, and Wendy Brewer have supported me, discussed the book, and helped with childcare throughout the many years of writing, research, and revision. In addition to the grandmothers to whom I dedicate this book, my late grandfathers Edward Slocum Brewer and Archer Harman were loving and supportive every day that I knew them. Many of these pages were written while those family members did the invaluable work of looking after our children and making all of us food. I am so thankful for Daniel Maloof, research assistant, who found an image that had alluded me at the British Library online during a pandemic. Cate Brown provided childcare, editing, and typing help during these years, and for that I am grateful.

This book was written alongside political activism in the past four years in particular, and I am grateful to the New Jersey family of social justice activists for helping me think about performance and voice in a contemporary movement of collaboration and street theater. I also want to thank the family of mothers in my New Jersey neighborhood and before that in Brooklyn who have helped support my children and me throughout this process.

Lucy McDiarmid offered unending help throughout the revision process, answering every email with invaluable advice. Mary McGlynn read many drafts and made suggestions that brought the most important moments and points to the surface and made me feel that I could actually say what I wanted to say. Amrita Ghosh, my co-author on another book about Tagore and Yeats, has helped me through the frustrations of writing and revision as a fellow writer, researcher, writing teacher, and parent, and I thank her from the bottom of my heart for her encouragement. Mary Burke helped me think about Synge from the moment I met her at Abby Bender's wedding, and Keri Walsh's encouragement about my reading of female performance helped bring Sara Allgood to life in the Epilogue. I have only briefly met Deirdre Toomey, Adrian Frazier, Ann Saddlemyer, Elizabeth Butler Cullingford, and R. F. Foster, but their books sat by my side these many years of writing, and I am grateful to them for the paths they have cleared with such beautiful writing into Yeats and Synge studies.

My colleagues at Seton Hall University, Donovan Sherman and Marianne Lloyd, have read so many emails and listened for hours while I discussed this project, offering unstinting support during writing and revision, and I thank them from the bottom of my heart. I am grateful to Angela Weisl, Mary Balkun, Karen Bloom Gevirtz, and Martha Carpentier of the Seton Hall English Department for helping me navigate the publication process, and to Peter Shoemaker, Dean of the College of Arts and Sciences at Seton Hall, for his support of the book and help with funding for research. My students over the years have listened to my own revision approaches while they work on their papers, and I thank them for that conversation. I thank Sara Bader and Nellie Perera for reading the earliest drafts and providing their suggestions, friendship, and support over the years. Meg Persichetti and Kristin Aswad let me hash out the most difficult arguments during long runs in the woods, and I thank them both for their friendship and generosity.

Finally, I dedicate this book to my two grandmothers, Mari Brainerd Harman, a naked swimmer into her nineties and challenger of social mores, and Elizabeth Lee Brewer, an artist who died before I was born, and to Jill McLean Taylor. As a teenager, I helped Jill research, and she showed me how to be a scholar. When Jill died, she left an unfinished book entitled *Jack MacLean Also Had Five Daughters* about her grandfather's daughters and the way that women are erased from history. Jill listened to my ideas and encouraged me to write from my earliest memories, and her eyes lit up when I told her about exploring new directions for this book shortly before her death when my children were small.

Contents

List of Illustrations

Introduction

"I am pouring out my heart to you in Deirdre the whole day long."
J. M. Synge to Molly Allgood, November 15, 1907.[1]

"I had a different conception. I did not wish to make my audience feel that 'Kathleen' called the young man to a hopeless sacrifice...I say to myself their death was victory. Ireland too will be victorious. I fill myself with joy."
Sara Allgood, March 1909, *The Weekly Freeman*.[2]

Whose name appears under the title of a play like W. B. Yeats's *Deirdre* or J. M. Synge's *Deirdre of the Sorrows*? The single-author answer does not tell the whole story, and this book examines the way that both plays, among other famous Abbey Theatre productions, have complicated histories of composition. Questioning how theater becomes text and who gets credit for written scripts forces us to reconsider the role of gender and performance in authorship. A terminally ill J. M. Synge wrote the quotation that begins this book in a letter to his fiancée, Molly Allgood, stage name Maire O'Neill. He died before completing *Deirdre of the Sorrows*, and in his bedridden and painful final days, Synge would watch Molly act out the most difficult parts of the play that he was composing for her; after watching her embody a scene, he would then revise or add material. After Synge's death in March 1909, Molly, along with Lady Gregory and W. B. Yeats, the surviving directors of the Abbey Theatre, completed the draft of the play, and Molly performed *Deirdre of the Sorrows* to great acclaim in 1910. Synge's version of the Deirdre story was an answer to Yeats's, AE's (George Russell) and Lady Gregory's efforts to imagine the myth, and his conception of the play and lead role had everything to do with his relationship with

---

[1] John Millington Synge and Maire O'Neill, *Letters to Molly: John Millington Synge to Maire O'Neill 1906–1909*, ed. Ann Saddlemyer (Cambridge, MA: Belknap Press of Harvard University Press, 1971), 214.
[2] Qtd. in John Kelly, "Ghost-Writing for Sara Allgood," in Warwick Gould, ed., *Essays in Honour of Eamonn Cantwell: Yeats Annual No. 20* (Cambridge: Open Book Publishing, 2017), 351.

Gender, Performance, and Authorship at the Abbey Theatre. Elizabeth Brewer Redwine, Oxford University Press (2021). © Elizabeth Brewer Redwine. DOI: 10.1093/oso/9780192896346.001.0001

Molly Allgood. The drafting and posthumous revision of this play reveal the central argument of my book: that the role of female performance in the plays of the Abbey needs a reassessment to counter a historical bias towards male authorship at the expense of female performance. Echoing Yeats's version of events, accepted history privileges male and upper-class ideas of authorship and occludes the contributions of female performers. I want to call critical attention to Molly Allgood's work on this and other Synge plays as part of this book about the overlooked importance of female performance to drafting and revising the plays of the Abbey. My project explores the power dynamics around gender and class that caused Molly Allgood and other actresses to be written out of histories of the Abbey and the Revival as I investigate the fraught line between performance and text, asking questions about how performance influences both the creation and revision of the texts that remain with us today. This book argues against patriarchal read-ings of literary history; repeatedly we see Yeats and Synge make a familiar rhetorical move. They praise a woman's role in forming a play, in fact calling attention to the collaborative nature of all of their projects, but this credit is difficult for us to hear due to the patriarchal inheritance of the way we define authorship.

What is the final "text" of a play? Many of these plays came out of thousands of pages of manuscripts that reflect anxieties about gender, identity, and performance and continue to be performed, so what we read as the "final version" remains an important issue for a study like this one. Yeats and Synge changed the texts of their plays constantly; a play like Yeats's *The Player Queen*, written and rewritten over the bulk of his lifetime, bearing the imprint of a number of actresses who contributed to the final text, is an example of a larger trend. Current productions of the plays of the Abbey reimagine the language and action in our contemporary context, and the performances of the past shadow the revivals. The concept of a final draft of a play, like the idea of the single author, needs reassessment as perfor-mance and production inflect the way that these plays arrive onstage and, as I shall discuss in the Epilogue, onscreen.[3] Who gets credit is not accidental;

---

[3] The idea of a play versus a performance is well thought out in Siddhartha Biswas, *Theatre Theory and Performance: A Critical Interrogation* (Newcastle upon Tyne: Cambridge Scholars Publishing, 2017); on page 15, Biswas posits that "the difference between theatre and a written text, or cinematic text, is that the theatrical text changes with each and every performance." I am also indebted here to Patrick Pavis, "From Text to Performance," in *Performing Texts*, ed. Michael Issacharoff and Robin F. Jones (Philadelphia: University of Pennsylvania Press, 1988). Pavis provides a helpful framework for understanding the complicated "ways in which a text culminates in a performance" (p. 86).

those with more power, due to gender and class,[4] strategically told a certain version of events, ignoring the contributions of actresses, as we shall see in the coming chapters. Upper-class men were more likely to write and to take credit for writing, and working-class women, due to education and cultural mores, tended to perform. These women did, however, affect these canonical texts in profound and important ways.

The second quotation, by Sara Allgood, Molly's sister and fellow Abbey actress, raises fraught questions about ownership and the plays of the Abbey, questions that still bear scrutiny. The inclusion of Sara Allgood's 1909 *Weekly Standard* article in the 2017 *Yeats Annual* as an example of "ventriloquism" and "ghost writing" shows the way that we need to question assumptions about authorship that undergird even the most recent and canonical Yeats criticism. John Kelly, to whom any Abbey Theatre scholar is indebted for his revelatory multi-volume *Collected Letters of W. B. Yeats*, includes the passage quoted above as part of his essay "Ghost-writing for Sara Allgood." Kelly argues that Yeats "ghost wrote" much of Allgood's published material. He takes Yeats at his word in a letter from Yeats to Gregory about Allgood. According to Yeats, the essay writing went like this: "I questioned her & got her to talk & made a rather charming peace [*sic*] of girlish self revelation."[5] Yeats goes on to say that he is "frustrated" because another editor, "Henderson," wrote a second interview with Allgood that is anathema to the story about the Abbey that Yeats wanted told.[6] Lady Gregory has nothing but sympathy for Yeats's complaint, responding with class-based assumptions and "rage" "that Miss Allgood should take [Henderson] as an equal guide with you on a literary question and fall so low." John Kelly goes on to argue that Henderson, editor of *The Weekly Standard*, "was clearly sweet on Allgood."[7] Henderson, Kelly explains, lost his job in 1911 because he lent Allgood a copy of her contract to help her advocate for better pay. Lady Gregory's anger is a bellwether for flare-ups about class, gender, and Irishness in performance at the Abbey; often even-keeled, her

---

[4] Discussion of "gender and class" here and throughout this book shows my indebtedness to Marjorie Howes, *Yeats's Nations: Gender, Class, and Irishness* (Cambridge: Cambridge University Press, 1996), in particular her exploration of how Yeats imagined Irishness as "specific configurations of gender and class" (p. 1).

[5] Kelly, "Ghost-Writing for Sara Allgood," 344–5.

[6] W. A. Henderson of the National Literary Society ended up, after much financial negotiation, as business manager at the Abbey from 1906 to 1907 and again in 1908. Class issues abound in Yeats's power struggles with Henderson here and elsewhere. Yeats reported that Henderson "sucked up vulgarity like a sponge" (qtd. in R. F. Foster, *W. B. Yeats: A Life: I. The Apprentice Mage*, Oxford: Oxford University Press, 1997, 349).

[7] Kelly, "Ghost-Writing for Sara Allgood," 346.

rare moments of fury respond to threats to her own power in interesting ways throughout the research for this project.[8]

Yeats's claims and Gregory's words warrant further examination; I would like to offer a different take on Allgood and to return credit to her by closely reading articles like this one alongside the manuscript of Allgood's "Memories." *The Weekly Standard* article was not, in fact, written solely by Henderson because it repeats what Allgood ended up writing in her version of events in "Memories" and in letters. Authorship for theater is layered and needs re-evaluation to recover the ways that these plays reached the stage, revealing the lost contributions of female performers. The chapters in this volume address the many ways that the author's name under the title of a published play hides the story of the complicated manner that the text interacts with the stage.

What interests me in the story above is the way that Yeats so confidently claims to write for Allgood then expresses frustration with Henderson's version of her voice. We do not know how much Henderson wrote of that article, but the entire part about *Cathleen Ni Houlihan* reappears in her "Memories" and in letters, so Sara Allgood probably wrote much of that herself, or Henderson transcribed from her words. All we have is Yeats's claim that he wrote the other passage. And his explanation of how he wrote this interview—that Allgood told him what to write and he wrote her words with his own edits—echoes what we know of how Gregory wrote much of the text that Yeats nominally produced in his own name at Coole, Lady Gregory's Big House near Galway.[9] Gregory's patronizing frustration that Allgood should "fall so low" encodes both gender and class critiques, lamenting that Sara Allgood should fall into a relationship with someone of the wrong class and treat Henderson as Yeats's "equal." In Gregory's critique is a sense that Allgood should have been grateful for the help

---

[8] R. F. Foster's biographies of Yeats (Volume I, *The Apprentice Mage* and Volume II, *The Arch-Poet*) trace the way that Lady Gregory's responses influenced Irish theater, in particular her rare moments of frustration and anger, usually over control of productions. James Pethica, "'A Young Man's Ghost': Lady Gregory and J. M. Synge." *Irish University Review* 34, no. 1 (2004): 1–20 explores the tensions between the three directors of the Abbey.

[9] Coole, Lady Gregory's ancestral home, looms large in the poems of Yeats, acting as a symbol of inherited wealth and culture and a haven for Yeats during Abbey rows. For context about the Big House in Irish culture, see Jacqueline Genet, *The Big House in Ireland: Reality and Representation,* (New York: Barnes & Noble, 1991) and for a description of the house and a brief history of the Gregory family and Coole, see Colin Smythe, *A Guide to Coole Park, Home of Lady Gregory* (Colin Smythe, 1973). Elizabeth Bowen, *Bowen's Court or Seven Winters* (London: Virago, 1942), though the story of a different house and family, gives an invaluable sense of the culture of the Irish Big House for the past four hundred years.

of those who came from a higher class than her and Henderson. Lady Gregory, throughout her career at the Abbey and the movement pre-dating that theater, also had to negotiate complicated collaborations fraught with questions of gender, class, and power, and this project examines her position as an upper-class woman creating text and performing on rare occasions as well. Her place as a "Lady" with a landed estate gave her access, but she, too, struggled, as I discuss, to see her words accredited to her. Throughout her "Memories", Allgood hints at using the power she had as a young woman and actress to acquire better pay and lead roles, so her use of the borrowed contract from Henderson is not surprising. It is important to note the way that directors Yeats and Gregory tried to use her voice and her identity as a working-class Catholic woman who had performed in the *Playboy* to argue for their own version of events. The "frustration" and "rage" that both directors express when Allgood, in their eyes, doesn't accept her place, is part of a pattern at the Abbey that requires discussion about authorship.

Allgood's position as a Dubliner who started out in Inghinidhe na hÉireann gave her credence with the public that Yeats and Gregory, for all of their power as members of a higher class, would never have. Sara Allgood makes a claim for her own interpretation of the role of her 1906 Cathleen in the quotation that starts this introduction. With "my," she makes clear who owned the role that night, and the "different" advises the reader that she is reinterpreting a canonical and mythic part. This story illustrates the directors' dependence on the voices of women. Both directors dismiss the possibility that Allgood wrote any part of Henderson's article, though archival research suggests that she did. And if she did write some or all of the article, then the two directors cannot interfere with her perspective; the story is not in their control, and her fears during the *Playboy* Riots and claim to *Cathleen ni Houlihan* through performance are out. An undercurrent of appropriation by a higher class runs through these letters; the subtext is that due to their class positions, Gregory and Yeats can make whatever claims they like. Posterity has taken them at their word, but I offer a counter-narrative of authorship at the Abbey, one that shifts the focus to the ways that the canonical texts attributed solely to Yeats and Synge could have reached neither the stage nor print without the contributions of actresses.

This work has broader implications for theater and gender studies, and scholars in both areas have helped me rethink authorship. Judith Hamera's *Dancing Communities: Performance, Difference, and Connection in the Global City* "argues that both concert dance and amateur practice are laboratories for examining and revisioning the myriad complex interrelations between gender, sexuality, race, class, and culture in urban life."[10] Authorship studies ask us to revisit how these links between performance and text are accredited. The early modern repertory approach is helpful as well, as early modern theater critics have shown "a willingness to approach plays in relation to the acting companies that staged them and the other works in those companies' repertories rather than simply as part of the oeuvre of a particular dramatist."[11] That field of study, inspired by Foucault's "What is An Author?" and Derrida's *Grammatology* as well as Barthes' *Death of the Author* troubles the bourgeois meaning of authorship. Most important to my rethinking of authorship at the Abbey is Foucault's discussion of the "system of ownership" around definitions of the author. Judith Butler's work in *Gender Trouble* and *Bodies that Matter* argues for "women" as a construct informed by questions of class, gender, and sexuality; her rethinking of the way gender is performed has been a helpful way to approach authorship, gender, and performance at the Abbey.

This project uses scholarship on the history of performance to question the material creation of theater at the Abbey. Books like *Moving Performances: Divas, Iconicity, and Remembering the Modern Stage*, by Jeanne Scheper, provide a model for using gender, feminist, and performance studies to recover the importance of bodies onstage. Her text proves how intersectional this work is, as she begins with "Salomania," a transnational craze for theatrical productions inspired by Wilde's play; Scheper argues that "Salome- as-cypher exposed faltering nineteenth-century colonial powers and patriarchy."[12] Her work here is to recover the role of four "divas" performing on the transnational stage: Aida Overton Walker, Loie Fuller, Libby Holman, and Josephine Baker. She argues that these women "challenged existing prescriptions for women onstage and off, as they performed their lives in the public eye." Certainly, the Irish women in the world of the Abbey did not deal with the racism that governed the reception of Walker and Baker, but Scheper's work recovering the contributions of female performance helped me structure my project, and she reveals the way that these women's bodies onstage reveal fissures in cultural ideas of gender and performance. Dorinne Kondo's *Worldmaking: Race, Performance, and the*

[10] Judith Hamera, *Dancing Communities: Performance, Difference, and Connection in the Global City* (Basingstoke: Palgrave Macmillan, 2007), 1.

[11] Tom Rutter, "Introduction: The Repertory-Based Approach," *Early Theatre*, 13(2): 121.

[12] Jeanne Scheper, *Moving Performances: Divas, Iconicity, and Remembering the Modern Stage* (New Brunswick, NJ: Rutgers University Press, 2016), 1.

Work of Creativity, though concerned with race, gender, and representation in contemporary theater, helpfully theorizes the way that theater is made, emphasizing the interactions between playwright, performer, audience, and critic.

Judith Hamera's discussion of what she calls "technique" in ballet is a useful way to think about the stage directions, repeated and changed over the more than one hundred years of producing the Irish plays of the Abbey. Hamera believes that "technique, like aesthetics, is a useful synecdoche for the complex webs of relations that link performers to particular subjectivities, practices, and to each other."[13] These "webs" are what Sara Allgood describes in her "Memories" as the "cabbages and kings" of the theater, arguing for theater as a collective act of creating art. Hamera's discussion of the way these relationships between past and present performance and between ballet dancers and choreographers raises questions about how actors and authors relate to each other creating works for the stage. The text that is crafted reflects and codes the performance, but the written play does not tell the whole story, and this book examines the complicated back and forth between text and performance.

Textual and manuscript scholarship has been central to my work on recovering the role of the actress in creating plays. Without Virginia Rohan's Cornell edition of the *Deirdre Manuscripts*, none of that chapter would have been possible; she includes all of Yeats's drafts and notes. Lucy McDiarmid's *At Home in the Revolution* questions the lines between home and sites of urban warfare with particular attention to class and gender, showing how to introduce a vital new reading of a much-told story by including a perspective that had not been considered by previous scholars. Roy Foster's *Vivid Faces* argues for the importance of individuals who bridged the worlds of theater and political work during the Revival and Rising, challenging boundaries between theater and revolution; Mary Trotter's *Ireland's National Theatres* troubles the line between the Abbey and the theaters of the street and other companies. Revealing the way that different identities intersect, Marjorie Howes's *Yeats's Nations: Gender, Class, and Irishness* allowed me to see the layered responses to actresses on the Abbey stage and beyond. Adrian Frazier's *The Adulterous Muse* asks for a reconsideration of the occluded parts of Maud Gonne's story; his *Hollywood Irish* focuses on the work of Abbey theater alumnae with John Ford in Hollywood; and his *Behind the*

---

[13] Hamera, *Dancing Communities*, 5.

Scenes: Yeats, Horniman, and the Struggle for the Abbey Theatre is a model for challenging versions of events passed down by Yeats. Devoted to the study of *Yeats's Collaborations*, the fifteenth *Yeats Annual*, published in 2003, offers new research on Yeats's work with his wife George, Lady Gregory, Douglass Hyde, and Frank O'Connor, but like other available scholarship, the book does not explore the way that gender, performance, and class affect authorship and the creation of theatrical texts. I hope to remove the barrier between writing and performance and investigate the ways that actresses helped create the texts of the plays at the Abbey that are so central to the ongoing critical discussion of Irish theater. James Pethica's work on Lady Gregory's contributions is an important precedent for challenging the monolithic great man theory of the Abbey, but there is currently no scholarship advocating for a rethinking of authorship at the Abbey that focuses on actresses.[14]

This book starts to recover a history of the contributions of female performers to the plays of Yeats and Synge. Much remains to be done. Yeats's work with dancers Margot Ruddock and Ninette de Valois, for example, is beyond the scope of my project, though Richard Allen Cave admirably recovers the collaborations between Yeats and de Valois in his *Collaborations*. In fact, Cave's volume provides a model for reading past stage performance and its influence on text because he stresses the importance of dance to Yeats's late theater and models the reading of bodies onstage.[15] Cave argues for "the debt we owe to the past history of performance." His writing on the dancing body and use of interviews and written records and photographs of those de Valois dances in the late dance plays she created with Yeats show how to write about the movements between text and performance in collaboration. In the early 1990s, C. L. Innes lamented the lack of female voices in the history of nationalism: "What has received comparably little attention until the last decade, however, is the role of Irish women in that struggle (for Irish identity and nationality) and how they themselves defined and sought to define 'the consciousness of the race.'"[16] Welcome publications from Deirdre Toomey, Lucy McDiarmid, Margaret

[14] James Pethica, "Patronage and Creative Exchange: Yeats, Lady Gregory, and the Economics of Indebtedness," *Yeats and Women*, ed. Deirdre Toomey (London: Palgrave Macmillan, 1992), 60.

[15] Richard Allen Cave, *Collaborations: Ninette De Valois and William Butler Yeats* (London: Dance Books, 2011), xviii.

[16] C. L. Innes, *Woman and Nation in Irish Literature and Society, 1880–1935* (Athens: University of Georgia Press, 1993), 3.

Ward, and Louise Ryan, among others, have changed the landscape of Irish studies since Innes's book, forcing a reconsideration of how women have functioned in Irish history and literature. This book builds on Innes's work and those who came after, exploring how the women performing at the Abbey shaped the plays they made famous, an area that Innes does not discuss. Margaret Ward and Elizabeth Coxhead have provided helpful research and arguments for the inclusion of female voices in the story of the Revival and ensuing revolutionary generation. More recently, Méabh Ní Fhuartháin's "Parish Halls, Dance Halls, and Marquees: Developing and Regulating Social-Dance Spaces, 1900–60" expands critical ideas about what constitutes theatre and focuses on "public-social dance spaces" as sites of performance that warrant close reading.

Who gets credit for playwrighting reflects the power dynamics in a theater and a culture. The story of authoritative texts at the Abbey continues to follow Yeats's lead, privileging male, upper middle-class Protestant writers because of a power structure that had everything to do with class position and gender. Yeats's version of events comes down through history in his canonical poems and essays, emphasizing his own role in theatrical creation and casting women, specifically Catholic, working-class women, as subordinate with Lady Gregory occupying an in-between position as unaccredited author, ghostwriter, collector of folktales, and hostess along with her acknowledged plays. Yeats also controlled Synge's legacy after that writer's death. Synge himself occluded Molly Allgood's role in creating his plays in an attempt to protect her from gossip because of his sensitivity to her position as a working-class Catholic actress engaged to an upper-class Protestant man. As I discuss in Chapter 3, that well-intentioned effort to save her reputation caused him to hide her contributions to his plays. Yeats's life's work was not only poetry and plays but directing how his art should be consumed and how the movement should be remembered in essays, letters, and speeches. He took on Synge's reputation as part of this project and tried to cast the actresses in their places, honoring them in ways that took away their role in the creation of texts.

At the same time, the class position of Yeats and Synge at the Abbey put them in a bind, a fascinating trap that I examine in this volume. The infamous image of Synge listening in on servant girls in his Preface to *The Playboy of the Western World* perfectly illustrates this position. Both Yeats and Synge needed to be the sole authors of their texts and hoped in different ways to influence ideas about Irish womanhood onstage but required access to women as both performers and co-authors to create those texts. The women they needed to work with were often working class and Catholic as the nominal authors sought a "real" Irishness. In other words, the much-maligned bodies and voices of these women allowed the writers to imagine and create the major roles of the Abbey's most canonical texts, and then the performances set them revising.

The figure of J. M Synge listening in on "servant girls"[17] through a crack in the wall has incited justified criticism—the image of the writer as voyeur violates the privacy of the women in the kitchen, turns their conversation into unintended public performance, and uses their language without permission. The experience, Synge argued, of transcribing *In the Shadow of the Glen* from eavesdropping led him to the idea that "all art is collaboration" with the voices of women at its source. As Yeats and Synge developed diverse female figures for the stage at the turn of the last century, they did not do so alone but with the active and often contentious participation of the women who inspired and/or performed those roles. Women who did not act the parts onstage influenced the plays as well; some actresses refused the roles after initial collaboration, and those debates found their way into both textual revision and performance. The central characters of the plays that incited the most debate over the last century are female. Reactions to performances, from the hubbub over soul-selling in *The Countess Cathleen* to the political impact of *Cathleen ni Houlihan* to the riots at the January 1907 production of *The Playboy of the Western World* and the rival interpretations of the Deirdre myth show how much was at stake in the performance of female Irish identity.

I argue in Chapter 3 that Synge's "Preface" questions accepted and limited ideas of authorship, challenging the traditional image of the solitary writer creating after inspiration from a passive muse. The "servant girls" do not just give him ideas for characters; instead he admits to actually writing their dialogue into their play. This form of collaboration reinterprets identity in the Irish Revival, as Synge well knew—the "Preface" tries to deflect charges of misrepresenting Irish women by setting up the girls in the kitchen as the source of the drama. Synge's version of writing the play leaves the audience and reader at a loss about whose voices they hear onstage. This is intentional; Synge knew that *The Playboy* was going to hit the stage like a thrown rock, setting off ripples in the press and the community in response to provocative images of Irish womanhood he'd built out of his letters and

---

[17] J. M. Synge, "Preface," *The Complete Works of J. M. Synge: Plays, Prose, and Poetry*, ed. Aidan Arrowsmith (Ware: Wordsworth Editions, 2008), 67.

relationship with Molly Allgood, or "my Pegeen Mike," as he called her.[18] Synge's claim for collaboration is strategic: he can't be blamed for what he transcribed through a crack in the door. The "servant girls" are a conduit to a way of being Irish and female that is cordoned off to him; what he could not say is how much of the play came from his behind-the-scenes controversial relationship with Molly Allgood.

The unpublished "Memories" of Abbey actress Sara Allgood contain their own argument for reassessing authorship at the Abbey and in theater and film. Often described as the provenance of mostly male Anglo-Irish writers (Lady Gregory's exceptional position is a focus here as well), the Abbey Theatre in fact offered productions that reflected the diverse perspectives of the performers and writers involved. My project argues for a refocusing on the contribution of actresses, but work also needs to be done on other seemingly peripheral characters who helped inspire and produce central roles. In her "Memories," Sara Allgood puts forth a different theory of authorship and asks that the Abbey be remembered not just for the writers but for all who took part in creating iconic roles. She singles out forgotten Abbey worker Miss Nellie Bushel, program distributor, ticket seller, and rescuer of abandoned Dublin babies. Mrs. Martin, the char-lady, also contributed to the plays in ways she never knew: "I think I modeled my Juno on her," claims Allgood.[19] Those figures and the later dancers and actresses of Yeats's life are beyond the scope of this project, as are the automatic writing experiments by George Yeats that contributed to *A Vision*, but Allgood argues, in shifting the focus to those women, for an approach to theater and performance studies that would echo in Judith Hamera's evocative description of practice and performance spaces as haunted:

> To stand in a dance studio is to occupy a haunted place and to write about what happens there is to confront a community's ghosts at every turn: company members, now gone, who became 'sad cases'; affairs and dalliances not to be talked about; fellow dancers who have died of AIDS; crippling depressions; physical breakdowns. There is enchantment too, of course, and fully as much, but whatever its emotional valences, the haunted studios index their ghosts by things like good feet or bad turns or the breathtaking backbend – corporeal, technical madeleines.

---

[18] Synge and O'Neill, *Letters to Molly*, 90.
[19] Sara Allgood, "Memories," unpublished manuscript, Berg Collection, New York Public Library, 49.

Like Hamera's dance studios, the Abbey stage holds the imprint, the evolving motion, of so many moments remembered in continued performance. Chapter 5 examines how the many Deirdres of the Revival built performance style one over the other; Maud Gonne's entrance in the 1902 *Cathleen ni Houlihan* brought street theater moves to the stage and continues to color performance and text; Yeats, accepting his Nobel Prize, sites images of actress' performing bodies that will "haunt me on my deathbed."[20]

Synge described collaboration as the use of woman's language, and Sara Allgood saw theater-writing as inseparable from theatrical production; I explore the various forms of collaboration between Yeats, Synge, and the major female figures at the Abbey. This book defines theatrical collaboration as the way that a woman inspired a writer to begin a play, the joint work of an actress and an author on creating a part or writing a text, rehearsals and productions that caused a writer to revise the text of a drama, and changes in staging made during and after a performance. These different forms of collaboration with a diverse group of women generated varied female roles that reflected the central question of the Abbey: what is an Irish woman? Also, how do the movements between writing and performing in groups affect the written plays that remain to us?

Gender, Performance, and Authorship at the Abbey follows a roughly chronological format because the chapters track the development of two ways of imagining women for the Irish stage—as iconic figures of nation and as realistic, individual characters. I explore the way that performances and collaborations affected these ideas of women in revivals and later productions. Theater is a public art, and the actresses and writers knew each other and watched one another's productions; in many cases they came from the same family of origin or ended up married to each other. Chapters reveal how, at the Abbey, each play responded to the years of earlier plays and to Inghinidhe na hÉireann, the female revolutionary theater organization that predated the Abbey. Revivals of earlier plays sent Yeats and Synge back to revise, so some chapters cover the same years as I discuss how a new version of an earlier drama changed a writer's and performer's goals for the plays they were writing or rehearsing.

Because Molly Allgood and Synge knew each other well, they created individualistic characters connected to the places of their births; the female roles in *The Playboy of the Western World* and *Deirdre of the Sorrows*

---

[20] W. B. Yeats, "The Irish Dramatic Movement," Nobel Lecture, December 15, 1923, https://www.nobelprize.org/prizes/literature/1923/yeats/lecture/.

resist representing symbolic ideas of Ireland. Synge and Molly used the peculiarities of Molly's language and personality, along with details of the landscape, to distance the plays from the earlier mythic work of Yeats and AE. Changes in Yeats's relationships with women dictated new characters and revisions of old ones. His work for Laura Armstrong and Maud Gonne set women up as powerful figures, reflecting his sense of the women's higher class and social autonomy. As he and Gonne began to disagree about Gonne's political work, conversion to Catholicism, and marriage to John MacBride, Yeats wrote *Deirdre*, a play about a woman distancing herself from the cares of daily life in an increasingly mythic and loaded figure of Ireland as a woman. For more than a decade, Yeats revised *Deirdre* to reflect his work with more than six actresses. Synge set out, with Molly, to revise their version of Deirdre. Synge's and Molly's *Deirdre of the Sorrows* is bound to the place of her birth and aware of the physicality of aging and death.

The intersections between class and gender onstage and in creating and casting roles contribute to my argument. Part of Yeats's claim to a position as a self-styled aristocrat meant that he needed the female performers of the Abbey to be subordinate to him; on the other hand, he collaborated most effectively with women who challenged his efforts to control the projects. Out of that controversy came his most far-reaching plays. The collaborations are as varied as the women and the playwrights themselves. My book provides a close reading of the actress's experience at the Abbey, mining letters, manuscripts, program notes, diaries, photographs, and film to argue for the neglected role of actresses in creating not only the performances but also the accepted texts of the Abbey.

A focus on the actresses and their work with Yeats and Synge forces a reconsideration of boundaries in the theater movement with Lady Gregory's complicated role as a major part of the story. Looking at the experience of these women, Inghinidhe na hÉireann and other lesser known female groups become inextricable from Abbey history and the story of performing the most important and controversial roles in the Revival. Years later, at the advent of the film industry into the 1930s and 1940s, Sara Allgood navigated stereotypical roles and different kinds of prejudice about how being older, female, and Irish played in American movies. The lessons learned dealing with prejudice at the Abbey stood her in good stead in Hollywood, and in those films, contemporary viewers can see traces of Abbey performance. The project ends with an Epilogue that closely reads the film performances still available to viewers that show how Sara Allgood brought the performance techniques that she honed at the Abbey to film.

Questions of Irish identity are central to this book: Inghinidhe was created for Irish women, led by Maud Gonne who had a complicated background, as she was both Irish and British. The daughter of a British army officer, she spent much of her life advocating for Irish causes and considered herself Irish. Yeats imported Florence Darragh to play Deirdre, courting controversy and claiming, all evidence to the contrary, that she was "an Irishwoman."[21] This claim raises fascinating questions about what Irishness meant to Yeats, as do his revealing and appalling comments about the bodies of working-class Catholic actresses like the Allgood sisters. Concerned that they did not have "sensitive bodies," Yeats justified importing British actresses who resembled Maud Gonne. Finally, Mrs. Patrick Campbell, a working-class, half- Italian British woman, challenged ideas of identity at the Abbey. Though British, her ability to collaborate with Abbey mainstays like Sara Allgood allowed her to save Yeats's flailing attempts to find a way to make his *Deirdre* a success. Sara Allgood's unpublished "Memories" offers a tribute to Mrs. Pat; the two of them were friends as old women in Hollywood, playing bit parts to pay the bills at the ends of their lives.

My project deals with different forms of co-authorship: the written contributions of Lady Gregory and Molly Allgood, revisions after suggestions in letters and from performance—Maud Gonne's stage direction are an example—and the politics of inspiration in the contributions of Laura Armstrong, Maud Gonne, Molly Allgood, Florence Darragh, and Mrs. Patrick Campbell. Central to my discussion are the theatrical experimentations with actresses like Florence Farr and Sara Allgood. This project began when I noticed the way that Yeats and Synge needed certain women to imagine and begin their plays. The contributions to manuscripts, so deftly chronicled by James Pethica in the case of Lady Gregory, are only part of the story here. Molly Allgood, for example, did complete the draft of Synge's *Deirdre of the Sorrows* with Lady Gregory and Yeats after Synge's death, though her co-authorship rarely comes into discussions of the play. Ronald Schuchard has told the important story in *The Last Minstrels* of the ways that Sara Allgood and Florence Farr experimented with bardic and lyric chanting elements to influence Yeats's playwriting and ideas of performance. This project looks into the actual contributions that women

---

[21] W. B. Yeats, *The Collected Letters of W. B. Yeats*, Vol. V, ed. John Kelly (Oxford: Clarendon Press, 1986), 450.

performers made to manuscripts. Another part of the story of authorship at the Abbey that remains unexplored, one I bring to this discussion of complicated forms of collaboration in performance, is the more amorphous way that corresponding with women, observing them perform, and discussing theatrical ideas led Yeats and Synge to create parts for and with actresses.

1

"She Set Me Writing My First Play"

Laura Armstrong and Yeats's Early Drama

"She interests me far more than Miss Gonne does and yet is only
[*sic*] as a myth and a symbol."[1]

Laura Armstrong was the first woman to inspire Yeats to write plays and
verse. Yeats's brief friendship with Armstrong in 1884 was responsible not
only for his initial serious interest in drama, but their relationship also
influenced Yeats as he began, soon after meeting her, to create his first
major female figures with her in mind in a series of short plays, *Vivien and
Time*, the revised *Time and the Witch Vivien*, *The Island of the Statues*, and
Mosada.[2] While the larger-than-life female characters that dominate each of
these plays celebrate Armstrong's unconventional strengths, their deaths
dramatize Yeats's ambivalence about both her upper-class status and her
female power. The works he wrote with Armstrong in mind stand as
important precedents in their examination of the links between class, gender, and performance. Yeats would bring the symbolic figures he began
imagining after meeting Armstrong to the stage for the rest of his life in
plays that both celebrate and limit female agency. Like the lives of many of
the actresses whose contributions I explore in this book, her role in Yeats's
literary and dramatic beginnings tells an important and neglected story
about Yeats and gender. Her influential relationship with the young writer
has been dismissed as a flirtation, and this chapter recovers the story of
Armstrong's impact on how Yeats first began to see himself as a writer.[3]

---

[1] William Butler Yeats, *The Collected Letters of W. B. Yeats*, Vol. I, ed. John Kelly and Eric
Domville (Oxford: Clarendon Press, 1986), 154.
[2] Though Yeats has composed a short verse play at sixteen in 1881 with a schoolmate, *Vivien
and Time* is the first full-length play he wrote for performance; Yeats himself always referred to
the work as his "first play." See Yeats, *Letters*, I, 154.
[3] R. F. Foster calls Armstrong "pretty, unstable, and already spoken for," in *W. B. Yeats: A
Life: I. The Apprentice Mage*, 2nd edition (Oxford: Oxford University Press, 1998), 34. David
Clarke calls her a "tantalizing witch" on page 3 of *W. B. Yeats and the Theatre of Desolate Reality*

Gender, Performance, and Authorship at the Abbey Theatre. Elizabeth Brewer Redwine, Oxford University Press
(2021). © Elizabeth Brewer Redwine. DOI: 10.1093/oso/9780192896346.003.0001

From a well-to-do neighboring family, Laura Armstrong had a big personality. A woman who flouted convention and used her social status to perform power publicly, Armstrong tended towards the theatrical and chafed against societal expectation. After her short friendship with Yeats, she married and disappears from the historical record with the exception of a few Yeats family mentions I will discuss later on. Her patterns of performance and pushing against convention made a deep imprint on Yeats and his ideas of gender and performance. When they met, she was already engaged and a few years older than the young would-be playwright. She was also a distant cousin from a wealthier branch of the family, reminding Yeats of what his own family had lost. Her letters show that she was uncomfortable with her fate, with succumbing to marriage at a young age, and that she had artistic ambitions, but the choices for a woman in her position were few. The little we know about her shows that she understood the performance of the forms of power she had, power that would disappear once she was married. And, once married, she appears to have continued to challenge expected behavior. Though she did not reappear in Yeats's life, her legacy affected his work for and with other women and performers in the years to come. Yeats's earliest drama has received little attention: George Bornstein bases his argument for *The Island of the Statues*, not *Vivien and Time*, as Yeats's first major work on its status as first publication: "*Island* was the first of his works to be published at all.[4] As such, it claims a special place in his development, the point of origin for all of the later work."[5] My emphasis is on the neglected origin of the original poem—a drama modeled on Yeats's vision of Armstrong. Writing theater for a specific woman is a thread that this book follows from this starting point through the creation of the Deirdre plays by Yeats and Synge.

Armstrong's influence predates Yeats's collaborations with more renowned women of the theater like Florence Farr, Mrs. Patrick Campbell, Florence Darragh, Ninette de Valois, and the figure who has occluded most

---

(Dublin: Dolmen, 1993), and Keith Aldritt, in *W. B. Yeats: The Man and the Milieu* (New York: Potter, 1997) calls Armstrong "a flirt and a tease" (p. 31).

[4] Devoted to the study of Yeats's collaborations, the fifteenth *Yeats Annual* offers groundbreaking research on Yeats's work with his wife George, Lady Gregory, Douglas Hyde, and Frank O'Connor, but this volume does not mention Armstrong's early influence. *Yeats's Collaborations: Yeats Annual No. 15: A Special Number*, ed. W. Chapman and Warwick Gould (London: Palgrave, 2002).

[5] William Butler Yeats, *The Early Poetry, Manuscript Materials, Vol. I*, ed. George Bornstein (Ithaca, NY: Cornell University Press, 1987), 9.

of these other women, Maud Gonne.[6] The tradition has been to read Maud Gonne as a precedent for Yeats's mythologizing of women, but I hope to show that Yeats was trying to make sense of Laura Armstrong's impact on his work when he met Maud Gonne and began turning the latter, too, into a "myth and a symbol." The women who would later inspire female characters in Yeats's plays share Armstrong's tendency to flout traditional gender roles both in their lives and in their relationships with Yeats. Armstrong's understanding of public performance also reappears in the other women who would set Yeats writing in the years to come. John Butler Yeats called Armstrong "the wicked heroine in Willie's only novel," referring to Margaret Leland in *John Sherman*, a manipulative character who rejects Victorian mores as well as life as a traditional wife to the hero in Sligo.[7] Armstrong, though, ended up trying to live out the traditional roles she challenged in her relationship with Yeats, though not without difficulty and unhappiness, from what we know about her later years. She started a pattern of women who refused to conform to traditional roles who inspired Yeats; Farr, a believer in non-monogamous love, abandoned a theater career to teach at a girl's school in Ceylon in 1912; Maud Gonne had two children out of wedlock and became a nationalist leader; Mrs. Patrick Campbell, Florence Darragh, and Ninette de Valois struggled to control the plays that they had created with Yeats and challenged society's rules in their lives as well.

Yeats's first meeting with Armstrong shows how she refused to adhere to their shared culture's rules for young women of her class; Elizabeth Butler Cullingford argues that in his first contact with Armstrong, Yeats was "metaphorically ravished by a Muse who displayed the traditionally masculine qualities of aggression and initiation."[8] The traditional gender roles of Victorian Anglo-Irish culture are reversed in this public revelatory moment,

---

[6] Further chapters will explore how each of these actresses collaborated with Yeats at different points in his career as a playwright: Farr worked with him on chanting verse lyrics and performed as Aleel, the male poet character, in *The Countess Cathleen* in 1889. Mrs. Patrick Campbell performed Yeats's *Deirdre* in 1908; actress Florence Darragh played the lead role in *Deirdre* and Dectora of *The Shadowy Waters* on tour in 1907; and Ninette de Valois, along with her company of dancers, performed *At the Hawk's Well* and *The Dreaming of the Bones* in 1926. Yeats also revised *The Only Jealousy of Emer* for de Valois as *Fighting the Waves* in 1929. Maud Gonne's role in Yeats's life has been discussed in countless texts including Yeats's own poems; see Adrian Frazier, *The Adulterous Muse: Maud Gonne, Lucien Millevoye, and W. B. Yeats* (Dublin: Lilliput, 2016) for a nuanced discussion of their relationship.

[7] This comment is in a letter in the Berg Collection in the New York Public Library; from John Butler Yeats to John Quinn, written December 3, 1917.

[8] Elizabeth Butler Cullingford, *Gender and History in Yeats's Love Poetry* (Cambridge: Cambridge University Press, 1993), 14.

and the muse descends upon the writer, altering everything with the force of her physicality and personality:

> I was climbing up a hill at Howth when I heard wheels behind me and a pony-carriage drew up beside me. A pretty girl was driving alone and without a hat. She told me her name and said we had friends in common and asked me to ride beside her. After that I saw a great deal of her and was soon in love. I did not *tell* her I was in love, however, because she was engaged. She had chosen me for her confidant and I learned all about her quarrels with her lover. Several times he broke the engagement off, and she fell ill, and friends had to make peace. Sometimes she would write to him three times a day, but she could not do without a confidant. She was a wild creature, a fine mimic, and given to bursts of religion. I had known her to weep at a sermon, call herself a sinful woman, and mimic it after.[9]

This first meeting, with Yeats as the powerless passenger, grew mythic in his memory and inseparable from his beginnings as an artist. Yeats's recollection of Armstrong's mercurial moods and knack for mimicry suggests that her voice and irreverence were as important as her prettiness. She writes often, and although these are letters to her on-again off-again fiancé, not poetry or plays, she sounds like a theater director in her way, demanding that friends act as go-betweens. Yeats fulfills the role of "confidant," audience to her dramas. Her unconventional attitude and self-identification as a "sinful woman" show her proclivity for playing with Victorian mores. She is "alone" and lacks a hat as she descends on the young Yeats, two signals that she bucks convention. Her higher social class remains powerful in Yeats's memory; poorer and a few years Armstrong's junior, he makes his way on foot until she overtakes him in her carriage, a "wild creature" linked to a non-human fairy world, and orders him to play the writer to her muse. Yeats wrote later that as a young man, "I was humiliated and wrote always proud, confident men and women." His memory is only partly right. The men in these works are weak, and only the women show confidence and pride. In memory, the men begin to gain power from the women.

Challenging gender roles in his friendship with Armstrong allowed Yeats to imagine non-traditional female and male characters in the plays; in both *Vivien and Time* and *The Island of the Statues*, the male characters fade, and

---

[9] Quoted in Foster, *The Apprentice Mage*, 37.

the powerful women court each other. In the first play Yeats wrote after meeting Armstrong, *Vivien and Time*, Vivien, the female lead, praises Asphodel, her female rival for the affections of Clarin, the play's insubstantial male character. With phrases like, "so fair," Vivien uses the language of traditional male courtiers for the play's other woman.[10] The young man, Clarin, is under Vivien's spell, powerless and childlike, and her control over him reflects the balance of power in Yeats's friendship with Armstrong. Clarin's position as both lesser courtier and largely silent poet underscores his weakness next to Vivien, a powerful witch, and, in the character of Clarin, Yeats questions the very gender structures inherent in the courtier tradition—in this case, the power dynamic shifts as the male courtier is the weakest character in the play. As he revised the play, Yeats removed Clarin altogether, focusing solely on two remaining characters: Vivien and a figure representing Time—the only character, as I discuss later, who can curb her power, perhaps a stand-in for the ticking hours until Armstrong would be married and disappear from Yeats's life and the world of acting and writing.

The two musicians who attempt to court Naschina at the beginning of *The Island of the Statues* upset her with their "shrill and loud" music and run in fear exclaiming *"Fly! Fly!"* when a hunter shoots an arrow nearby.[11] In *Island*, the Enchantress professes her love to Naschina, a young woman disguised as a shepherd: "There's little I'd refuse thee dearest youth."[12] The power of the Enchantress in *Island* has paralyzed men into statues, and Naschina, after complaining about the lack of powerful males ("No one in Arcadia is courageous") sets off for the island to recover her male lover, Almintor, who has been turned to stone. Before leaving on his doomed quest to impress Naschina, Almintor had offered to bring her a lynx's fur; a disappointed Naschina replies, taking on a traditionally male role and rebuffing his efforts, "methinks I myself could shoot a great grey lynx."[13] She succeeds in rescuing Almintor by seducing The Enchantress into freeing the statues. The Enchantress, who has effortlessly turned male warriors and archers into stone, loses her power quickly to Naschina, begging her, "deign to kiss / My lips, fair youth."[14] Naschina complies, and saves Almintor as well as the forest of stone ex-warriors on the island, who proclaim her their leader, a title she insists on sharing with Almintor. Naschina and The

---

[10] See Cullingford, *Gender and History*, for an overview of Yeats's use of the courtier tradition.

[11] William Butler Yeats, *The Variorum Edition of the Poems of W. B. Yeats*, ed. Peter Alt and Russell K. Alspach (New York: Macmillan, 1957), 649.

[12] Ibid., 669.   [13] Ibid., 650.   [14] Ibid., 669.

Enchantress challenge each other's power in this play while the male characters stand by, frozen and silent.

Only one letter survives from what was, according to Yeats, a more extensive correspondence, and this piece of writing shows that Armstrong and Yeats wrote to each other as Vivien and Clarin, the names of the characters they used in *Vivien and Time*. Yeats is forming his ideas about what it means to be a poet at this time, and writing for a demanding, dramatic, and intelligent women who needs him to read aloud hints at future collaboration through performance as well as arguments over ownership and power. Armstrong wields power over Yeats, who found, from 1882 until well into advanced age, the position of passive suitor inspiring. He would write this power dynamic into many of his early plays about enchantresses and powerless, immature male characters like Clarin in *Vivien and Time* and Almintor in *The Island of the Statues*. In a show of her financial and class status, Armstrong records conducting some of her interactions with Yeats through her maid. According to Foster, "after meeting they corresponded in a high falutin' way,"[15] but the pretensions in their friendship re-emerge in the development of Yeats's theatrical characters, and that performance over letter is an important precedent for later collaborations between Yeats and actresses. The following letter from Armstrong to Yeats shows how the two performed for each other as dramatist and actress, with the actress dictating the terms of the relationship. Here, she allows him to imagine himself a poet. Yeats and Armstrong prepared for a performance of *Vivien and Time* that summer and performed the play "in a local judge's house in Howth, in the home of the family's landlord."[16] This first Yeatsian theatrical production was only possible with Armstrong. Her unavailability and forcefulness argue for her contribution to Yeats's vision of powerful female characters; the writer of this letter is anything but a passive muse:

10.8.84

My dear Clarin, What can I say to you for having been so rude to you—in not being at home when you called and I had asked you? I am really very sorry about it. I hope you will forgive me. It so happened that I was positively obliged to go out at the hour I had appointed for you to come but it was only to a house quite close to here—and I had told our maid to send me over word when you came—she did so (but I find since it was just

[15] Foster, *The Apprentice Mage*, 34.
[16] Terence Brown, *The Life of W. B. Yeats: A Critical Biography* (Oxford: Blackwell, 1999), 27.

before you went!) and I was rising to leave the room—I looked out of the window and to my great disappointment saw my Clarin leaving No. 60. It was too bad—and I am indeed sorry I missed you—I like your poems more than I can say—but I should like to hear you read them. I have not nearly finished them. Could you come some afternoon—and read a little to me—I shall be in Tuesday afternoon. I promise! So you can come? I should have written to you sooner but I have been away from home. Pray excuse my silence. Trusting to see "the poet"—and with kind regards. Believe me. Ever yours "Vivien."[17]

Writing a month before her marriage, Armstrong certainly transgresses the boundaries of accepted behavior for a Victorian, Anglo-Irish bride-to-be, and the claimed possession ("my Clarin") of both her confidant and the play's characters suggests that she delighted in her roles of controlling actress and muse. Indeed, she directs Yeats throughout the letter ("I had asked you . . . I had appointed you to come") when she is not directing her maid. Armstrong appears never to be at home, either visiting neighbors or "away" for longer periods; her mobility is central to her self-presentation in these months before her wedding. Looking down on him from the window of her large home, she repeats the moment of their first meeting when she observed him from high up in her carriage; in both scenes she is the one in control. Though she loves the poems, she has not finished reading them and requires Yeats to come perform them aloud. Armstrong frames "the poet" in quotation marks, creating a character for Yeats, and their habit of redefining themselves helped him take on, in these early years, the role of public poet and playwright that was to serve him so well until his death.[18]

Trying to make sense of Maud Gonne's effect on him shortly after their first meeting in 1889, Yeats focused instead on the lingering impact of her precursor. In a letter to Katherine Tynan, he attributes Gonne's "borrowed interest" to her similarities with Armstrong, though she lacks Armstrong's "half insane genius." His memories of the earlier friendship quickly eclipse impressions of Gonne:

As for the rest she [Gonne] had a borrowed interest, reminding me of Laura Armstrong without Laura's wild dash of half insane genius. Laura is

---

[17] Yeats, *Letters*, I, 154.   [18] Ibid., 154.

to me always a pleasant memory she woke me from the metallic sleep of science and set me writing my first play. Do not mistake me she is only as a myth and a symbol. Will you forgive me for having talked of her—She interests me far more than Miss. Gonne does and yet is only as a myth and a symbol. I heard from her about two years ago and am trying to find out where she is now in order to send her "Oisin." "Time and the Witch Vivien" was written for her to act. "The Island of the Statues" was begun with the same notion though it soon grew beyond the scope of drawing room acting. The part of the enchantress in both poems was written for her. She used to sign her letters "Vivien."[19]

In Yeats's memory, he is completely passive, indeed, unconscious, until Armstrong wakes him, and even after this awakening, she controls the beginning of his work as a dramatist; he remembers having no choice in starting to write the plays. His description of meeting Gonne ("I was twenty-three when the troubling of my life began")[20] is an effort to experience that awakening again. Most important to my argument, he imagines Armstrong, in a phrase he is compelled here to repeat, as a "myth and a symbol." In this letter, Yeats hopes to track her down and send her the plays that he created for her. He created witches and enchantresses as the major characters for his first plays, mythical and symbolical figures that express both his attraction to and discomfort with Armstrong's power. The reference to "drawing room" theatricals shows, as does Armstrong's letter demanding he come read the poems, that the two performed amateur productions as Yeats wrote and revised those first plays.

Five years after their collaboration on these first plays, Yeats returns to his image of Laura Armstrong to begin to develop his idea of Maud Gonne; he would soon rewrite the controlling enchantresses of his early plays into roles inspired not only by Gonne but also by his memory of Armstrong and the earliest female characters in his work. Gonne, for her part, recognized the power of these early heroines based on her predecessor. Guiding Yeats to create a particular kind of role for herself, Gonne reacted to *The Island of the*

---

[19]   Ibid., 155n.

[20]   Yeats met Gonne, as I discuss in Chapter 2, in 1889 when she descended on the Yeats family home and argued politics and the use of force with the poets father, her pet monkey playing on the rug. The meeting started Yeats on numerous plays and poems, as he reworked Gonne in Armstrong's image. See William Butler Yeats, *Memoirs* (New York: Macmillan, 1972), 40.

Statues with appreciation of the Enchantress though she "hated Naschina," the play's less mythical female character.[21]

Though they began with women who celebrate their power over men, *Time and the Witch Vivien*, *Mosada*, and *The Island of the Statues* take the lead female character's death as their main subject and gaze at the slow process of a mythical woman dying into a world far removed from reality, a no-place that makes her speech impossible. Intersections between class and gender were an important part both of Yeats's performance with Armstrong and his ambivalence about her power.[22] Beginning with Armstrong, the financial freedom and unconventional lifestyles of the women who inspired Yeats both put them in a position to influence the writer and allowed him to imagine powerful women in alternative, mythical settings. Each of the female protagonists, Vivien, the Enchantress, and Mosada, possesses magical power and controls the rest of the cast until the final scene. *Time and the Witch Vivien* takes place in a "marble-flagged, pillared room," complete with "magical instruments" and a "fountain"; *Mosada* is set in "a Moorish room"[23] and *The Island of the Statues* is introduced as "An Arcadian Faery Tale."[24] An odd shift occurs, however, in Yeats's idea of these women after he begins writing. He establishes the magical strength of each protagonist and the setting as otherworldly, then dramatizes, in detail, her death. His gaze at the death of the female lead in the final scene of each play expresses his conflicted response both to the real woman's high social position and to her influence on his work. Elizabeth Butler Cullingford argues that Yeats's courtier poetry for these women masks actual power differences, and "follows tradition in reversing the normal distribution of sexual power."[25] I contend, however, that social position and wealth gave the women Yeats collaborated with freedoms, albeit short-lived, that the poet, for all of his status as an Anglo-Irish man, lacked due to his family's straitened economic circumstances. In the case of Laura Armstrong, soon to marry a solicitor in September 1884, impending marriage not only made her a safely unattainable object of desire for the young Yeats, but the ineluctable approaching change in her status allowed him to imagine her nearing death in the works

---

[21] Quoted in George Bornstein, *Mosada and The Island of the Statues: Manuscript Materials* (Ithaca, NY: Cornell University Press, 1994), 12.

[22] Any discussion of class and gender in Ireland is indebted to Marjorie Howes, *Yeats's Nations: Gender, Class, and Irishness* (Cambridge: Cambridge University Press, 1996).

[23] Yeats, *Poems*, 690.   [24] Quoted in Foster, *The Apprentice Mage*, 87.

[25] Cullingford, *Gender and History*, 25.

he wrote with her in mind. And marriage would mean the end of the kind of power she wielded as a well to do young woman riding around Howth alone.

In one of the plays inspired by Armstrong, *Mosada*, first published in *The Dublin University Review* in 1886, the method of the title character's suicide is telling: she "sucks poison from the ring," choosing to reach death through a symbol of marriage.[26] Because his mother, Susan Yeats, fell into a debilitating depression after marrying his father, marriage was a kind of death in Yeats's childhood home. Dying heroines in his plays avoid the humiliation of Susan Yeats's decrepit end. Beginning with Armstrong, Yeats chose to collaborate with powerful Anglo-Irish women who, in contrast to his mother, enjoyed financial freedom and lacked domestic ties. Later in life, he would remember his early vision of women as distant from the reality of his mother and sisters: "When I thought of women they were modelled on those in my favourite poems and loved in brief tragedy, or, like the girl in *The Revolt of Islam*, accompanied their lovers through all manner of wild places, lawless women without homes or children."[27] Though none of the men in these early plays is strong enough to be a lover, the women are powerful in part because they lack domestic ties. Yeats wrote for Laura Armstrong a few months before her September 1884 marriage, while her short-lived independent status and economic class allowed her to enjoy a brief period of relative freedom. The change in her life loomed, though, and, consequently, Yeats's mythical plays about women dying depicted an imagined escape for powerful women like Armstrong and expressed his own fears of female authority.

Setting the plays in either mythical or remote romantic lands, Yeats distanced the characters from prosaic financial and familial concerns. While class divisions are clear in these plays and defined along gender lines, the characters live in worlds with no evidence of money; preoccupied by class, Yeats avoided writing about the major problems in his own home. John Butler Yeats gave up his ambition to become a solicitor soon after marrying Susan Pollexfen, deciding instead on a career as a portrait painter, and his difficulty finishing commissioned portraits left the Yeats family in constant debt.[28] Land reforms prevented the family from living on other forms of income, and W. B. Yeats grew up in an atmosphere of financial

---

[26] Yeats, *Poems*, 700.

[27] W. B. Yeats, *Autobiographies* (London: Macmillan, 1955), 463.

[28] For more on the Yeats's precarious financial situation in the 1880s, see Deirdre Toomey, "Away," in *Yeats and Women*, ed. Deirdre Toomey (New York: Macmillan, 1997), 135–67.

instability that precipitated his mother's mental and emotional withdrawal. Deirdre Toomey sums up the reasons for the severity of Susan Yeats's emotional problems: "Susan Yeats suffered from financial instability—fields and houses vanishing into a bottomless pit – her husband's marital alienation, the death of two children."[29] The family moved, Toomey reminds us, every other year until Yeats was twelve, often because of problems paying the rent.[30] According to Terence Brown, "in the stratified, genteel world of Protestant Dublin, Yeats's status was unquestionably anomalous."[31] The Yeats family was caught between financial need and social expectation, and this tension comes out in the plays and in Yeats's relationship with Armstrong.

The Yeats family troubles reflected larger social upheaval: changes to the landlord system had a direct effect on Yeats's already precarious financial situation. Tenants at the Yeats family estate stopped paying rent while John Butler Yeats, still incapable of completing enough portraits to support the family, failed to meet monthly payments on their Dublin house.[32] John Butler Yeats believed that an Anglo-Irish gentleman should not concern himself with money: "In my young days a gentleman did not bother about either his health or his finances, now we are all miserable bourgeois—like George Moore and such like timorous souls!"[33] Though he joked about becoming "bourgeois," Yeats's father behaved as if he lived in the Arcadian land of his son's early plays, artistic settings with no evidence of financial struggle, and modeled for his son a form of escape into art.

In *Vivien and Time*, the first play that Yeats wrote for Armstrong, the female title character refuses a traditionally maternal role, expressing both Yeats's ideal of a free Armstrong and his anxiety about his increasingly housebound and distant mother. Yeats emphasizes Vivien's anti-maternal status in the play by contrasting her with her domestic female foil, Asphodel. The play follows a love triangle made up of Vivien, an enchantress, Clarin, a young male musician, and Asphodel, his prosaic love interest. The familiar trio that began with *Vivien and Time* would recur in Yeats's better-known later plays as Fand, Cuchulain, and Emer in *The Only Jealousy of Emer* and Cathleen ni Houlihan, Michael, and Delia in *Cathleen ni Houlihan*.

[29] Ibid., 140.   [30] Ibid., 138.   [31] Brown, *The Life of W. B. Yeats*, 27.
[32] Foster, *The Apprentice Mage*, 30.
[33] John Butler Yeats, *Letters to His Son W. B. Yeats and Others 1869–1892* (London: Faber and Faber), 84.

In all three plays, a man is forced to choose between a prosaic domestic woman of the community (Asphodel, Emer, and Delia), and an other-worldly, threatening figure (Vivien, Fand, and Cathleen ni Houlihan). Vivien's manipulative actions towards the Page, a young child, separate her from conventional Victorian Irish womanhood and put her, "the goblin queen," in league with the child-stealing spirits of "The Stolen Child," *The Land of Heart's Desire*, and the evil witches and stepmothers of Grimm's Fairy Tales.[34] Like Cathleen ni Houlihan, she takes strength from youthful male figures for her own ends. Calling the young boy "my child," she tricks him into uttering a spell on Clarin and Asphodel, Vivien's rival. The heroine chooses to enchant and trick both the children and her love interest, Clarin. In the Yeats home, the maternal figure already showed signs of collapse: though she would not suffer her first debilitating stroke for three more years, Susan Yeats was withdrawing from her children and rarely left the house in the mid-1880s as the family's financial state became increasingly insecure. Armstrong, then, in contrast to the women in his troubled home, fulfilled Yeats's image of a woman without the daily tedium of money worries and domestic ties, and he wrote his first heroines out of that anti-maternal idea.

Fixating on the female lead's narration of moments leading up to the end of life, Yeats's early plays both translate the already mythological women into death and show their final lack of control for all their early power. The action of the plays, though set in fantastical lands, cannot follow these characters into death. Yeats became increasingly fascinated by this transition into silence, rewriting *Vivien and Time* as the shorter *Time and the Witch Vivien*, a version that pares the action of the play down to Vivien's death. In the revised title, Time comes first and holds the ultimate power. As she plays chess with Time and watches his hourglass run out, Vivien expresses each step towards her own mortality: "The passing of those little grains is slow upon my soul, old Time."[35] Losing the game, Vivien nears death against her will: "Check once more."[36] She refuses to die, and her reasons list her efforts to control public and private life: "I must be careful now. I have such plots / such war plots, peace plots, love plots – every side."[37] (Countering the stereotype of the romantic heroine, Vivien lists war before peace, and love comes last.) Her words follow and choreograph her every reaction as she moves closer to death:

---

[34] Clarke, *Theatre of Desolate Reality*, 23.   [35] Yeats, *Poems*, 722.   [36] Ibid.
[37] Ibid.

> Vivien: Ah! How bright your eyes. How swift your moves.
> How still it is! I hear the carp go splash,
> And now and then a bubble rise. I hear
> A bird walk upon the doorstep. [She plays.]
> Time: Check once more.[38]

Vivien's senses, just before death, are attuned to the details of her environment.[39] She ends her life with the line, "I cannot go into the bloodless land,"[40] but her refusal only emphasizes her final powerlessness as soon as she dies. These first plays prefigure the same scenes that resurface throughout Yeats's playwrighting life; his Deirdre, as I discuss in Chapter 5, ends the play with a chess game as she attempts to control the last moments of time before certain death.

The Enchantress in *The Island of the Statues* considers herself safe from time in the land of charmed statues she has created; she says to Naschina, "I could gaze upon thine eyes' clear grey; / Gaze on till ragged / Time himself decay."[41] The play, however, sets up her imperviousness to time only to focus intently on her departure from life at the end, a fate she fights: "I dream!—I cannot die!—No! No!"[42] Like Vivien and Mosada, though, the Enchantress cannot control her descent into death and, with lines like "Ah, subtle and slow, / The warmth of life is chilling," chronicles every sensation of her slow departure. Lest we imagine her living in another form or gaining a new kind of power after death, Yeats emphasizes the finality of her ending and its unwelcome nature. She repeatedly laments that "soulless a fairy dies" into a death that is "horrible! And foul, foul!" Her formerly powerful language, however, has no effect on her fate, and she finally moves offstage to die alone while Naschina comments, before turning to awaken the men/ statues, "Great sobs her being shake."

Like Vivien and the Enchantress, Mosada begins exulting in her power and beauty before death slowly takes her strength. In the 1889 version of the play, published in *The Wandering of Oisin and Other Poems*, Mosada declares her strength at the play's start: "Ah! Now I'm Eastern hearted once again, / And while they gather around my beckoning arms, / I'll sing

---

[38] Ibid.

[39] In Yeats's last play, the 1939 *The Death of Cuchulain*, completed in the last months of his life, the play's hero also shows heightened sensitivity in his final moments and describes a birdlike figure, "a soft, feathery shape," just before his death. See *The Collected Plays of W. B. Yeats* (New York: Macmillan, 1953), 444.

[40] Yeats, *Poems*, 722.   [41] Ibid., 671–2.   [42] Ibid., 675.

the songs that dusky lovers sing."[43] A precursor to Yeats's exotic, feminine Ireland, this heroine, described in the list of characters as "a Moorish lady," emphasizes her otherness from the play's first lines.[44] The play takes place during the Spanish Inquisition, and Inquisitors interrupt Mosada's speech and sentence her to death. Cola, a messenger, attempts to take her place, but, like Clarin and various other ineffectual male poet-lovers to come in Yeats's oeuvre, he fails. His loyalties are divided, as he had earlier informed on Mosada, and he owes his love to an enchantment reminiscent of Vivien's effect on the Page and Cathleen ni Houlihan's power over Michael: "she kissed the child with poisonous lips, and he is pining since."[45] His divided allegiance reveals Yeats's ambivalence about his own poet-lover position, and Mosada's instantaneous power over Cola repeats Yeats's response to his first sight of Armstrong. Like Clarin and Michael, he lacks even the power to choose his mate; her frightening sexual advances make this decision for him. Cola's position is as peripheral as Yeats's role of confidant in Armstrong's life. After taking "the poison drop," Mosada speaks for three pages, detailing her death before finally dying. An apple blossom (the flower Yeats would later associate with Maud Gonne[46]) wafts into her cell, and as she holds it against her fingers, she describes the contrast with her skin: "they've grown blue around the nails. / My blossom, I am dying, and the stars / Are dying too."[47] (This conflation of the dying women and the heavens also returns in Yeats's "pre-mortem" elegies for Gonne.[48]) The unblinking focus on the physical manifestations of Mosada's death, like the Enchantress's final lines, shows Yeats's obsession with a mythical woman's mortality: Mosada narrates her loss of physical power with "I cannot even crawl."[49] In a complete reversal of Laura Armstrong's heightened power in her first meeting with Yeats, Mosada is weighted in death, reduced to the level of the ground.

The female performer narrates and performs both her claim to power and her death, speaking until language meets mortality. Yeats brought this trope

---

[43] William Butler Yeats, *The Wandering of Oisin and Other Poems* (London: Paul Trench and Co., 1889), 476. For a discussion of Orientalism in Irish literature, see Joseph Lennon, *Irish Orientalism: A Literary and Intellectual History* (Syracuse, NY: Syracuse University Press, 2004). For a discussion of *Mosada*, see p. 254.

[44] Yeats, *Poems*, 689. Yeats and Gonne would later communicate in dreams reminiscent of *Mosada*'s Orientalism; in 1891 Gonne wrote to him, to his delight and interest, of a dream "where they had been (in a past life) brother and sister, sold into slavery in Arabia." See Foster, *The Apprentice Mage*, 114.

[45] Yeats, *Poems*, 696.   [46] Ibid., 700.   [47] Ibid., 700.

[48] Jahan Ramazani, *Yeats and the Poetry of Death: Elegy, Self-Elegy, and the Sublime* (New Haven, CT: Yale University Press, 1990), 50.

[49] Yeats, *Poems*, 700.

into his poems as well, but his love elegies contain only his own speech; the speaker in the poems is the courtier/lover, describing the woman's death. The lyrics that Yeats would write for Maud Gonne have received much more attention than these early plays because poetry and the figure of Gonne are central to the story of Yeats. I would like to examine two of these poems in terms of my argument that death in earlier plays is influenced by Armstrong. Jahan Ramazani calls Yeats's need to write elegies for a living Maud Gonne the "aggressive absenting of the beloved" by an "elegist [who] in some sense wills the death he mourns."[50] Ramazani provides an overview of this pattern in Yeats's poetry and helpfully argues for the "extraordinary extent" of Yeats's "dependence on the beloved's death and absence for the life of his poetry." Building on the work of Ramazani, I argue for the connection between these verses and Yeats's early plays and the anxieties about female influence that might have led Yeats to this poetic stance. Yeats wrote "He Wishes His Beloved Were Dead" in 1898, initially exulting in the power of the beloved, who has "the will of the wild birds," and expands to the heavens: "[your] hair was bound and wound / About the stars and moon."[51] The end of the poem, like the final moments of the plays for Armstrong, brutally limits the beloved's power, and imagines her contained in death in a sharp contrast to her early universal presence:

> O would, beloved, that you lay
> Under the dock-leaves in the ground
> While lights were paling one by one.[52]

Yeats admires the inspiring "will" of the woman and then betrays a fear of her power in a desire to curtail that strength and fix her in mortality. He comes back, in this poem, to the language of the plays he wrote in the 1880s, dramas that enacted the death of the "wild" female figures inspired by Armstrong.

A few years later, in 1891, Yeats wrote "A Dream of Death" for Maud Gonne after hearing rumors that she was gravely ill in France. Yeats sent Gonne the completed poem, originally entitled "An Epitaph," and Gonne wrote in her autobiography in the mocking tone reminiscent of Armstrong's letters to Yeats, "I was getting steadily better and amused when Willie sent me a poem, my epitaph he had written with much feeling."[53] The woman in the poem dies far from home, "in a strange place"; unconventionally

---

[50] Ramazani, *Poetry of Death*, 18.   [51] Yeats, *Poems*, 176.   [52] Ibid.
[53] Maud Gonne, *A Servant of the Queen* (London: Victor Gollancz, 1938), 147.

traveling alone "near no accustomed hand," and remains buried below an unlabeled cross until the poet visits her grave and inscribes "She was more beautiful than thy first love / But now lies under boards."[54] Ramazani connects this final line with Yeats's memory of Armstrong.[55] In this eerie image, the poem reprimands the traveling woman and recalls both the earlier poem and Mosada's focus on the physical manifestations of death: "they nailed the boards above her face, / The peasants of that land."[56] Maud Gonne, whose income from a family inheritance allowed her unusual mobility and freedom for a turn-of-the-century woman, married John MacBride in 1902, and in a draft of a distraught letter, Yeats urges her to rethink her decision, figuring her impending marriage as a death: "but Maud Gonne is about to pass away."[57] He ends the pleading letter with "For [it] is not only the truth & your friends but your own soul that you are about to betray." A terror of the effect of marriage on a woman's identity, forged in those early years losing his mother to depressed silence and Armstrong to a socially appropriate but unhappy match, resurfaces in those letters to Gonne.

The mix of marriage and death in Yeats's work—a connection that would culminate in his final dramas, *Purgatory* (1938) and *The Death of Cuchulain* (1939), began with his plays for Laura Armstrong. Yeats had, in fact, been right in imagining marriage as an unhappy fate for Laura Armstrong: John Butler Yeats wrote to his daughter Susan Mary Yeats twenty years after the planned performance of *Vivien and Time* that after divorcing her first husband, Armstrong married a Welsh gardener, "a very decent and intelligent man that she so henpecked that he was forced to leave her, allowing her £120 a year, though she told everyone she was a widow with two children."[58] Though she appeared carefree during the summer of 1884, marriage did signal a major change for Laura Armstrong. In the end, her fate mirrored Susan Pollexfen Yeats's decline: her class position and financial security eroded after she married. Secrecy and misrepresentation end Armstrong's story for the Yeats family, showing repercussions for women who did not play by prescribed rules. Social pressure had also pushed the Yeats children to keep Susan's mental illness out of public view, and Maud Gonne, as I discuss elsewhere in this book, had to pretend her first two children were wards because they were born out of wedlock.[59]

[54] Yeats, *Poems*, 123.   [55] Ramazani, *Poetry of Death*, 18.   [56] Yeats, *Poems*, 123.
[57] Maud Gonne, *The Gonne–Yeats Letters: 1893–1938*, ed. Anna MacBride White and A. Norman Jeffares (New York: Norton, 1993), 165.
[58] Yeats, *Letters*, I, 155n.
[59] For the story of Maud Gonne's secret life, see Frazier, *The Adulterous Muse*.

The early plays that Yeats wrote for Armstrong show no connection between women and Ireland; both national Ireland and local Sligo are conspicuous for their absences from *Mosada*, *The Island of the Statues*, and the Vivien plays. Marjorie Howes points out that Yeats's "engagement" with gender and nation "ranges from exaggeration to appropriation to resistance" throughout his career.[60] When he did begin to try to dramatize an idea of Ireland in his writing, Yeats would turn to the imagery and language he had used to describe Armstrong's effect on him. His first efforts for the stage dramatize mythical women struggling with mortality, a theme that reveals his conflicted reaction to female power. In plays and poems that figure Ireland as a woman, Yeats would negotiate between a detailed, local sense of place and a mythic version of nation, building on the symbolic female figures he created after meeting Armstrong. In 1884, however, Yeats began writing for women before bringing Ireland into his work, setting his dramas in imaginary, distant locations—Vivien's palace, an enchanted island, an Orientalized "Moorish" village. He would soon begin to imagine his nation in similar terms, as mythic and symbolic like the female characters he created for his earliest plays, and the lines between these kinds of female figures and Ireland would blur. In his fraught relationship with Armstrong, the precedent for the rest of the women who would collaborate with Yeats, struggles with strong women and the dramatization of impending death begin in Yeats's writing and life, due to her insistence on the performance of power dynamics from that fateful moment on the Howth road.

---

[60] Howes, *Yeats's Nations*, 7.

2

"A Play She Could Act in Dublin"

Maud Gonne's Cathleens

In late November 1918, sixteen years after playing the title role in Yeats and Lady Gregory's *Cathleen ni Houlihan*, a sickly Maud Gonne arrived at her house, No. 73 St. Stephens Green, disguised as a poor old woman and accompanied by her two children. Re-enacting the plot of the play in real life, she demanded entrance and shelter of the family inside. Her request brought danger: she was in Ireland illegally after transfer in late October from Holloway Gaol, where she was incarcerated for Republican activities, to a nursing home for ill health. She had walked out of the nursing home and escaped to Ireland. Yeats and George, his pregnant wife, had taken over Gonne's house for the autumn, and George was battling influenza at the height of the 1918 epidemic. Gonne dressed as an old peasant woman in costume to pass through the border and operate in Dublin unobserved.[1] In this complicated offstage re-enactment of *Cathleen ni Houlihan*, what Yeats's sister Lily called "the 'arrested on her deathbed' tableau," Gonne played both Cathleen ni Houlihan and returned absentee landlord.[2]

---

[1] Maud Gonne had been interned in Holloway Gaol with Constance Markievicz and Cathleen Clarke on charges that they had been part of a German plot against England. She suffered health problems in jail and worried there about her young son Sean. After six months, she was sent to a sanatorium—she escaped in disguise. Yeats had been using his influence to try and secure her release. For more on this episode, see R. F. Foster, *W. B. Yeats: A Life: II. The Arch-Poet* (Oxford: Oxford University Press, 2003), 135–7. Two contributions to the 9th Yeats Annual, *Yeats and Women*, have also been helpful here. In "Labyrinths: Yeats and Maud Gonne," Deirdre Toomey's footnote describes this episode and the debate about the effect of Yeats's refusal to give Gonne entry, and in "Secret Communion: Yeats's Sexual Destiny," John Harwood takes issue with Marjorie Perloff's reading of "A Prayer for My Daughter" as a reaction to Gonne's 1918 visit to the home on Stephen's Green. Perloff's essay, "'Between Hatred and Desire': Sexuality and Subterfuge in 'A Prayer for My Daughter'" appeared in the 7th Yeats Annual. Ann Saddlemyer's *Becoming George: The Life of Mrs. W. B. Yeats* (Oxford: Oxford University Press, 2002) discusses the episode on pp. 196–7. On p. 171 of *Viral Modernism: The Influenza Pandemic and Interwar Literature* (New York: Columbia University Press, 2019), Elizabeth Outka describes Gonne's efforts to gain entry. Anne Margaret Daniel's helpful "Moura is in Holloway: A Famous 'Prophylactic Love Poem' by W.B. Yeats" can be found in *The Times Literary Supplement*, January 29, 2016, no. 5887, 14–15.

[2] Qtd. in Foster, *The Arch-Poet*, 136.

Gender, Performance, and Authorship at the Abbey Theatre. Elizabeth Brewer Redwine, Oxford University Press (2021). © Elizabeth Brewer Redwine. DOI: 10.1093/oso/9780192896346.003.0002

Yeats had convinced Gonne to allow him to rent the lodgings with the promise, "should you be released and allowed to live in Ireland we will move out while strangers would not."[3] The charged term, "strangers," aligns Yeats and Gonne in the language of the 1902 *Cathleen ni Houlihan* they and Lady Gregory created together. By renting to Yeats, Gonne would avoid what the poor old woman, the play's title character, called "strangers in the house."[4] That night in 1918, Maud Gonne and William Butler Yeats performed, again, the tensions in the final scene of *Cathleen ni Houlihan*, a moment fraught with contested ideas of maternity and national responsibility. Like Cathleen ni Houlihan, a physically weakened Gonne appeared unexpectedly at the door, seeking allegiance and sacrifice from the family inside. In a gesture typical of Gonne's flair for the dramatic, the moment tested her long friendship with Yeats and their history as collaborators on the 1902 production of the play. And Yeats refused in an effort to protect George, though Gonne was furious, calling her old friend "an unpatriotic coward."[5] Yeats chose to protect the actual future mother inside instead of aligning himself with Gonne, an iconic figure from the past personifying a nationalism he found increasingly distant from his own beliefs. Gonne also arrived with her own children, so the role of mother and iconic symbol of nation are intertwined in this doorway tableau; though nationalist orthodoxy had tried to separate the physical, biological mother from the amorphous and spiritual Mother Ireland, the two conflate in this moment.

So many mother images compete in this story, and Gonne knew exactly what she was doing appealing to Yeats at this moment. Deploying her own class and financial powers here, her actions emphasize that despite her status as an illegal visitor she is the homeowner and landlord in the scenario. In other words, she is both pulling rank as the landowner and asking for Yeats's support in a dangerous mission as an Irish Republican operative. She is also an actual mother seeking shelter and asylum under political duress. Her "unpatriotic" jibe shows how political this moment was for her; this demand was a test that Yeats failed. She and Yeats were not arguing simply as old friends, but she was re-enacting their years of collaboration and disagreement over the role of women, mothers, and rebellion in Ireland and the line between the political and the personal or familial. Yeats goes back on his

---

[3] Gonne, *The Gonne–Yeats Letters*, 396.

[4] W. B. Yeats, *The Collected Works of W. B. Yeats, II, The Plays*, ed. David Clark and Robin E. Clark (New York: Palgrave Macmillan, 2001), 88.

[5] J. Londraville and R. Londraville (eds.), *The Letters of John Quinn and Maud Gonne MacBride*, n.d. September 1918, 216.

earlier agreement and is not willing to sacrifice his domestic safety for a possibly contagious Gonne-as-female-Ireland. Gonne found lodging with other friends and was soon at work on Constance Markievicz's successful campaign for Irish Parliament. The story gains symmetry with Gonne working at the end with Markievicz, another woman whose increasingly political persona challenged Yeats's ideals of gender, class, and Irishness. The two upper-class Anglo-Irishwomen had recently shared a jail cell for Republican activities.[6]

This chapter asks how Yeats's misreading of Gonne's female Irishness in the first Cathleen play contributed to the 1902 production of his second effort as both artists tried to make use of each other's voices in nationalist debate onstage. Yeats himself acknowledged both Lady Gregory's and Maud Gonne's roles in the creation of this play, and, as we shall see in later chapters, the contributions of many other actresses to his oeuvre. There is a privilege to these off-the-cuff remarks; due to his status as an established Anglo-Irish male author, Yeats could afford to be generous, if obfuscating, about the ways that Lady Gregory, Maud Gonne, and the women of the nationalist theater group Inghinidhe na hÉireann contributed to *Cathleen ni Houlihan*. This chapter will take Yeats at his word about this many-authored play, exploring how Maud Gonne and Inghinidhe influenced *Cathleen*, a text that came to the Abbey as the work of both Lady Gregory and Yeats. As I discuss in the section on Gonne and Inghinidhe, Mary Trotter's *Ireland's National Theatres: Political Performance and the Origins of the Irish Dramatic Movement* has provided helpful arguments for the importance of Maud Gonne and Inghinidhe to this and other productions. Antoinette Quinn's "Cathleen ni Houlihan Writes Back: Maud Gonne and Irish Nationalist Theatre" puts Gonne's performance in the 1902 premier of *Cathleen ni Houlihan* in the context of Gonne's other political work, the Inghinidhe na hÉireann performance of *In the Shadow of the Glen*, and the group's productions of Gonne's play, *Dawn*. Quinn focuses on *Dawn* as a response to the narratives of both Synge's and Gregory and Yeats's plays in that it brings together the local and national concerns of the women in the cottage, and she puts Gonne's play in the context of Gonne's political writing and newspaper coverage of Mayo. My goal in this chapter is to argue for Gonne as another creator of *Cathleen ni Houlihan* after Yeats's failed attempt to write a vehicle for her in *The Countess Cathleen*.

---

[6] For more on Constance Markievicz and Maud Gonne's political activism and imprisonment, see *The Prison Letters of Constance Markievicz*, ed. Esther Roper (London: Virago, 1987).

Lady Gregory, as James Pethica has shown, wrote most of the script that Gonne and Inghinidhe would enact on the Abbey stage in 1902. Aisling Carlin charts the controversies that led to Pethica's assessment in 1988; Pethica used both manuscript research and Lady Gregory's other writing to prove Gregory's contribution to the play.[7] Elizabeth Coxhead had made this assertion as early as 1962, noting that when Gregory's family members encouraged her to "stake her claim" as co-author of the play, "she always refused with a smile, saying that should could not take from (Yeats) any part of what had proved, after all, his one real popular success." Typically, this statement shows Lady Gregory claiming in private and contains a back-handed compliment that reflects Yeats's years of struggle to create plays that could find audiences at the Abbey. Much of Yeats's theatrical writing and folktales came from Gregory's translations. Deirdre Toomey and Pethica argue convincingly that the majority of the writing for the play, the parts that take place inside the cottage and the language of the family, were written by Lady Gregory. Without Lady Gregory's contribution, then, the play would have been a short ballad with a refrain, like Yeats's early 1887 "King Goll: A Legend." Gregory's language turns Yeats's ballad, the repeated lines of the title character, into a play, fleshing out family relationships, marriage plans, and the whole world that the young man would be renouncing to join Cathleen.

Lady Gregory had spent many years inside of cottages, recovering the stories and translations that would be used by herself and by Yeats to do the work of the Revival theater movement, bringing early Irish stories back into circulation on the stage as a counterweight to British images of the Irish as lazy and thoughtless.[8] George Moore, who had an axe to grind after a falling out with Yeats over their difficulties collaborating on the play *Diarmuid and Grania*, sums up Lady Gregory's work with Yeats in this way:

Well, if one had the courage to put on a tramp's jacket and wander through the country, sleeping in hovels, eating American bacon, and lying five in a bed, one might be able to write the dialect naturally; but I don't think that

[7] Carlin goes on to argue for Yeats's part in the collaboration. See Aisling Carlin, "'To make others see my dream as I had seen it,' Yeats's Aesthetics in *Cathleen Ni Houlihan*," *Yeats's Mask: Yeats Annual No. 19*, ed. Margaret Mills Harper and Warwick Gould (London: Open Book Publishers), 65–76.

[8] *Apes and Angels: The Irishman in Victorian Caricature, Revised Edition* (Washington, DC: Smithsonian Books, 1997) by L. P. Curtis, a revision of his 1972 work, remains an excellent overview of the way that Victorian Caricature stereotyped Irish people both in Britain and in Irish imported content.

one can acquire the dialect by going out to walk with Lady Gregory. She goes into the cottage and listens to the story, takes it down while you wait outside, sitting on a bit of wall. Yeats, like an old jackdaw, and then filching her manuscript to put style upon it, just as you want to put style on me.[9]

Moore's frustration is clear, and he is out to skewer Yeats's claims to authenticity or identity in his critique of "naturally" learning to write in dialect by working off of Gregory's translations. But his memory of Yeats and Gregory at Coole reminds us how much Lady Gregory did to recover the stories of Galway and the families living in the environs of Coole. Her work on *Cathleen ni Houlihan* shows that she was familiar with the interiors of rural houses and the concerns of mothers, and this very real and unheralded experience grounds the text of the play. Her writing in that initial script created a version of a play initially conceived for Gonne that would give Gonne and Inghinidhe the language for their tableaux-infused 1902 interpretation.

Inghinidhe na hÉireann, or Daughters of Ireland, began in response to rules in nationalist and Republican groups that prohibited women from joining. Started by Maud Gonne in 1899, Inghinidhe included both Protestant and Catholic women from all classes in Dublin. In the words of member, author, and Abbey actress Ella Young:

The Society is composed of girls who work hard all day in shops and offices owned for the most part by pro-British masters who may at any moment discharge them for 'treasonous activities.' To be dismissed in such wise means the semi-starvation of long-continued unemployment. These girls dare it, and subscribe, from not too abundant wages, generous amounts for the hire of halls to be used as classrooms and for theatre rehearsals.[10]

Young stresses the very real dangers to the young women who worked during the day and then joined Inghinidhe in the evenings for theatrical and educational events. These women were forced to live double lives, keeping their evening activities from their employers, performing even when they were not on stage. Stage performance, then, would come after days of hiding one's true identity from employers and, often, family. Focusing on financial danger and the willingness of these women to part with some of their wages for the

---

[9] George Moore, *The Collected Works of George Moore*, (New York: Appleton, 1911), 261.

[10] Qtd. in Kevin Whelan, *1916 in Ireland: Revolution and Counterrevolution in International Context* (Durham, NC: Duke University Press, 2018), 19.

group, Young emphasizes the sacrifices made by working-class young women in Inghinidhe.

The question of who creates theater needs revisiting especially in terms of the roots of the Abbey. Mary Trotter builds a case for Maud Gonne's and Inghinidhe's importance to the early Irish dramatic movement; she explains that the women's work in the famous 1902 production has been devalued, and she writes against the prevailing interest in the written script, emphasizing the Inghinidhe members' "vital roles as producers, financiers, ticket sellers, trainers, and actors." This recovery of the role of Inghinidhe forces us to recognize how the Abbey's history has been "gendered," as Trotter argues, privileging the writing of men like Yeats, George Moore, and the Fay brothers, obscuring Lady Gregory's contributions as well as the group work of Inghinidhe na hÉireann and the individual women who lead these groups.[11] Building on the work of Trotter, this chapter argues that the question of authorship around that night and those performances requires a reassessment. Closely reading the performative aspects of Maud Gonne's political persona, Trotter argues that Gonne was effective as an "extraordinary woman," someone who was able to move in nationalist circles often reserved for men, speaking publicly, and using her body to physically block evictions due to her privilege, height, and larger-than-life persona. The work of Inghinidhe, led by Gonne, had moved from semi-private performances of tableaux, like the Antient Concert Rooms 1901 series depicting women in Irish myth and history, to the most public Dublin protest in living memory, the 1900 Patriotic Children's Treat. Inghinidhe used the funds from that response to Queen Victoria's visit to start the group, and, as Trotter argues, the Patriotic Children's Treat both deployed images of motherhood and showed the strength of organizing in a brand new organization. As the *United Irishman* noted of Inghinidhe, in Trotter's epigraph to her chapter on the group, "while others have been talking, the women have been working."[12] The group would bring this energy and sense of ownership to the production of *Cathleen ni Houlihan*. Above all, Inghinidhe and Gonne understood the power of stagecraft and spectacle to shift opinions and to educate; their ability, in that 1902 production, to make a nationalist statement that continues to resound one hundred and nineteen years later shows the women of that group taking control of the message.

[11] Mary Trotter, *Ireland's National Theatres: Political Performance and the Origins of the Irish Dramatic Movement* (Syracuse, NY: Syracuse University Press, 2001), 74.
[12] Qtd. in ibid., 73.

Tensions around what it meant to be an Irish woman in the revolutionary movement of the early twentieth century animated the collaborations between Yeats and Gonne leading up to and beyond the April 1902 premier of *Cathleen ni Houlihan*. That performance focused on the contrasting claims of the domestic mother figures inside the cottage, Bridget and Delia, and Mother Ireland or *Cathleen ni Houlihan*. Two women in the cottage create a female community, generation to generation, and exist in historical time; solitary Cathleen lives beyond time, subsuming all male sacrificial figures who come near her and lose their individuality. In the play, when the Poor Old Woman arrives at the door demanding the sacrifice of the young man within, she requires death for her own rebirth: rather than producing children, she devours the young in the name of the nation. The play dramatizes a divide in nationalism's orthodoxy about a woman's proper role in the movement. Organizations like the Gaelic League expected women to raise their children in the tradition of nationalism at the hearth, domestically remaining within the cottage. Nationalist groups, most of them all male until well into the first decades of the twentieth century, also swore their allegiance to an imagined Mother Ireland, an ideal of land and nation calling them away from the real, domestic women in their lives to die for Irish freedom. They swore to protect the ideal of the domestic mother, so the maternity in question faced an imagined future of sacrifice built on past death and an ongoing enactment of the nation with a domestic female cottage interior as its source. The 1902 production of *Cathleen ni Houlihan* dramatized this divided view of motherhood due to the contributions of Maud Gonne and Inghinidhe na hÉireann.

This is a story of ownership and privilege; Maud Gonne had to trade on her remarkable appearance for power, but that part of the Yeats/Gonne history has been well documented; indeed, many have followed Yeats's lead and spoken of Gonne's beauty and "great height" as the central point about who she was and what kind of power she wielded.[13] She was also a consummate organizer and knew how to deploy not just her image but also the dates and histories of Irish rebellion; because of her connections to an England she hated, she also understood how best to use theatrical performance—onstage and off—to combat British public relations in Ireland. In Yeats's theatrical writing for and with Gonne, the passivity of a woman receiving poetry as a muse implodes as Gonne feels she owns the role of Cathleen ni Houlihan,

---

[13] Qtd. in A. Norman Jeffares and A. S. Knowland, *A Commentary on the Plays of W. B. Yeats* (London: Macmillan, 1975), 29.

having rejected Yeats's earlier effort to write *The Countess Cathleen* for her. Adrian Frazier has documented how much facts simply did not matter to Gonne as she created her persona from the 1890s into old age.[14] And Jahan Ramazani writes about Yeats's "aggressive absenting of the beloved" when Gonne's power became too strong and the poet needed to imagine her in elegy.[15] From her earliest, effective political actions from France in the 1890s with visits to Russia, Ireland, and England, Gonne created a shifting persona and autobiography that she was Irish, that she had family in Ireland, and that she was single and without children. (This is a summary of her extensive descriptions of an apocryphal biography told to the French press and made up, as Frazier shows, out of whole cloth.) She had a genius for this kind of fiction and an uncanny ability to put forth an effective image in the face of facts that showed a different version of her identity. Inghinidhe na hÉireann and that 1902 production of *Cathleen ni Houlihan* show how her ability to create political theater, both onstage and off, capitalized on her knowledge of how to influence people through a carefully cultivated image.

In 1902, the women of Inghinidhe na hÉireann changed *Cathleen ni Houlihan*'s staging to draw attention to the contrast between two kinds of women, the domestic mother and the magnetic nationalist ideal. In real life, the divisions were not so neat. As Maria Tymoczko has argued, Gonne and the women of Inghinidhe na hÉireann changed the ending of the play, bringing their experience in street performance and tableaux onto the Abbey stage. Gonne wrote to Yeats a month before the premier:

> We rehearsed Kathleen tonight, it went splendidly all but the end. It doesn't make a good curtain – We are all of the opinion that Michael ought to go right out of the door instead of standing HESITATING. It doesn't seem clear if he doesn't go out. If he goes out Delia can throw herself on Bridget's shoulder in tears which makes a much better end. Please write at once and say if we may do that. *Russell* and Miss Young & the Fays & all the actors want it & think it is much better indeed necessary.[16]

---

[14] For Frazier's summary of Gonne's apocryphal versions of herself for the French press, see his *The Adulterous Muse: Maud Gonne, Lucien Millevoye, and W. B. Yeats* (Dublin: Lilliput, 2016), 100–1.

[15] Jahan Ramazani, "The Elegiac Love Poems: A Woman Dead and Gon(n)e," in *Yeats's Poetry, Drama, and Prose: Authoritative Texts, Contexts, Criticism* (New York: Norton, 2000), 350.

[16] Gonne, *The Gonne–Yeats Letters*, 150.

Marshaling the opinions of those who were present, Gonne pulls rank in this letter, suggesting that the performers know the play better than the writer. Though she pretends to ask for permission, her request is more an effort to correct Yeats. The moment of stasis and tableau at the end should be, Gonne argues, for the women to perform, not the young man. Clarity was most important to Gonne and the women of Inghinidhe na hÉireann; because of their experience with political street theater, they heightened the contrast between the women inside the cottage and the figure outside. These two changes in staging—Michael's quick departure and the forceful embrace between Bridget and Delia—focused attention both on the power of Cathleen and the loss of a son and husband to the two women left behind. Yeats's text directed that "Michael breaks away from Delia, stands for a second at the door, then rushes out, following the old woman's voice. Bridget takes Delia, who is crying silently, into her arms."[17] In the 1902 production, the moment was starker because Maud Gonne and Inghinidhe na hÉireann removed Michael's ambivalence and focused the final image of the play on the embrace between Delia and Bridget; the luring figure outside pulls stronger, and those remaining perform a more affective form of silent loss, one rooted in the tableaux traditions of their street theater (Figure 2.1). Not coincidentally, all three founding members of Inghinidhe na hÉireann in the play, Gonne, Máire T. Quinn, and Máire Nic Shiubhlaigh, would go on to disagree vehemently with Yeats over ideas of Irishness, performance, gender, and ownership, and resign from the Abbey, but in 1902 all worked together to bring Cathleen to the stage.[18]

Before turning to a close reading of the 1902 production and Yeats's failed effort to write an initial play for her, The Countess Cathleen, one that she rejected, a close look at maternity in these plays shows how the performance illustrated loss. Critics have written much about Mother Ireland and sacrifice to the Shan Van Vocht, but one woman on that stage had a young son who had died, and the story of Cathleen ni Houlihan, after all, is one of the loss of son. Máire Nic Shiubhlaigh, who played Delia, the jilted bride to be, had no children, and neither did Máire T. Quinn who played Michael's mother. The one onstage who had experienced maternal loss was Maud Gonne, whose infant son Georges had died of meningitis in France in 1893.

---

[17] W. B. Yeats, The Collected Works of W. B. Yeats, II, The Plays, ed. David Clark and Robin E. Clark (New York: Palgrave Macmillan, 2001), 93.

[18] For an overview of the disagreements that led to these actresses' departure from the Abbey, see Adrian Frazier, Behind the Scenes: Yeats, Horniman, and the Struggle for the Abbey Theatre (Berkeley: University of California Press, 1990).

Figure 2.1 Queen Maeve of Connaught and her daughter Finbarr (Miss Elise McGowan and Davidson) in Gaelic Tableaux at Belfast, June 1898, from a Belfast group that worked with Inghinidhe

Source: Appeared in *The Gentlewoman*, Courtesy of the British Library.

In later years, Sara Allgood would take on the part of Cathleen ni Houlihan and make it her own. Allgood would go onto lose a child, as I discuss in the Epilogue, while on tour in Australia to the Spanish Influenza in 1918, and Lady Gregory, who wrote much of the play, would lose her son Robert in World War I. Maternal loss was part of the fabric of women's lives at this time, whatever their class position, but in the 1902 production, only Gonne represented that secret loss, known to Yeats, onstage. Yeats also began writing poetry of escape as a young man, as I discuss in the Introduction and as Deirdre Toomey argues, in response to the loss of his younger brother and the devastating impact of that death on his mother.[19] Yeats had written

---

[19] Deidre Toomey, "Away," in Deirdre Toomey, ed., *Yeats and Women* (New York: Palgrave Macmillan, 1997), 135–67.

poems about Gonne's loss as well, though he seems to have believed Gonne's story that the baby was adopted by her. As Frazier notes, one of Yeats's early poems, "The Glove and the Cloak," reveals that Gonne kept a memento of her son with her always and held it tightly when she spoke on platforms, linking the physical loss of a mother to the performance of nationalist female iconography.[20] Yeats wrote the poem in 1893, and Gonne asked him not to publish it. The secret of her loss is written into both of the Cathleen plays, particularly the second one, and the performance of 1902. Though the poem mentions a glove, Gonne in fact kept a little bootie of Georges' with her and gripped it when she spoke to crowds. In her will, when she died in 1953, she requested to be buried with Georges's baby shoes. Since she often spoke of the loss of children in evictions, perhaps this piece of Georges's clothing reminded her of a personal stake in sparing other mothers.[21] Speaking from platforms and clinging to her son's baby bootie, Gonne linked the public persona of Irish female activism and her heartbreaking experience as a mother, one that would resurface, as secrets do, in *Cathleen ni Houlihan*.

Gonne always identified with the figure of the woman of the Sidhe, so one would expect her to emphasize Cathleen's power. Why, though, would Gonne and the other actresses revise the ending to heighten the audience's sympathy with the plight of the realistic, domestic mother Bridget, and the cheated Delia? Gonne preferred Yeats's fantastic versions of womanhood and "hated Naschina," the more prosaic heroine of *The Island of the Statues*.[22] Yeats himself pushed the simplified reading of Gonne as love object, not organizer or artistic collaborator, and the revision has stuck. Gonne's desire to play the role of female Irish avenger made the part of Cathleen ni Houlihan attractive to her, but her interest in embodying a mythic figure coincided with a defense of those in the cottage. In altering the final scene to draw attention to the embrace between Delia and Bridget, the abandoned bride and mother of the house, Gonne and the women of Inghinidhe na hÉireann challenged the very iconic images that they exploited,

---

[20] Frazier discusses this episode and includes the poem in *The Adulterous Muse*, 120.

[21] Caoimhe Nic Dháibhéid's article, " 'This Is a Case in Which Irish National Considerations Must Be Taken into Account': The Breakdown of the MacBride–Gonne Marriage, 1904–8," *Irish Historical Studies* 37, no. 146 (2010): 241–64 is helpful on maternity, misogyny, and Irish nationalism. She explores the way that the divorce between Maud Gonne and John MacBride reveals fissures in the nationalist movement around fears and resentment of female power. Gonne's controversial motherhood is also at issue in this article that chronicles Gonne's efforts to retain custody of her children.

[22] Yeats, *The Collected Letters of W. B. Yeats*, Vol. I, ed. John Kelly and Eric Domville (Oxford: Clarendon Press, 1986), 134.

dramatizing both sides of the debate on Irish nationalist womanhood. Inghinidhe's production stressed loss along with celebrated sacrifice. Antoinette Quinn sums up the contrast between the kinds of mothers imagined by nationalist organizations like the Gaelic League: "it idealized mother and home as the repository of spiritual, moral, and affective values and it constructed women as bearers and cultural reproducers of the future nation."[23] A year after the premier of *Cathleen ni Houlihan*, Patrick Pearse defended the role of the cottage-bound mother raising her baby with nationalist ideals and the Irish language, arguing that if "the Gaelic League could get a thorough grip of the cradles all over the country, and keep that grip, its work would be assured."[24] Pearse and the other members of the League also praised sacrifice to a maternal symbol of nationhood, and many were moved by performances of *Cathleen ni Houlihan*. Motherhood and attendant fears about women's sexuality and biological national identity were continually under review in the world of Irish nationalism and theater, from the Cathleen plays to Yeats's 1938 play *Purgatory*, where the unraveling of a nation and a family into murder is due to a woman making the wrong choice in a man. If *Cathleen ni Houlihan* stands for Mother Ireland, she vies with the actual and future mothers onstage, Bridget and Delia. Elizabeth Butler Cullingford sums up the difference: "Yeats distinguished carefully between the terrible claims of Mother Ireland and the protective response of a biological mother . . . unwilling to sacrifice for her country."[25] A close look at the way that Gonne and Inghinidhe performers changed the stagecraft in the play raises questions about who made that distinction so forceful onstage—Yeats or the actresses. James Joyce famously parodied the youth-devouring figure of Cathleen ni Houlihan or Mother Ireland as "the old sow that eats her farrow" in *A Portrait of the Artist as a Young Man*; the play contains its own critique, and Gonne focused the audience's attention on the divided images of motherhood on the stage.[26]

Inghinidhe na hÉireann's work on *Cathleen ni Houlihan* reflected their experience portraying nationalist ideas of motherhood in earlier productions. When Gonne arrived in Dublin to try and work for the nationalist

---

[23] Antoinette Quinn, "Cathleen ni Houlihan Writes Back: Maud Gonne and the Irish National Theatre," in *Gender and Sexuality in Modern Ireland*, ed. Anthony Bradley and Maryann Gialanella Valuilis (Amherst: University of Massachusetts Press, 1997), 41.

[24] Qtd. in ibid., 42.

[25] Elizabeth Butler Cullingford, *Gender and History in Yeats's Love Poetry* (Syracuse, NY: Syracuse University Press, 1996), 67.

[26] James Joyce, *A Portrait of the Artist as a Young Man* (New York: B. W. Huebsch, 1916), 238.

cause, Michael Davitt thought her a British spy because of her English background, and she was not, as a woman, allowed to join groups like The Celtic Literary Society or The Contemporary Club. John O'Leary and Tim Harrington initially saw her value only in terms of publicity and propaganda. Because of this exclusion, female nationalists like Gonne and her group turned to performance in their nationalist work. Inghinidhe na hÉireann's theater both exploited and reclaimed traditional nationalist ideas of motherhood. Many of the actresses in their ranks, like the Allgood sisters, excelled at portraying cottage-bound Irish women while Gonne played larger-than-life magical nationalist icons.[27] Ella Young, a member of the group, describes Gonne reading *The Legend of Red Hugh* as the curtain rose for Milligan's 1901 play; Gonne was

> sitting in an ancient carved chair, with an illuminated parchment book on her knee. She had a splendid robe of brocaded white poplin with wide sleeves, and two little pages in medieval dress of black velvet held tall wax candles on either side of her. The stage was strewn with green rushes and branchlets of blossomed heather. Maud Gonne has a sun-radiance about her. The quality of her beauty dulled the candle flames.[28]

This curtain-raiser dramatizes tensions around Irishness, class, and gender. There is no claim to Irishness like an ancient one, and that throne-like "carved chair" and "splendid robe" are regal and assert both identity and authority. The only male figures onstage are "two little pages in medieval dress," so again we are in what Yeats would call the land of "the noble and the beggar man," an apocryphal ancient world, Orientalized by that Irish present of modernity and industrialization. Gonne knew how to make use of her classic image to claim a link to an essential female Irishness. The candles, the boys, and the rumored loss of her son would also suggest a link to the Virgin Mary, and the bringing of Irish vegetation inside blurred the lines, as Inghinidhe would do with props in later plays, between the natural outside world of Ireland and the stage. That heather and the boys suggested fertility and maternity as well as upper-class status, and the only power on the stage

---

[27] Further chapters will stress the typecasting that contributed to the Allgood sisters' relegation to cottage-bound female roles and their successful campaigns to be taken seriously in iconic roles.

[28] Margaret Ward, *Maud Gonne: A Life* (Ontario: n.p., 1990), 67.

is female. The 1902 *Cathleen*, performed a year later, would build on the power of these earlier images of Gonne commanding the stage in tableau.

Gonne and her group were adept at creating and performing iconic nationalist female figures onstage and on the Dublin streets, and all their changes to *Cathleen ni Houlihan* in 1902 led to more stillness, blurring the line between plays of action and tableau. The image Young describes above calls to mind Gonne's insistence on drawing attention to herself as Cathleen ni Houlihan by sitting after entering the cottage; Gonne rejected George Moore's suggestion that Cathleen walk around the house "which I think would have spoilt it."[29] After hearing this opinion from Gonne, Yeats wrote to Gregory, on March 22, confirming that, in his absence, Gonne's ideas would prevail:

> Moore writes to me, by the by, that...he wants Cathleen ny Hoolihan not to sit down...However I have told Miss Gonne, to whom I have sent Moore's letter to do as she likes. One must judge of these things on the stage. I shall go over and see for myself on Wednesday.[30]

A stationary Cathleen ni Houlihan, Gonne believed, would be more impressive to the audience and balance the final tableau of Delia and Bridget. Yeats's awareness of the importance of the scene's visual effect helped Gonne to influence the performance. She wrote to Yeats that "we have kept your stage directions to their own, not Moore's satisfaction."[31] Here, Gonne has convinced Yeats of her own idea for the stage and then reported to him that the stage directions will be to her and her groups' "satisfaction," using a royal "we" for Inghinidhe as was her habit.

The tension between female figures that Inghinidhe na hÉireann and Gonne brought to the stage in 1902 characterized not only Gonne's arrival in Stephens Green in 1918 but also Yeats's first memory of her. Yeats, as I discuss in the Introduction, described his first meeting with Gonne as a revelation: in his version of the January 1889 encounter, a powerful, otherworldly figure from outside descends on the Yeats home to pull him into the orbit of nationalist activities and unrequited love. This meeting previewed the scenes of 1902 onstage and 1918 in Stephens Green—in all three moments, a demanding female presence arrives to trouble those inside and

---

[29] Gonne, *The Gonne–Yeats Letters*, 151.   [30] Yeats, *Collected Letters*, Vol. II, 162.
[31] Gonne, *The Gonne–Yeats Letters*, 151.

claim a young man in contrast to the domestic female activity indoors, though in the Yeats home, a figure awaited upstairs with her own link to other worlds. In 1889, the divide between Gonne and the women in the Yeats home was striking. His industrious sisters, unimpressed with Gonne's airs, believed she came to convert him to her cause under the pretext of visiting John Butler Yeats, while Yeats's housebound mother waited upstairs, debilitated by depression years after losing a young son. Deirdre Toomey argues that Yeats imagined his mother's illness as a link to a fairy world in "Away," so her presence in another part of the house suggests an underlying link to powerful, troubled Irish maternity.

The day Gonne stopped in at the family home in 1889, Yeats referred to his housebound mother's illness to Tynan in a letter as if this was the normal state for the family: "She is as usual, that is to say feeble and unable to go out of doors or move about much."[32] Yeats's memories of meeting Gonne contrast her beauty with the ordinary domestic life of his own home and his own family secret, also based in the death of a child. His mother's debilitating illness was brought on in part by her own loss, of her three-year-old son, Robert, in 1873 as well as the financial stress of marriage to a portrait painter who struggled to complete commissions. Yeats wrote in his *Memoirs* about the way that Gonne, building on his earlier obsession with Laura Armstrong, symbolized for him a separate female identity from his mother: "it was natural to command myself by claiming a very public talent, for her beauty as I saw it in those days seemed incompatible with private, intimate life."[33] This memory separates life into two spheres—the "public" and the "private" or "intimate"—Yeats would divide the female figures and language in his play along the same lines. From the beginning of her friendship with Yeats, Gonne aligned herself with public performance, helping to bring his theater out of drawing rooms. The play betrayed Yeats's growing ambivalence about conflicting images of Irish motherhood; in 1918, the converting young girl of 1889 and the liberator of 1902 would be recast as threatening invader and sent away, though she was his old friend, compatriot, and landlord. Yeats and Gonne, after twenty-three years of wrestling with their roles in Irish political and dramatic circles, were reading from different scripts of the same play and focused on the survival of different maternal figures.

---

[32] W. B. Yeats, *The Letters of W. B. Yeats*, ed. Alan Wade (London: R. Hard-Davis, 1954), 107.
[33] W. B. Yeats, *Memoirs: An Autobiography—First Draft, Journal*, ed. Denis Donoghue (New York: Macmillan, 1974), 41.

Though Gonne would never play the title role, she and Yeats collaborated on *The Countess Cathleen* before more fruitfully working together on *Cathleen ni Houlihan*, and the earlier play began to divide female figures along the same lines dramatized in *Cathleen ni Houlihan*. Yeats claimed that Gonne requested the role of what was to be *The Countess Cathleen* as part of her public political activities: "She spoke to me of her wish for a play she could act in Dublin."[34] Immediately after that January 1889 meeting, Gonne and Yeats began dining together, discussing nationalist and artistic issues as well as the best way to dramatize *The Countess Cathleen*. Like *Cathleen ni Houlihan*, the earlier Cathleen play is driven by threatening outside forces. *The Countess Cathleen* takes place in an invaded cottage and a plundered Big House. Mary welcomes Cathleen, a returning countess, into her cottage, and her husband Shemus calls in merchants, supernatural like Cathleen ni Houlihan, but foreign and satanic; these outsiders also demand the souls of the inhabitants. This initial collaboration between Yeats and Gonne would remain unrequited because Gonne, finding the role of the countess too distant from her political work, refused to play the part in 1891. Out of this rejection, Yeats not only revised the play for forty-five years but also learned of her ideas about performance and successfully created another role for her. In the second Cathleen play, he cast Gonne as a supernatural version of Mother Ireland, one the young man chooses to follow, leaving the maternal inside of the cottage.

Central to both plays is the question: Who is the outsider, or the "stranger"? In both plays, Yeats and Gonne struggled to create versions of Irish nationalism that would include their own backgrounds, Anglo-Irish and British-born, respectively. Yeats's fears as a member of the declining Anglo-Irish class influenced *The Countess Cathleen*; the more successfully collaborative *Cathleen ni Houlihan* reveals his discomfort with nationalist orthodoxy, both celebrating and warning of a nationalism that devours all men without regard to their background. The foreign merchants of *The Countess Cathleen* invade the declining Big House to steal riches and souls. In *Cathleen ni Houlihan*, the powerful figure, now female, enters a cottage and not only disrupts the transfer of money for a wedding but also steals the family's promising young man. The plays reflect the dual fears of Yeats and Gonne, the first dramatizing anxiety about both foreign invasion of an increasingly mercantile Ireland and peasants overtaking a ruined

---

[34] Ibid.

Big House and the second about "strangers" in a colonial context. The "others" in the first play are Catholic peasants and foreign invaders, and the root of the evil is a focus on earthly goods. In the final scene of the first Cathleen play, the countess must choose between the demands of the supernatural and national—the sacrifice of her soul for the tenants—and the needs of Oona, her foster mother, who begs her not to deal with the merchants. Cathleen occupies a strange position in her connections to others: though Oona is her foster mother, Cathleen lacks familial ties except to the old house. Unlike the family in the cottage, this first Cathleen, like her successor, *Cathleen ni Houlihan*, is removed from family continuity, in a pattern that resurfaces in *Deirdre*. At the end of the play, maternal Oona mourns Cathleen's departure verbally and physically, a precursor to Delia and Bridget's sorrow: "[*casting herself face downwards on the floor*]. O Maker of all, protect her from the demons. And if a soul must be lost, take mine."[35] Inspired by Yeats's observations of Maud Gonne with her devoted French governess, Oona follows Cathleen to glorious death: "The years like black oxen tread the world, / And God the herdsman goads them on behind, / And I am broken by their passing feet."[36] (That Gonne's closest mother figures were governesses and maids points to the class differences between her and Yeats. Both were Anglo-Irish, but Gonne's family, like Laura Armstrong's, was financially more secure and could afford to hire governesses.) The first Cathleen play, like the 1902 performance of *Cathleen ni Houlihan*, ends with a mother figure left behind.

Yeats failed to write a role for Gonne in *The Countess Cathleen*, in part, because they separated after a collaborative beginning—a parting that was as shocking as their initial meeting to Yeats: "Suddenly she was called back to France...I stayed on in Ireland, probably at Sligo with my uncle, George Pollexfen, finishing *The Countess Cathleen* that had become the symbolical song of my pity."[37] Yeats was marvelously adept at ignoring increasing hints at Gonne's involvement with Lucien Millevoye, the right-wing French activist with whom she would have a son, Georges, who died in 1863, and then her daughter Iseult. The passive "was called back to France" reveals his desire not to wonder who did the calling. After discussing the play with Gonne and losing her to France, Yeats began to image her as a symbol, repeating the shift in his idea of Laura Armstrong five years earlier. The play also coincides with the years when Yeats was writing poems like "A Dream

---

[35]   Yeats, *Collected Works, Plays*, 93.   [36]   Ibid.   [37]   Yeats, *Memoirs*, 47.

of Death" in 1891, another misreading of Gonne that I discuss in Chapter 1, who, alive and well with her lover in France, responded with surprise when she received the poem.[38] At the end of *The Countess Cathleen* and in the poems of this time, Yeats imagines Gonne dead; the first play envisions her as a sacrifice though in the second the young man sacrifices himself to her. In her absence, along with writing her death into plays and poems, Yeats knitted the text and Gonne to his ideal Ireland of Sligo. The end to their initial collaboration and his return to Sligo explain the play's local setting and the inclusion of geographical symbols like Knocknarae and Maeve's cairn. Though Gonne refused the part of *The Countess Cathleen* in 1891, Yeats began, in a tug-of-war over her image that was to continue throughout their lives, to write their shared history more specifically into the play in spite of her decision to remove herself from the project.

The refusal jolted Yeats's idea of the part, contributing to his difficulties completing a version for the stage. Michael Sidnell comments on the play: "He becomes Kevin in the 1892 version and was Aleel in all later ones. However, under all three names the identity of the character is much transformed by the tribulations of the author's love for Maud Gonne, which were being written into the play almost as soon as they were felt in life."[39] Sidnell mentions this tendency, this need in Yeats to write his changing vision of Gonne, orchestrated by her, "into the play," but stops there; most scholarship on Gonne and *The Countess Cathleen* takes Yeats at his word that his "love" needs no examination or discussion. These changes to the young poet character, resulting from Gonne's rejection, would bring the play farther from the one she would act as Yeats began to collaborate more successfully with Florence Farr. And Farr would play Aleel, bending the genders of the roles in the play. Yeats continued to include his ideas of Gonne in the project even as she distanced herself from the role; as the Cornell editors note, her sickness in France coincided with the addition of Cathleen's need for rest.[40]

Though circumspect about reading biography into the play, Michael Sidnell does go on to trace changes in the political overtones of *The Countess Cathleen* drafts in relation to Maud Gonne's work against evictions. In 1897, Gonne advocated stealing as a morally sound choice for the starving in a

[38] Maud Gonne MacBride, *A Servant of the Queen* (London: Victor Gollancz, 1938), 147.
[39] Michael Sidnell, *The Countess Cathleen: Manuscript Materials* (Ithaca, NY: Cornell University Press, 1999), xlviii.
[40] Ibid., xlviv.

pamphlet distributed in Kerry. This position shocked Kerry residents, though she built her argument on memories of 1847 when people starved to death while ships full of food were anchored nearby in the harbor. Sidnell follows the trail of influence between Gonne, Yeats, and history:

> Probably Yeats had 1847 in mind when he first wrote the scene. Maud Gonne may have had *The Countess Cathleen* in mind when she addressed the peasants of Kerry. Yeats surely remembered the Maud Gonne of 1897 when he revised that play in later years. But whatever the relationship between Yeats's fictional heroine and Maud Gonne, Cathleen's speech and the pamphlet do indicate that Yeats's play was by no means so remote from ordinary life and topical events as has been suggested.[41]

Yeats likely remembered Gonne's work in Kerry while revising the first Cathleen play, and her leadership against evictions would certainly have influenced his ideas of both Cathleens. While Yeats worked to bring *The Countess Cathleen* to the Abbey stage in 1899, ten years after beginning the play for Gonne, she fought evictions in Mayo. Like Gonne, *The Countess Cathleen* dedicated herself to relief for the poor, claiming that "from this day on I'll have no sorrow of my own."[42] Yeats continued to revise the play to reflect their friendship, bringing his idea of Gonne and her actions into a project she had abandoned.

Yeats and Gonne would disagree in their memoirs about the history of creating *The Countess Cathleen*, and their different perspectives reflect their changing ideas about connections between art and nationalism. Two days after their first meeting in 1889, Yeats wrote to John O'Leary, in a letter full of his first impressions of Maud Gonne: "I have long been intending to write [a poetic drama] founded on 'Countess Cathleen O'Shea' in the folk lore book."[43] (He had been talking of writing a drama based on the story for a year but required meeting Gonne to begin.) Yeats remembered that he and Maud Gonne had discussed the project: "I told her of a story I had found when compiling my *Fair and Folktales of the Irish Peasantry*, and offered to write for her the play I have called *The Countess Cathleen*."[44] It is worth noting the difference between writing love poetry for Gonne, an important genre for Yeats, and writing plays for her to act. Gonne knew that the love poems helped her image as Yeats's love object and muse, but these poems

[41] Ibid., 176.   [42] Yeats, *Collected Works, Plays*, 93.
[43] Yeats, *Letters of W. B. Yeats*, 108.   [44] Yeats, *Memoirs*, 41.

are private utterances for public consumption. The plays bring her into the process of creating the text and the performance.

In the days after their first meeting, Yeats and Gonne met daily to discuss Ireland, nationalism, and art: "I think that I dined with her every day during her stay in London of perhaps nine days, and there was something so exuberant in her ways that it seemed natural she should give her hours in overflowing abundance...and she were now returning to Paris where their home was." These daily discussions ("I saw her day after day") pushed Yeats into what Foster calls "a ferment of writing" drafts of *The Countess Cathleen*, and this pattern is one familiar from his response to Laura Armstrong, a way that Yeats reacted to women throughout his life.[45] The dedication to the first edition stood as a reminder to Gonne of her role in the first days of writing the play: "I Dedicate this play to my friend Miss Maud Gonne At Whose Suggestion It Was Planned Out And Began Some Three Years Ago."[46] The mechanics of this form of credit are illustrative: Yeats credits her and uses her up to a point. The passive voice makes the creation of the play amorphous and asks us to examine what it means to suggest that a play be planned out and started. Also, as the play in revision drifted from any kind of nationalism that Gonne would support and became embroiled in class issues and sectarianism, Yeats used the dedication as a reminder to Gonne, readers, and audiences that the play had started with nationalist and feminist credentials to bring Maud Gonne in as a "planner" of the play who suggested the idea aligns the play with early forms of nationalism despite the controversy over its portrayals of Catholic people and the Countess. Yeats, in this dedication, makes a rhetorical move we see repeated throughout his career: he acknowledges the role of a woman, usually a performer, often a more fervent nationalist, in the creation of a play. That literary history has taken its time hearing these hints has much to do with the systemic ways that we think about authorship. Men in Ireland at this time were usually the ones credited with writing the texts, but women, from Lady Gregory to Maud Gonne to the printing work of the Yeats sisters, had much to do with how those texts reached both stage and printing houses. Though my focus is on Gonne's contributions and performance, it is worth repeating that Lady Gregory, as James Pethica has shown, wrote the lion's share of *Cathleen ni Houlihan*. The fact that Yeats did not see these women, due to their gender, as a threat to his authorship means that he made these offhand comments

[45] Ibid.   [46] Yeats, *Collected Works, Plays*, 57.

often. By "muse," he often meant co-author, performer, and source of inspiration. And if Yeats used Gonne, she used him too; this planning out of the play was an attempt to turn his infatuation into a vehicle for her self-image and hopes for a role in Irish politics.

While Yeats remembered the play's inception as a collaborative few weeks with Gonne, she distanced herself from *The Countess Cathleen* in her autobiography. Gonne's explanation of refusing the part reveals her idea of performance as necessarily tied to politics and of acting as embodying a part. Though Gonne would later decide that the role was too separate from her political work, Yeats tried to write her ideas on identity into the role of the Countess. The audience is introduced to the Countess in terms of her ability to experience for others; Oona comments that "Sorrows she's but read of in a book, / Weigh on her mind as if they had been her own."[47] This description circumvents questions of voice and identity through art; the Countess, an absentee landlord, is as affected by stories of the poor as though she had experienced them. The Countess is not only a perfect reader—she is an ideal actor. Yeats stresses the importance of theater and spoken poetry, emphasizing Gonne's ability to transform the solitary act of reading into empathy and action, tools of the actor's trade. In this version of Gonne's position in Ireland, her social status has no effect on her ability to sympathize with the poor. Gonne's idea of embodying personas rather than performing parts finds expression in the first role that Yeats wrote for her. These ideas would allow her to transform herself into *Cathleen ni Houlihan* for the 1902 Abbey audience eleven years after refusing the first Cathleen role.

As the version of Irish female heroism in *The Countess Cathleen* and her own image diverged, Gonne revised her role in the story of the play's inception, claiming that Yeats presented her with a completed work and interrupted her political activities with the women of Inghinidhe na hÉireann. She recalled, in her autobiography, that during "one of our late nights in my rooms over Morrow's Library" with Inghinidhe na hÉireann members Alice Milligan and Anna Johnson, editors of The Shan Von Voght and future collaborators on the 1902 *Cathleen ni Houlihan*,

Willie Yeats had read his play, *The Countess Cathleen*; he wanted it produced in Dublin and he wanted me to play in it. He said that he had written the part of the Countess Cathleen for me and I must act in it. I was

[47] Ibid., 32.

severely tempted for the play fascinated me and I loved acting, but just because I loved the stage so much, I had made the stern resolve never to act. I was afraid it would absorb me too much to the detriment of my work. I knew my own weakness, and how, when I first got interested in anything, I was capable of forgetting everything else, – house-building, evicted tenants, political prisoners, even the fight against the British Empire, might all disappear in the glory of the stage; it was the only form of self-discipline I consciously practiced.[48]

Here, "acting" is not part of what she calls her "work" but would take her energies away from her political projects. The reasons Gonne gives for her refusal to act show her attempt to write herself out of the first Cathleen play and into the history of the play she did choose, as her work on the second Cathleen follows in her autobiography. Though she attempts to contrast the two plays, the memory of one brings up the other in *A Servant of the Queen*. In an effort to clarify her role in Irish history as primarily political rather than artistic, she downplays her work in formal theater in her autobiography. She prefers instead to dwell on the lectures and more visual, populist approaches to theater like tableaux vivants and magic lantern shows she produced with Inghinidhe na hÉireann. Though she would include her early interest in theater in her autobiography, Gonne does not mention her contributions to the first version of *The Countess Cathleen* in *A Servant of the Queen*.

Gonne strategically claims that she refused *The Countess Cathleen* because her political work took precedent, but her role in *Cathleen ni Houlihan* clearly fulfilled her definition of theater as activism, as a means to a political end. In *A Servant of the Queen*, Gonne explains the exception she made both in agreeing to act as Cathleen ni Houlihan and in teaching theater to Inghinidhe students. She refused to act in plays that could be differentiated from political activities like advocacy for "house-building, evicted tenants, political prisoners, even the fight against the British Empire" (SQ 176). Her idea of *Cathleen ni Houlihan*, then, differed from Yeats's in that she saw the play as part of a larger project of political activism, and the changes that she and the other producers and actors made incorporated aspects of street theater into the 1902 production. Indeed, her insistence on changing the play so that the title character stands still in the doorway would have reminded the audience of Gonne as a speaker in front of a nationalist

[48] Maud Gonne, *The Autobiography of Maud Gonne: A Servant of the Queen*, ed. A Norman Jeffares and Anna MacBride White (Chicago, IL: University of Chicago Press, 1995), 176.

crowd and as a figure blocking evictions in the doorways of Mayo in 1898, a moment covered extensively by the nationalist press.

When she discusses drama in her autobiography, Gonne dwells on the political and historical moment; her most detailed description of Inghinidhe na hÉireann's magic lantern shows begins with a cursory summary of the pictures only to introduce an extensive description of police brutality during Queen Victoria's royal visit:

> I had obtained a window in the National Club in Parnell Square from which, on a huge screen, Pat O'Brien's photos of the Eviction scenes could be shown and the photos of the men who, during Victoria's reign, had been executed or died in prison... I fancy that, taken by surprise at the demonstration in Dame Street and summoned from all quarters to cope with it, the police had never noticed the magic lantern show and now, patrolling the city, had suddenly discovered it and had made a wild baton charge on the few harmless women and children who were still looking at it.[49]

Gonne does not separate the dramatic work of Inghinidhe na hÉireann from political activism and unrest. Her understanding of the political potential of these populist forms of street theater had evolved in the nine years between meeting Yeats and requesting a role in one of his plays and 1889, the year of the magic lantern shows described above for The Jubilee Riots and the beginning of Inghinidhe. And the use of "wild" for the police neatly switches the colonial narrative of the "wild Irish," while the "harmless women and children" in the audience become the victims, attacked by the police who had finally noticed the political activism performed under their noses.

Gonne set out to embody and become the role of Cathleen ni Houlihan rather than perform the part, and perhaps this is why she does not include the 1902 performance or her political street theater in her vow to avoid acting quoted above. An excerpt from a letter Gonne wrote to Yeats in 1902 while preparing to perform as Cathleen shows her pride in becoming Mother Ireland; she not only played the part but set out to merge her own identity with the role. Informing Yeats of her costume choices, she wrote:

> Tomorrow Sunday is the first dress rehearsal. I have a beautiful untidy grey wig, a torn grey flannel dress exactly like the old women wear in the west,

---

[49] Ibid., 218.

bare feet & a big blue hooded cloak. You would give me a penny on the street if you saw me & I look 60 at least. Let me know when you are coming over.[50]

This excerpt from the letter repeats a common tendency in the Revival theater world to bring documentary artifacts to the stage in an effort prove identity. In fact, this habit showed the insecurity surrounding identity and Irishness on the Irish stage especially among the Ascendancy directors, performers, and writers. The irony of the woman known for her beautiful wardrobe taking on the identity of an "old woman" of the West is not lost on Gonne, and she feels no concern about appropriating a role not hers. Instead, she congratulates herself on becoming this new identity. And her final sentence is vintage Gonne; rather than invite Yeats, she demands that he let her know in advance when he arrives. She requests his presence so that he can come to her house to see her development of the role through costume.

After deciding to play the role of Cathleen ni Houlihan in the winter of 1902 (Figure 2.2), Gonne immediately took over the part and began to make changes both to the role and the production as a whole to reflect her theatrical and political needs. Fay remembered working with Gonne and Inghinidhe na hÉireann: "It was under the auspices of Miss Gonne's society that our performance was formally given."[51] Gonne's tone in a letter to Yeats of February 1902 reflects her effort to control the production:

Did you write him [Fay] that I would act the part of Cathleen? Have you got another copy that you could let me as I would like to learn the words here & then go over them with you in London... Easter I think would be the best time for the plays but I will write Fay as soon as I hear from you – What have you arranged with him.[52]

She informs Yeats of her detailed ideas for her costume ("I think I had better wear a long black dress") and dictates the time of their meetings: "If it is convenient for you I will come to see you about *4 on Thursday afternoon* & we can go over Cathleen ni Houlihan together."[53] Her language is consistent;

---

[50] Gonne, *The Gonne–Yeats Letters*, 152.
[51] William George Fay and Catherine MacFarlane Carswell, *The Fays of the Abbey Theatre: An Autobiographical Record* (London: Rich and Cowan, 1935), 119.
[52] Ibid., 147–8.   [53] Ibid., 107.

Figure 2.2 Maud Gonne as Cathleen ni Houlihan in the April 2, 1902 premier of that play at St. Theresa's Hall, Clarendon Street, Dublin
Source: Courtesy of the Abbey Theatre Archive.

she never asks for advice on the role. On the contrary, she claims ownership, and her goal in going over the play with Yeats is to further influence his idea of the production and the text. She insists that the play be performed on Easter in an effort to control the work's symbolism and emotional force. A professional lecturer who specialized in employing nationalist symbolism, Gonne requested the Easter date for the premier in hopes of building the play into Republican folk history and, perhaps, to align the story with another that tells of a lost son and renewed hope. Though not a countess, Gonne was independently wealthy and enjoyed freedom of movement at this time that Yeats, a much poorer artist, did not, and her class position comes out in these letters. Yeats chose a woman above him in social class, as he would when he wrote about both Armstrong and the Gore Booth sisters, and Gonne's social position and unconventional upbringing gave her the tone she uses in the letters to him. In these early works, as with Armstrong, Yeats needs a woman who will challenge his perceptions before he can begin and to push him to revise.

In 1918, Gonne would test this ability to pass as an actual elderly Irishwoman in her effort to escape the authorities and re-enter Dublin. Though she succeeded in deceiving the border guards, her 1918 performance at the doorway in Stephens Green did not gain the hoped-for response from Yeats. Gonne had refused to play his Countess Cathleen in 1891; Yeats would reject the role of sacrificial young man in her re-enactment of *Cathleen ni Houlihan* in 1918.

An excerpt from *A Servant of the Queen* reveals Gonne's early propensity for becoming not only an iconic liberator but also the figure of innocent Irish femininity, as always, in the name of a political cause. Visiting Russia in 1887 as a spy for Millevoye, her performance of Irish female identity allowed her to overtake a rival Russian emissary also attempting to reach the Tsar:

> I also found that my difficulties were beginning because the obliging officials had reserved a special carriage for me and the Russian, and before the train was out of the station he was on his knees telling me of his great joy in meeting such a beautiful and wonderful lady. I had my revolver in my pocket, but the young Russian was altogether too nice and sympathetic for me to wish to do anything so rude as to produce it. Instead I took his hand and told him I too was happy to meet a Russian like him, who, I felt, could understand an Irish girl; that I had always believed that Russians were understanding people and not like others, Englishmen or Frenchmen, who looked on women in a vulgar way; that in my country the women were very free because friendship between men and women should be beautiful and not commonplace. The appeal to national honor worked.[54]

So, apparently, did Gonne's assumption of the role of innocent "Irish girl"; she based her "appeal to national honor" on stereotypes, and a virginal and independent idea of femininity distinguishes this claim to female Irishness from the more iconic figures she would later personify. Her use of the "Irish girl" to save herself from a dangerous situation shows her Irishness as an attribute to be claimed and cultivated.

Gonne would even more successfully perform the other side of the innocent "Irish girl" when she personified the woman of the Sidhe in Donegal and Mayo. Her language is striking as she remembers embodying the supernatural female avenger in various campaigns against landlords: "In Donegal, being the woman of the Sidhe had helped me to put evicted families back in their homes and release prisoners. I hoped that being the woman of the prophecies in Mayo would help me to stop the famine."[55] As she would in the 1902 production of *Cathleen ni Houlihan*, she saw herself not as playing a role in these campaigns but as actually becoming the iconic

---

[54] Gonne, *A Servant of the Queen*, 79.   [55] Ibid., 253.

characters. Blurring the line between the material and the imaginary allowed the wealthy, English-born Gonne to claim representation of the Irish poor. This personification of supernatural female Ireland was so important to Gonne that she began her autobiography with a vision she saw after working with the Mayo poor in 1899, two years before Yeats and Lady Gregory wrote *Cathleen ni Houlihan*: "Then I saw a tall, beautiful woman with dark hair blown on the wind and I knew it was Cathleen ni Houlihan."[56] Her image of Cathleen ni Houlihan as a figure she could embody would influence Yeats's idea of the character and push her to accept the role, a part she could take on as she "became" the woman of the Sidhe in her political work.

Yeats's response to Gonne's performance is telling, revealing tensions around ownership and representation and re-claiming Gonne as an object of beauty. The contrast between Gonne's youthful stature and realistic make-up delighted Yeats, dramatizing the mythic and the real on one stage:

> Miss Maud Gonne played very finely, and her great height made Cathleen seem a fine being fallen into our mortal infirmity. Since then the part has been twice played in America by women who insisted on keeping their young faces, and one of these when she came to the door dropped her cloak, as I have been told, and showed a white satin dress embroidered with shamrocks... The most beautiful woman of our time, when she played my Cathleen, 'made up' centuries old, and never should the part be played but with a like sincerity.[57]

Yeats's "my" does protest too much after identifying Gonne so strongly with the role. Gonne's interpretation influenced Yeats's idea both of her role and of the larger structure of the play. This quotation shows the effect of Gonne's interpretation of the performance on his idea of theater: his thoughts on the face of the main character preview his interest not only in realism but in masked theater as well. Gonne's interpretation of the role was an embodiment not a performance; playgoers like Joseph Holloway found the "creepy realism" of her Cathleen unnerving.[58] The renowned beauty hiding underneath the façade was both fascinating and disturbing to audiences.

---

[56] Ibid., 9.

[57] Qtd. in Jeffares and Knowland, *Commentary on the Plays of W. B. Yeats*, 29–30.

[58] Joseph Holloway, *Joseph Holloway's Abbey Theatre: A Selection from His Unpublished Journal: Impressions of a Dublin Play-Goer*, ed. Robert Hogan and Michael J. O'Neill (Carbondale: Southern Illinois University Press; London: Feffer & Simmons, 1967), 17.

Reflecting Gonne's effort to become the role, most audience members and critics, like the writer for *The All Ireland Review*, saw the part as a simple extension of Gonne's political activities:

> Miss Gonne, as Cathleen ni Houlihan, cannot be considered as an actress in the sense of a person who produces a certain effect by means of an illusion in portraying the character created by the author... No hiding personality, it was just Maud Gonne the well-known Nationalist agitator, addressing not the actors, as is usual in a drama, but the audience, speaking to them just as she might in Beresford Place or Phoenix Park, the only difference was that the words were not her own.[59]

The reviewer echoes Gonne's take on theater, interpreting her acting as part of her political work lecturing, setting up magic lantern shows, and performing tableaux vivants. He links her performance with specific moments from her political history and redefines what it means to be an actress on the Abbey stage.

Playgoers in 1902 began an oral tradition about the part as played by Gonne; Shaw commented "When I see that play I feel it might lead a man to do something foolish,"[60] and Fay equated the role with the person: "As president of Inghinidhe na hÉireann, Miss Gonne was in fact what Cathleen ni Houlihan was in symbol. Never again will there be such a splendid Cathleen as she."[61] Stephen Gwynn found the way that Gonne blurred the line between performance and personification in her role as Cathleen disquieting:

> The effect of Cathleen ni Houlihan on me was that I went home asking myself if such plays should be produced unless one was prepared for people to go out to shoot and be shot. Yeats was not alone responsible; no doubt but Lady Gregory had helped him to get all the peasant speech so perfect; but above all Miss Gonne's impersonation had stirred the audience as I have never seen another audience stirred.[62]

Gwynn's account stresses the importance of Gonne's interpretation of the title role and the effect of her performance, or as he calls it, "impersonation"

---

[59] Qtd. in Paige Reynolds, *Modernism, Drama, and the Audience for Irish Spectacle* (Cambridge: Cambridge University Press, 2007), 27.

[60] Lady Augusta Gregory, *Seventy Years* (Gerrard's Cross: Colin Smythe, 1970), 444.

[61] Fay and MacFarlane Carswell, *Fays of the Abbey Theatre*, 113.

[62] David B. Ross, *Critical Companion to W. B. Yeats* (New York: Facts on File, 2009), 148.

on the audience. He stresses the collaborative work that led to the production and argues for Gonne's contribution to the play's impact. These reviews perform a strange absolution, arguing that the male audience is as blameless as the man who is hypnotically led to his death and to violent sacrifice by Gonne's Cathleen. This response shows that Gonne had gained control of the message from the stage. The play has had the effect she worked for, and her experience with nationalist street theater contributed to a Cathleen that blurs the line between politics and drama and incites the violent response that Gonne supported.

Máire Nic Shiubhlaigh remembered Gonne's uncanny ability to live the part of Cathleen onstage in her memoirs, *The Splendid Years*. Nic Shiubhlaigh's memories of Gonne's performance emphasize both Gonne's success in becoming the role and the contrast between her beauty and evocation of an old woman:

> How many who were there that night will forget the Cathleen ni Houlihan of Maud Gonne, her rich golden hair, willow-like figure, pale sensitive face, and burning eyes, as she spoke the closing lines of the Old Woman turning out through the cottage door...Watching her, one could readily under- stand the reputation she enjoyed as the most beautiful woman in Ireland, the inspiration of the whole revolutionary movement. She was the most exquisitely fashioned creature I have ever seen. Her beauty was *startling*. Yeats wrote *Cathleen ni Houlihan* especially for her, and there were few in the audience who did not see why. In her, the youth of the country saw all that was magnificent in Ireland. She was the very personification of the figure she played onstage.[63]

Gonne brought her public role as political activist to the part and melded, in the mind of the audience, her work outside of the theater with her realization of the role. A member of Inghinidhe na hÉireann, Máire Nic Shiubhlaigh played Delia Cahill in the April 1902 production; as one of the domestic women in the cottage, she likely took part in the decision to change the blocking at the play's final scene. One of the women who collaborated with Gonne, Nic Shiubhlaigh's memory of the performance reveals a goal of the production in keeping with Gonne's idea of theater as political. The women of Inghinidhe na hÉireann, as they had in Milligan's play, worked to create

---

[63] Máire Nic Shiubhlaigh, *The Splendid Years* (Dublin: James Duffy, 2016), 19.

this impression of Gonne as the embodiment of the role, the actual woman, and the inspiration for political action all at once. Two years later, Nic Shiubhlaigh played the title role, and her memory of taking on the part proves Gonne's lasting effect on the play:

> That night I played *Cathleen ni Houlihan* for the first time. This made the occasion doubly memorable for me. I suppose every player has a favourite part. This was mine. From the very first appearance of the company in 1902, I had hoped that I would some day appear as the Poor Old Woman in Yeats's play. People have said that through the years my playing of that part has been creditable, but I would like it known that every time I have played Cathleen I have modeled my performance on the one given originally by Maud Gonne. Although I have seen many actresses play Cathleen since, I have yet to know of a performance which surpassed hers in the little stage in St. Theresa's Hall.[64]

Nic Shiubhlaigh attempts to play the role as Gonne did because she sees Cathleen ni Houlihan not as a fictional character but as a mythic figure who was also Maud Gonne. Gonne's interpretation of the role as a persona to become not just to perform affected the blocking, speech patterns, and costume for the role for years to come. Nic Shiubhlaigh's memory also shows how performance history affects the way plays come down to us through the years and argues that this play is inseparable from its premier in 1902.

Both Yeats and Gonne would not only remember their work on *The Countess Cathleen* differently; they would also revise their roles in the premier and writing of *Cathleen ni Houlihan*. As Yeats's appeal to the audience as "the author of Cathleen ni Houlihan" during the Playboy Riots five years later attests, much was at stake in the ownership of the 1902 production. The play could help Yeats's nationalist credentials when audiences began to react against what they saw as the Abbey's elitism, but the call to sacrifice in the play also alarmed Yeats, and he would wonder, thirty-seven years later in the last year of his life, "Did that play of mine send out / Certain men the English shot?"[65]

---

[64] Ibid., 60.
[65] W. B. Yeats, *Poems* (London: Fisher Unwin, 1899), 392. The conversation is not over; Paul Muldoon deflates Yeats's attempt to take credit along with guilt for the Easter Rising by answering, nearly fifty years after Yeats posed the question, "certainly not / If Yeats had saved his pencil lead, / Would certain men have stayed in bed?" Paul Muldoon's tone in the poem, "7 Middagh Street," from *Meeting the British* (Winston-Salem, NC: Wake Forest University Press,

Gonne would try to control the play after the 1902 production while Yeats worked to reclaim *Cathleen ni Houlihan* from her more Republican interpretation; she played the part again in October and November of 1902. The argument over control of the play had everything to do with the changing politics of Yeats, Gonne, and Fay. A threatening letter Gonne wrote in September 1903, as she and Yeats disagreed about Synge's *In the Shadow of the Glen*, illustrates the tension surrounding ownership of the part:

> As for playing *Cathleen*. It is published, there is no copyright, any society has the right to play it *besides* you gave it to me for the use of any of the National Societies & particularly said it might be played by any of them & was not to be considered Fay's particular property. With Miss Quinn & Diggs & Conally and another girl whose name I can't remember just now but who I know acts well. I think it will be quite completely played but enough of all this.[66]

In this passage, Gonne does not ask for permission, but claims the part as hers to give, belonging to her as well as any other actor or theater groups interested in performing the piece. The "you gave it to me" suggests that she believes that Yeats has relinquished all ownership of the play and performances. The letter shows Gonne's belief that plays belong to actors not authors, an idea that reflects her experience collaborating with Inghinidhe na hÉireann on street performances that would not be credited with specific authors. And "enough of all this" attempts to finish the argument in her favor; the play is hers and can be acted, she believes, for the political ends of the performers.

Though she would re-assert control over the play as it suited her political ends, Gonne appealed to Yeats on the future of the part when she wanted to pass it on to another actor. The tone of the 1903 letter sounds like a parent consulting a spouse about a child, reminding us that Gonne and Yeats, like Gregory and Yeats, referred to their work together as children:[67]

1987), reveals frustration with Yeats's attempt to insert himself into the history of the Rising when the poet, during Easter Week 1916, was comfortably ensconced in the Cotswolds. What the poetic argument across a century misses is the role of women, Gregory, Gonne, and the Inghinidhe performers, in the creation of that play that inspired the audience, perhaps, to violence.

[66] Gonne, *The Gonne–Yeats Letters*, 175.

[67] For their correspondence referring to Yeats's poems as their children, see Gonne, *The Gonne–Yeats Letters*, 302.

Miss Quinn writes to ask me if I will let her understudy & if necessary play Cathleen ni Houlihan. She says she doesn't think she would be let do it unless you & I agreed. As far as I am concerned I am delighted she should because I can't possibly act often. 1st because I am away from Dublin and 2nd because I don't want to get too much in the habit of acting it wouldn't do good for my work.[68]

Though ostensibly preparing to pass along the part, Gonne retains some control; she has both chosen a successor and decided when to give up mastery of the play. A year after the production, she began to see *Cathleen ni Houlihan* as separate from her political work and reverted to her earlier opinion that theater impinged on her activism, a convenient argument that she had used rejecting the role of *The Countess Cathleen* twelve years earlier, though her distance from theater only encompassed actual stage performance. Every one of her speeches and organized demonstrations was theatrical, with shades of the earlier Cathleens. She welcomed the chance to pass on the part for the stage but maintained a connection between herself and the image of *Cathleen ni Houlihan*; it had been useful to her in the past and would be again in the future.

A year after the production, Yeats tried to distance himself from the play's radical politics, citing the dream source of the plot and the collaborative nature of the project. Though both Yeats and Gonne had pursued Republican politics at the turn of the century, Yeats's ideas about issues like the use of force were already changing while Gonne became increasingly dedicated to hardline Republicanism. As their views changed, they revised each other and their collaborative project, *Cathleen ni Houlihan*. Gonne and Inghinidhe na hÉireann had made the 1902 production a call to arms that also demanded that the audience appreciate the cost of sacrifice. In 1903, Yeats would try to reclaim control of *Cathleen ni Houlihan*, a figure created out of collaboration that had come to signify an Irish identity he no longer wholeheartedly supported:

I am a Nationalist, and certain of my intimate friends have made Irish politics the business of their lives, and this made certain thoughts habitual with me, and an accident made these thoughts take fire in such a way that I could give them dramatic expression. I had a very vivid dream one night,

---

[68] Ibid., 161.

and I made Cathleen ni Houlihan out of this dream. But if some external necessity had forced me to write nothing but drama with an obviously patriotic intention, instead of letting my work shape itself under the casual impulses of dreams and daily thoughts, I would have lost, in a short time, the power to write movingly upon any theme. I could have aroused opinion, but I could not have touched the heart.[69]

Dividing the audience's response along the lines of "opinion" and "heart," Yeats again separates the public and the private, the interior and the exterior. He gives his "intimate friends" much responsibility in influencing his ideas on the play, from its inception to the performance and tries to walk a fine line, restating his nationalist allegiances while holding his dream and the influences of others accountable for the more radical aspects of the play. Research does show that "I made Cathleen ni Houlihan out of that dream" represents a collaborative effort as solitary, as if he fashioned his dream into the play without Lady Gregory writing most of the dialogue and Gonne and Inghinidhe revising the stage directions. He argues above that the best art is not written solely with patriotic intentions, and it is this definition of art as separate from politics that resulted in disagreements with Gonne.

Cathleen ni Houlihan not only came out of Yeats's struggle to imagine Gonne as the Countess Cathleen, but also resulted from collaborations with a diverse group of artists and nationalists. The figure of Cathleen was created not by Yeats alone, but by Gregory, Yeats, Gonne, the Fays, and the other Inghinidhe na hÉireann women who produced the influential 1902 production, a premier that continues to sway interpretations of the play. From its inception, Cathleen ni Houlihan was a product of collaboration, rooted in Yeats's discussions with Gonne about The Countess Cathleen and bringing the imagined Irelands of Lady Gregory, Yeats, Gonne, and the Inghinidhe na hÉireann performers onto the stage in 1902.

James Pethica has established Lady Gregory's important contributions to the written dialogue in Cathleen ni Houlihan. Another collaborator, Maud Gonne, also deserves attention for her contributions to the play not simply as Yeats's love object. Remembering the 1902 Cathleen ni Houlihan, Yeats emphasized Gonne's role because of the success of her production after their thwarted collaboration on The Countess Cathleen. Gonne took over control of the 1902 premier after Yeats created the script with Lady Gregory. Yeats's

---

[69] W. B. Yeats, *Explorations* (New York: Macmillan, 1962), 116.

letters to Gregory in the spring of 1902 bear this out; he tells her that Gonne's ideas of the staging should prevail—Gonne must be allowed to "do as she likes."[70] Though Yeats often remembered Gonne's performative work on the production, critics have focused on Gregory's written collaboration. The different ways of speaking in the play came from Gregory's idea of local speech, the ballad tradition, and the imagery of Yeats's love poetry for Gonne, while the stark physical language of the play in performance grew out of Inghinidhe na hÉireann's political theater.

Correspondence between Yeats and Gonne, even after the 1902 performance, shows Gonne convinced that she remains an important partner in the theater venture until the September 1903 split over the portrayal of women in Synge's *In the Shadow of the Glen*. As one of three Vice Presidents of the Irish National Theatre Society, she considered *Cathleen ni Houlihan* as part of her early nationalist work with Yeats on book distribution, the 1798 Celebrations, and the Castle of the Heroes. She freely offered her advice on Russell's *Deirdre*, which would share billing with *Cathleen ni Houlihan*: "The last act goes very well. The dresses and scenery are very good. Let me know when you are coming over."[71] After Yeats sent her *In the Seven Woods*, she counseled him on the ending of the play, *On Baile's Strand*, that appeared in the volume. Again, she proved sensitive to staging final scenes: "The Cuchulain play is very much improved since I heard it, but I can't help regretting one of the previous endings, when the body of the young man was brought in, & Cuchulain recognized him as he lay dying. This ending is more original but less strong I think."[72] She goes onto advise him that if he writes a nationalist play with Gregory, he should "sign it" to help his reputation as a nationalist. Gonne remained interested both in Yeats's work and in his public image after the 1902 production, and though their political commitments pulled them in increasingly different directions, they continued to work together in creating art for the stage even as their ideas of nationalism and female roles diverged.

Writing from Paris in January 1914 after receiving a copy of Gregory's *Our Irish Theatre*, Gonne attempts a casual last word on who is responsible for the play and makes sure that Yeats knows she could correct the record if she chose. (The "Our" must have rankled; by "our," Yeats and Gregory did not mean a theater belonging to all but to a theater managed by the

---

[70] W. B. Yeats, *The Collected Letters of W. B. Yeats*, Vol. III, 1901–1904, ed. John Kelly and Ronald Schuchard (Oxford: Clarendon Press, 1994), 162.
[71] Gonne, *The Gonne–Yeats Letters*, 151.   [72] Ibid., 175.

directors, and there was not a place for Gonne in that version of the founding.) In tossing off a claim that she does not care who gets credit for the play, Gonne asserts ownership:

> I received a letter asking me if I wouldn't like to have the real facts about Inghinidhe na hÉireann's connection with the starting of Irish plays & Samhain festivals & with the 1st performance of Cathleen ni Houlihan made public, I replied I did not think it worth while. I have never minded other people taking credit for my work why should I this time? – but I must say I was amused when I remembered how I engaged Fay for Inghinidhe na hÉireann to stage & produce for those first performances & Russell painted most of the scenery, that Lady Gregory thought it worth while to mention the small cheque she sent to Russell *some time* after, when they had the Camden St Hall – She was not I think once on our committee at that time but as far as I am concerned I don't mind & refused to give the facts for publication.[73]

Gonne claims to approach theater and political work, the founding of this now seminal play and the Irish dramatic movement, as a project with many authors. She wants to believe that authorship and ownership are not important and that she has an anti-colonial idea of who claims the beginning and the production, that this was a group effort. At the same time, she lays a very clear claim, one against Gregory's version of events, and one that reminds Yeats about her financial power then and now and her monetary claim on the production especially against Gregory. Though she reports her decision not to publicize this version of history—what she calls "the facts"—the letter contains a not-so-veiled threat. She is being approached; her public wants "the real facts," and at any moment, she could correct the record about whose play this is. Throughout the history of their friendship, Gonne and Yeats would argue like this about authorship, female performance, and nationalism, rewriting and performing the tensions in that 1902 production again and again, like the ghost love affair in the background lantern show productions in Yeats's 1938 play, *Purgatory*. In that night of November 1918, Gonne appealed to Yeats on the grounds of her own maternal status: "It is monstrous to refuse me to return to my home...Wherever I am, I must have Iseult and Seagan with me."[74] Rival versions of Irish motherhood animate the decades of disagreements and collaborations between Yeats and Gonne.

---

[73] Ibid., 336.   [74] Ibid., 399.

3

My Pegeen Mike

Ownership and Performance in *The Playboy*

John Synge wrote his relationship with Molly Allgood into drafts of *The Playboy of the Western World*, revised to reflect their partnership and her suggestions, and then rewrote after watching her rehearsals and performance and discussing the text. The tensions in their relationship reflected the limitations of their society as their engagement transgressed social bounds: Synge was of the landed Anglo-Irish aristocracy and Molly Allgood came from a struggling working-class Dublin tenement family on the edge of poverty. She was raised a practicing Catholic by her mother in secret though her father was Protestant. The 1907 production of *The Playboy of the Western World* shows how one version of a play in process reached the stage, and the over one hundred years since that premier have produced countless descriptions and critical assessments, but Synge's fiancée Molly Allgood's role creating a play about two artists limited by their surrounding culture requires more discussion. This is a play about collaboration and role-playing in a community that is desperate for change while fearfully policing its residents. In the following two chapters, I use the archival and theoretical sources that remain to us to build an argument for Molly Allgood as a serious artist whose contributions to the two most important characters and plays of Synge's oeuvre are overdue for critical assessment.[1]

---

[1] Molly Allgood received some recent fictional treatment in Joseph O'Connor's historical novel *Ghost Light*, published in 2010. O'Connor re-imagines the creation of Synge's later plays, the relationship between Synge and Molly, and Molly's old age and demise in a work of historical fiction, told from Molly's point of view. Leszek Drong's "Mnemofictions: Rewriting the Past in *Ghost Light* by Joseph O'Connor" argues that in the absence of Molly's side of the correspondence, "history is powerless to tell us the whole truth about their relationship. We are left with fiction and the truth(s) it has to offer." Though the "whole truth" of the past and of a story like Molly's is, of course, always out of the reach of the contemporary moment, archival and textual evidence does prove Molly Allgood's significant influence on the drafts of *The Playboy* as Synge built and revised not only Pegeen but the dynamic between the two main characters through discussions with Molly. O'Connor writes of *The Playboy*: "A lovechild in a country of murderous pieties, its unrecognised second parent is Molly Allgood." Refocusing the lens on the impact of Molly on the text and performance show that *The Playboy of the Western*

Gender, Performance, and Authorship at the Abbey Theatre. Elizabeth Brewer Redwine, Oxford University Press (2021). © Elizabeth Brewer Redwine. DOI: 10.1093/oso/9780192896346.003.0003

Molly Allgood's looks, unfortunately, have been a focus of much writing about her relationship with Synge, rather than her power as an actor and contributor to scripts of the Revival. Following the lead of her contemporaries, many recent writers also use class-based language to describe her work on the stage and her relationship with Synge. In his canonical 2000 biography, *Fool of the Family: A Life of J. M. Synge*, W. J. McCormack, echoing Elizabeth Coxhead, introduces Molly Allgood and the sole chapter devoted to her relationship with Synge in these words:

> Hers was a heartbreaking prettiness more dangerous than classical beauty, and she had a combination of virginal Irish innocence and strong 'come-hither' well calculated to drive men mad.[2]

McCormack defines Molly in a seminal biography of the playwright strictly by the level and kind of her attraction to men, using language from Elizabeth Coxhead's 1965 *Daughters of Erin* without attempting to update Coxhead's description. The phrase "virginal Irish innocence" brings her sexual experience or supposed lack thereof into the discussion, and her looks are "dangerous" and threatening.

How did the Allgoods' very real financial needs dovetail with their political and dramatic ambitions? This is a thread I will follow into the Epilogue on Sara Allgood and American film. For women born into a large Dublin tenement family, becoming a writer was out of the question. Their creativity and art came out in the form of theater, but this does not mean that they had no role in creating and, in some cases, co-writing many of the plays. What many critics have described as "an element of calculation" that pushed Molly and Sara Allgood to "theatre (as) a way out of the unhappy domestic mess of the Allgood family" was, in fact, as Anthony Roche and Adrian Frazier have discussed, theatrical genius in two women who lived in poverty. The Allgoods needed jobs; there is nothing calculating about attempting to make a living when one is working class and has a large family to support, and it is worth noting that this is not a term used for men in the

---

World would not have been possible without Molly's words and personality. While a fictional account of their relationship is welcome to address the way that Molly Allgood gets occluded in discussions of *The Playboy*, archival and textual evidence, as I argue in this chapter, show her role in the creation of that play.

[2] W. J. McCormack, *Fool of the Family: A Life of J. M. Synge* (New York: New York University Press, 2000), 288.

theater, ever, though McCormack uses it twice in the first paragraphs of his section on Synge and Molly Allgood.

Nearly every critic of Irish theater from 1907 until today has told his or her version of the story of *The Playboy of the Western World* and the "eight nights at the Abbey" set off by the explosive premier on January 26, 1907.[3] What gets less attention is the crafting of the play, a story of Molly and Synge creating a drama about two frustrated storytellers living in a stultifying place with limited options. And at the Abbey, the actors, directors, and stagehands were all observing each other's behavior, including Synge's "shockingly unsuitable" interest in Molly Allgood.[4] The neglect of the actresses is not a coincidence. In my argument, the entire drama surrounding the drama of the *Playboy* premier focused on one flashpoint: the intersection of class and gender, but critics and historians even in recent years tend to devote more ink to the Trinity students in the stalls than the women on the stage. This chapter investigates the way the play took shape alongside the relationship between Synge and Molly and then follows the development and experience of the role as Molly played the part of Pegeen Mike in 1907 (Figure 3.1). Central to my argument is the way that previous critics have been unable to see Molly as anything other than a distraction, when the real story is her work to create this role and, as I explore in the next chapter, *Deirdre of the Sorrows*, the play she completed after Synge's death.

The work of women, especially Catholic, working-class women, in the context of the Abbey, remains invisible, occluded by critical perspectives that favor the male, Anglo-Irish gaze, and due to a lack of the kind of evidence that privileges that focus on male, written work at the expense of female performance.[5] The reasons for the lack of evidence are also steeped in assumptions about women and language. Molly Allgood's letters are gone, and the reason is likely Synge's very real fears for her reputation and her earning power should both sides of their correspondence come to light. We need only look at recent critical dismissals of Allgood due to her relationship with Synge to see that his fears were well founded. The architecture of influence, of a woman like Molly helping an educated, Ascendancy man like Synge to create a role, is harder to see when the focus is on text not performance. And the predominantly male audience gets more print and

---

[3] Any discussion of the *Playboy* riots must rest on the work of Ben Levitas in his *The Theatre of Nation: Irish Drama and Cultural Nationalism, 1890–1916* (Oxford: Clarendon Press, 2002).

[4] Joseph O'Connor, "The Playboy and his Muse," *Prospect Magazine*, May 25, 2010.

[5] As I discuss in Chapters 2 and 5, Lady Gregory's position as an Anglo-Irish woman who collected folk tales and wrote many of the plays of the Abbey is integral to this story as well.

Figure 3.1 Molly Allgood as Pegeen Mike in *The Playboy of the Western World*, January 1907, Abbey Theatre

Source: Courtesy of the Abbey Theatre Archive.

attention, even more than a century after that famous week of the *Playboy* premier, than the woman on the stage, a female figure risking all to bring the words and actions she had helped create to performance.

The relationship between Synge and Molly is well-documented in Ann Saddlemyer's *Letters to Molly* and shows a collaborative exchange of ideas about theater, gender, class, and Irishness from their first days when she was 19 and he 36 to his death three years later in 1909. Except in the not infrequent moments where Molly scribbled in frustration on Synge's letters, we only have Synge's side of the correspondence; in seeking to protect her reputation, ironically, Synge likely destroyed the letters that would have proved her role in creating these plays. At the same time, we can see in his responses to her letters how Molly guided his writing and their relationship and how her ideas shaped his creation and revision of many of his later plays, *The Playboy of the Western World* and *Deirdre of the Sorrows* in particular.

What gets saved and why is an important part of this story. As Saddlemyer notes in her Introduction to *The Letters of J. M. Synge*, Synge was an amateur archivist. He preferred to read primary sources rather than historical texts, and he saved his diaries, letters, and writings of and about the Aran Islanders. His penchant for saving sources for future researchers makes the disappearance of Molly's letters that much more remarkable. His fears for Molly's reputation must have been strong for him to destroy her part of the correspondence while keeping his own. He must have known that the stakes were higher for her. His archival bent also gives ballast to the argument that much of the language and ideas in his theater come from his habit of listening to primary sources, the women in the kitchen or the woman he hoped to marry, almost always women and almost always of a lower social class in a class-bound society.

Due to the play's development between two artists, *The Playboy of the Western World* dramatizes collaboration through the linguistic duet of Pegeen Mike and Christy Mahon. The play is not only, as so many critics have argued, the story of an artist discovering his calling but also, and more importantly, a drama of two would-be artists creating imagery together through language and trying to find their way out of a stultifying and judgmental society.[6] This mutual discovery distinguishes *The Playboy* from the works that Synge wrote before meeting Molly and brings their view of themselves as fellow creators of theater to the stage. In this chapter, I refocus the critical lens on both leads and their relationship as central to a play created by a couple dealing with the strain of a limiting society. By the time he wrote *Deirdre of the Sorrows*, the character based on Molly had

---

[6] Seamus Deane's "Synge and Heroism," in *Celtic Revivals: Essays in Modern Irish Literature, 1880–1980* (Winston-Salem: Wake Forest University Press, 1985) celebrates Christy's use of language to create himself on pp. 51–62.

subsumed the importance of the male characters around her; manuscripts and letters show how Pegeen's character grew more central and forceful as Synge contended with Molly's larger than life personality. In other words, what McCormack and other critics see as "calculating" was in fact the behavior of an artist who expected Synge to incorporate her ideas about character into his plays.

The story of these collaborations throughout this book addresses the question: why did the playwrights choose specific women as collaborative writers and actresses? In the case of Synge and Molly, their relationship followed a pattern: Synge was the consummate eavesdropper and observer of women, particularly women from the serving, tenement, or rural classes, and Molly had a knack for language, performance, and stagecraft as well as a big personality, all of which he wrote into Pegeen Mike. Though the image of the Anglo-Irish upper-class artist eavesdropping on the servant girls has rightly invited more than a century of critiques, Synge valued access and strove to find authentic voices, and Molly's voice fascinated him. Of course, the voices came through him, so his perspective would alter what reached the stage. But in the case of *The Playboy*, those servant girls' voices are also mediated by his extensive discussions of the role with Molly Allgood, a woman who came from tenement Dublin and who had spent time in an orphanage when her family was in desperate financial straits after her father's death. Her perspective, so far from Synge's own upper-class Anglo-Irish background, was necessary to the creation of the role and the play. Synge learned much about family and community observing women on his travels, and watching Molly negotiate the world of the Abbey with her sister and many of her siblings working on and off the stage showed him how to write a Pegeen who is both of the village and desperate for a separate life.

From his early transcription of "servant women" language to his plays that feature Molly and Sara Allgood knitting, keeping house, feeding people, and dealing with the minutiae of daily work, Synge's project is to make the invisible labor of women visible. Eavan Boland has written movingly about the unseen daily tasks of women in suburban Dublin, a topic traditionally seen as unfit for Irish poetry.[7] Synge began the work of foregrounding that kind of toil, and knowing and corresponding with Molly, a woman who

---

[7] Eavan Boland's *Object Lessons: The Life of the Woman and the Poet in Our Time* (Manchester: Carcanet, 1995) challenges monolithic ideas of poetry as rooted in male spaces in cities rather than domestic suburbia and chronicles her ability to start to see herself as a poet.

always had to work out of necessity, pushed Synge to re-imagine a first scene where Pegeen Mike is combining the tasks of work and writing, putting together a list of orders for a Wine and Spirit Dealer and for new clothing for herself. Synge's and Molly's goal in this initial scene is to foreground the importance of female work; Pegeen is the only character whose work we see onstage for most of the play, and, like Molly Allgood, she is of necessity entrepreneurial, perhaps a better word than "calculating" for a woman who looks out for herself out of necessity.

Synge understood early that through observing and listening in on women he could access the kind of Irish life that remained occluded to him due to his class and gender, as well as the strict codes of early twentieth-century Ireland. Synge's interest in imagining female experience contributed to characterization in early plays like *In the Shadow of the Glen* and *Riders to the Sea*, and he filled his youthful travel writings with observations of unknown women as a way to try and understand place and culture. Observing women closely became Synge's method for reading a place, a habit that informs all of his plays. Before visiting the Aran Islands in 1898, Synge's prose about traveling in Europe included many such portraits, filled with empathy as he tried to imagine the inaccessible lives of women from backgrounds very different from his own. A description from *Via Vecchia*, written in 1893, is typical both in its sympathy and in its lack of male figures: "Do flowers mourn like women for their briefness? In Luxembourg I see also girls from eighteen to twenty in the blossom of their beauty, and women with a few babies who are withered."[8] Here, he tries to understand experience outside his own, and motherhood seems both powerful and toxic.

Next to the women's ability to produce children, Synge sees the male province of artistic creation as futile: "We are less fortunate than women. The frailest suckling is robust besides the offspring we have borne in travail darker than a woman's and all our honor and glory is in the shadow of a dream."[9] There is some envy here; Synge realizes that female experience, especially outside of his own class, is inaccessible to him, but he tries, through observation, to find a way to understand the reality of the woman on the train. Unlike Yeats, who freely imagined the lives of women without that research, Synge understood the limits of his own perspective. The observation also suggests that the labors of birth and certain kinds of work

---

[8] J. M. Synge, *Collected Works: Vol. 2, Prose*, ed. Alan Price (London: Oxford University Press, 1962), 23.

[9] Ibid.

have a connection to the real that Synge hopes for in his own art. Book after book have lambasted Synge for appropriation in these moments, but his efforts at empathy translate to full female characters in his plays. Meeting Molly allowed him to get beyond observation and to use her language, perspective, and history in creating characters that reflected their work together.

Molly Allgood's place in creating the plays of the Abbey requires our attention, and so do her precursors; in particular, a nameless young woman who got the idea of The Playboy started for Synge. Synge's habit of observing women in his travels eventually gave him his first model for Pegeen Mike: on a trip to West Kerry in 1905, Synge stayed in a cottage on Great Blasket Island and found a model for Christy's love interest in the hostess.[10] He not only observed this young woman, however, but began to discuss both his work and the community with her. In other words, Synge had begun to listen and converse rather than just observing from afar. She struck him immediately as unusual:

> His (the host's) eldest daughter, a young woman of about twenty, who manages the house, shook hands with me also, and then, without asking if we were hungry, began making us tea in a metal tea-pot and frying rashers of bacon. She is a small, beautifully-formed woman, with brown hair and eyes – instead of the black hair and blue eyes that are common in these parts, where the woman's work is so hard. Her sister, who lives in the house also, is a bonny girl of about eighteen, full of humor and spirits.[11]

Like a changeling, his name for Molly, the "little hostess" stands out from the rest of the women in her community but is also of the community, and, like Molly, she comes from a close but economically strapped family, toils all day, and is attended by a sister. Synge acknowledges the difficulty of their daily work. How different these portraits are from Yeats's habit of defining Gonne as one in a long line of heroic women standing for a feminized idea of nation. Instead, Synge grounds the female figures he writes for the stage in the particular, the women he observed and then the one he knew best, and his writings show that he grappled with the limits of his own understanding.

---

[10] David H. Greene and Edward M. Stephens, J. M. Synge 1871–1909, revised edition (New York: New York University Press, 1989), 203.

[11] J. M. Synge, In Wicklow; West Kerry; The Congested Districts; Under Ether (Boston, MA: J. W. Luce, 1912), 71.

Synge, in these descriptions and in his eventual relationship with Molly, is always after the specific, the particular place, the actual woman, as much as he can understand that individual, and part of this form of observation comes down to his fascination with female work. On the Blaskets, the hostess settles him in his room at night as Pegeen does Christy, and in most of the descriptions, she works to provide food for the family and Synge himself. (Synge, a man who lived for most of his life with his mother, enjoyed these attentions.) She inspired Synge to write a poem that begins: "You've plucked a curlew, drawn a hen / Washed the shirts of seven men."[12] The poem focuses on her methodical, uncomplaining attitude to work and ends with release in song and dance, and in a departure from his earlier descriptions of women, the poem concerns her actions rather than her beauty. While he wrote in the cottage, she asked him about the people he corresponded with, and as he began to know the people on the island, she became a liaison, explaining the people's names and relationships, and he told her about characters in Europe and on the mainland.[13] What fascinated Synge, here and in the famous eavesdropping episode, is both the intimate conversation and the specificity of female labor, two aspects of his future relationship with Molly that animate *The Playboy*. The work of the woman of the Blaskets, the actions of her small body constantly acting to sustain the house and those around her, is what Synge observes and brings into his poem. The women in his plays, most particularly in *Riders to the Sea*, work with their hands, and that kind of action translates into his female characters in ways that link the women to the stage and to the land as anti-romantic workers, investors in survival, in the community, their physical surround-ings, and the real. Death and loss become grounded in the physical and the real as well due to this investment in female work in the text.

In this early and formative relationship on Great Blasket, Synge is always aware of his own position as an outsider, a role familiar to him in his own family. Unlike the mercurial and shape-shifting Yeats, Synge was never confused about his own position and did not dress up or play roles, but he

---

[12] This treatment of birds critiques Yeats's swans, linnets, and white birds of his Maud Gonne fantasies in poems like "White Birds." For more on this Yeats poem and his tendency to imagine women as birds, see A. Norman Jeffares and A. S. Knowland, *A Commentary on the Plays of W. B. Yeats* (London: Macmillan, 1975), 36. Synge challenges bird imagery in Yeats's 1899 poem, "He Reproves the Curlew," a Romantic notion of bird and nature in stark contrast to Synge's imagery here.

[13] Molly would also serve as a liaison to the working-class world of Dublin through her family and upbringing and, as I discuss later on, to the folk memories and more rural history of her grandmother Harold.

did listen in and observe keenly; John Masefield remembers "His place was outside the circle, gravely watching, gravely summing up, with a brilliant malice, the fools and wise ones inside." Yeats built his muse-fueled inspiration from Dante, Homer, and the ancient world. Performing a relationship with cues from romance was not Synge's style; getting to know a particular person, often as a path into a different way of living and speaking, was. With the young woman on Great Blasket, he reveled in attention and intimacy and recreated this feeling for Christy, "expanding with delight at the first confidential talk he has ever had with a woman."[14] That intimate, particular conversation is central to Synge in his connection with this woman, and Molly's specific voice and individual character and history would inspire him in their correspondence as well. After he left the island and returned to town on the mainland, he missed "our little hostess" and the life of the island, but, like Christy, at the end of the play, he realized that he belonged outside the community: "By this time they are wandering back from the head of the cliff and are gathering in the kitchen where the little queen has sanded the floor, and filled the water crock and pushed the nets into a corner. Yet I know even while I was there I was an interloper only, a refugee in the garden between four seas."[15] In memory, she is already elevated from hostess to queen, but what, to borrow a phrase from Yeats, he "delights to imagine" is her specific tasks at that time in the evening, the list of actions, like stage directions, that continue the work of the island; and that imagining is rooted in what he actually saw.[16] The "little hostess" of The Great Blaskets contributed her distant experiences to the isolated and cottage-bound Pegeen. Whatever the issues of appropriation around Synge's obsession with watching, listening, and writing the work of women, he understood his own position, "an interloper only."

Synge wrote Molly's industriousness into Pegeen Mike, who asks, "give me courage in the doing of my work,"[17] as she minds the store, orders the items for the business and her trousseau, and fills Christy's glass. She attempts to identify him, settling on a tinker, and challenges him to define himself. In the face of all her doing on the stage since the raising of the curtain, she claims, "You did nothing at all." Though she lives with her father, Pegeen is, as defined by the Widow Quin, "an orphaned girl," and

---

[14] J. M. Synge, The Playboy of the Western World: A Comedy in Three Acts (Boston, MA: J. W. Luce, 1911), 32.

[15] Synge, Collected Works, Vol. 2, Prose, 258.

[16] William Butler Yeats, Poems (London: Fisher Unwin, 1899), 294.

[17] Synge, Playboy, 18.

Molly Allgood spent time in an orphanage due to family economic hardship after her father's death. The Allgood family story is important here, and in the revisions of the drafts of the play that set the Widow Quin apart, that develop her and Pegeen Mike alongside one another, Synge writes from his knowledge of the two sisters, Sara and Molly Allgood, their language, jealousies, closeness, self-sufficiency, required of them for survival, and their sense of being trapped. This is a play about women defined by work, loss, and the desire for language and the men of action that they create in their minds.

In his *Autobiography*, Synge credits women with influencing his narrative sense from his early childhood: "If I could know the dates of my nurses I could trace the whole course of my opening memory, but they are lost."[18] Importantly, he needs specific dates; he has no interest in collapsing the women who cared for him into a monolithic, stereotypical ideal of working-class caretaking femininity. Not having the details means that the memories "are lost"—he refuses to make up the characters without a factual basis. And he does not hope for knowledge of his more wealthy relations or his mother's upper-class friends; instead he couches his access to memory through his nurses, and his earliest knowledge of the world is mitigated through their perspective and, like any decent archival researcher, he wants the particular dates. This way of accessing language and reality, from infancy, would inform his later way of writing female characters.

Ann Saddlemyer, in *Synge and the Nature of Women*, argues that Synge was able to build his drama around female characters because of his many women friends: "It is from this wide range of companionship culminating in his successful courtship of Molly, that Synge, once he had found his métier, drew his powerful characterization of women."[19] He lived, off and on, with his mother for much of his life, and, though he had a reputation for intense privacy and withdrawal from social interactions, as Masefield points out, he was often open with women: "When I turn over my memories of him, it seems that his grave courtesy was only gay when he was talking to women. His talk to women had a lightness and charm."[20] As a child, Synge developed an intense friendship with his cousin Florence Ross, and their interactions bear the mark of the collaborative relationships with women he would seek

---

[18] Synge, *Collected Works, Vol. 2, Prose*, 4.
[19] Ann Saddlemyer, *Synge and the Nature of Women*, in *Women in Irish Legend, Life, and Literature*, ed. S. F. Gallagher (Gerard's Cross: Colin Smythe, 1983), 72.
[20] John Masefield, *John M. Synge* (Letchworth: Garden City Press, 1916), 9.

as an adult. The two divided their time between the empirical study of insects and storytelling, and discussed sex directly "with the attitude of folktales" that he would bring to his plays.[21]

That early focus on scientific study with Ross became more physical and sexual with Molly. The years working with Molly Allgood must have brought back memories of this young collaboration; the early connection to Florence Ross certainly made an indelible impression: "I loved her with a curious affection that I cannot pretend to analyze and I told her ... that she was to be my wife. She was not displeased."[22] Synge wrote a passage about the connection between Ross and his scientific pursuits that reveals that from a young age he experienced the joy of discovery as collaborative: "I remember telling her—or intending to tell her—that each egg I found gave three distinct moments of rapture: the finding of the nest, the insertion of the egg successfully in my collection, and, lastly, the greatest, exhibiting it to her." In this description of Ross' importance to his sense of achievement, he suggests that accomplishments did not seem real to him unless a female friend acknowledged the work. Like many of his relationships with women, this collaborative friendship with Florence Ross continued for his whole life, and he helped her with her writing in adulthood. In 1907, he wrote pedantically to Molly, "F. Ross has got her article on Skerries quite clear and good now after three corrections. Why won't you do the same?"[23] Women who interested Synge were fellow-writers and artists, far from ornamental figures in his life.

The stories and words that contributed to *The Playboy of the Western World* took a complex route to the stage, beginning with a tale told to Synge while he traveled and observations of women he met in a rural area and ending with a part rewritten for Molly Allgood. The tale that became the play was oral, then written, then oral, overheard by rural Irish, penned by Synge, and performed by Molly and the company. Synge's famous *Preface* makes no secret of the many-authored nature of this play. The women he overheard in the kitchen were trapped as well by their class, gender, and surroundings, and they used the story telling as a way out.

In Yeats's Introduction to *The Well of the Saints*, he recounts his advice to Synge when they met in Paris in December of 1896. Whether or not these

---

[21] Synge, *Collected Works, Vol. 2, Prose*, 7.   [22] Ibid., 8.
[23] J. M. Synge and Maire O'Neill, *Letters to Molly: John Millington Synge to Maire O'Neill, 1906–1909*, ed. Ann Saddlemyer (Cambridge, MA: Belknap Press of Harvard University Press, 1971), 217 (hereafter *LM*).

exact words were spoken is anyone's guess; Yeats always attempted to create his own versions of Synge for public consumption, and his effort here is to insert himself into a performance about creating a drama based on a particular kind of Irish identity. It is more likely that Yeats gave that advice in 1899 after Synge returned from Aran, but the mythology around the plays is important.[24] Yeats seeks some form of authenticity in the face of attack. If he sent Synge with the idea of putting an unknown Irish life in art, the story has the power of discovery. Yeats gives himself some great lines:

> I said, "Give up Paris. You will never create anything by reading Racine, and Arthur Simons will always be the better critic of French literature. Go to the Arran Islands. Live there as if you were one of the people themselves; express a life that has never found expression."[25]

Yeats reveals his own idea of identity here; because Synge is Irish, he seems to think that the young writer can become like the people of Aran and express their existence. Synge's interpretation, however, always acknowledged the distance between his experience and background and that of the islanders, but nonetheless he attempted to bring their language and community to the stage, refusing a sanitized version. An Anglo-Irishman of independent means could never live on the islands as the islanders did, and Synge realizes that as he watches the work of the women who keep the community going. In other words, the Aran Island life did not find full expression on that stage in 1907. What reached the Abbey was Synge's version of an old story reworked over a thousand pages and two and a half years into a reflection of his challenging relationship with Molly Allgood, a fellow artist.

The trail of the play from primary sources on Synge's travels is well-documented. To celebrate the play's 110-year anniversary, in January 2017, Nicholas Grene and James Little created "The Journey of the *Playboy*," a comprehensive online exhibit with images, maps, and manuscripts that is a

---

[24] Yeats recounts in his introduction to "Well of the Saints" his purported own role in sending Synge to the Aran Islands. The online exhibit, *The Journey of "The Playboy"* offers archival images of this and other moments in Synge's decision to travel to Aran: see https://artsandculture.google.com/exhibit/-gKSf51FMvvgKg. The exhibit also offers invaluable images and first-hand accounts from the first drafts of *The Playboy* to more recent productions.

[25] W. B. Yeats, *The Collected Works of W. B. Yeats, IV, Early Essays*, ed. Richard J. Finneran and George Bornstein (New York: Palgrave Macmillan, 2007), 217.

Figure 3.2 Synge's photograph of the McDonough cottage where he stayed in Inishmaan, including livestock, a child, and a woman turning in a doorway to work

Source: Courtesy of Trinity College Dublin.

boon to scholars, interested readers, and audience members.[26] There is some mention of the evolution of the characters the Widow Quin and Pegeen Mike, but the emphasis is on the development of the play through travel, not the actresses in the premier who influenced the writing and 1907 revisions. My focus is on the specific ways that women figured into collaboration with locals on his travels, and how these women were precursors for Synge's relationship with Molly and on Molly's work creating Pegeen Mike.

Synge first heard the story of a man hidden by locals after killing his father on his 1898 visit to Patrick McDonough's house in Inishmaan.[27] Synge documented the trip, as was his habit, with photographs (Figure 3.2). In

---

[26] "The Journey of 'The Playboy'", curated by Nicholas Grene and James Little, The Library of Trinity College Dublin, https://artsandculture.google.com/exhibit/the-journey-of-the-playboy-trinity-college-dublin-library/-gKSf51FMvvgKg?hl=en.

[27] Synge was not the only Anglo-Irish writer of the Revival to visit the McDonough home. Padraig Pearse also visited the family, and it is interesting to speculate on how this one family influenced the writing of a major play of the revival as well as Pearse's vision of a Western Ireland that required sacrifice.

the images, as in the photographs of his trips to West Kerry between 1903 and 1906, women stand at doorways with children and livestock because what interested Synge and what he chose to document was the community of women at work. Even the Widow Quin's dramatic breastfeeding of a lamb and then eating it, a tale Synge heard in West Kerry and recorded for later use in his notebook, is the story of a woman in extremis, doing the work she must do to feed and maintain her livestock and her household in a food scarce community, and using her own body to do so. The story caused an uproar at the Abbey and challenges the sacrosanct ideals of "the poor old woman," the sacred image of a nation as an ethereal woman requiring blood sacrifice for rebirth.[28] In fact, the Widow Quin sacrifices the sacred Cathleen ni Houlihan image of an older woman throughout the play; still a sexual being, she tries to seduce Christy into living with her for comfort and sighs over the "gallant hairy fellows" on the ships she sees passing on the coast.

Mary Burke provides context on Synge's use of folk elements and the complex negotiations of identity writing for the Irish stage: "The dramatist's linking of tinkers, tramps, and islanders to pre-Celtic peoples emerges from his desire to stress Ireland's genetic and cultural diversity during an era in which ultra-nationalism seized the terms 'Gael' and 'Celt' as equivalents of 'Irish.'"[29] Yeats professed to send Synge to a part of Ireland that would recover some essential version of Irishness, and in fashioning himself and Molly as outsiders, Synge challenged the orthodox tenets of what it meant to be Irish. In particular, he questioned both Irish femininity and the relationship of that image to Irish masculinity. Challenging the sacred images of Irish womanhood and manhood through engaging in folk research brought his plays to the stage like cultural time bombs. In another attempt to ratify the link between his plays and folk culture, Synge and Molly would ensure that actual clothing and set pieces from Aran would constitute set design.

Like many productions at the Abbey, this one plays scenes over a layer of loss. Pegeen has lost her mother, and the Widow Quin has "buried her children and destroyed her man."[30] Refusing the by-then stereotypical figure of the tragic woman of the cottage with loss visited upon her, the Widow Quin emphasizes her own agency. She "buried" and "destroyed," and both actions are figured as work. In an effort to woo Christy, she speaks as if she is

---

[28] W. B. Yeats, *The Collected Works of W. B. Yeats, II, The Plays*, ed. David Clark and Robin E. Clark (New York: Palgrave Macmillan, 2001), 83. For an exploration of the implications of *Cathleen ni Houlihan* and an overview of critical discussions of this figure, see Chapter 2.

[29] Mary Burke, *"Tinkers": Synge and the Cultural History of the Irish Traveller* (Oxford: Oxford University Press, 2009), 112.

[30] Synge, *Playboy*, 38.

applying for a job, casting herself as a solitary worker, like most of the women in the world of Synge: "When you see me contriving in my little gardens, Christy Mahon, you'll swear the Lord God formed me to be living lone, and that there isn't my match in Mayo for thatching, or mowing, or shearing a sheep."[31] The Widow Quin is the consummate worker and lives alone, supporting herself independently. She does not need a man for traditionally male farm chores, and her desire for Christy is sexual. Her character further upends ideas of the maternal aging Irish mother when she confesses to nursing a black ram who, when eaten, might have "elements of a Christian"[32] in it, based on the Kerry story above. The questions of identity and motherhood erupt here, stunning Christy to silence. The quilt that the Widow Quin uses for Christy is one she's "after quilting a while since with my own two hands" as she accomplishes all the work of her farm. In the beginning of Act II, mirroring Act I, Christy polishes books and lists items as Pegeen did at the start. This is the first time a man is working on the stage, and Christy is only able to function in this more practical way after Pegeen gives him a sense of identity and purpose. He mentions his own beauty, not hers; he is the one commodified here.

As Synge explained the role of Pegeen for Molly and worked to bring their collaboration into Pegeen's relationship with Christy Mahon, he created a play with two heroes. Seamus Deane, like many critics, focuses on Christy at the expense of Pegeen. Although Pegeen rivals Christy in her linguistic abilities, Deane ignores the main female character, focusing solely on Christy as an example of a certain kind of hero in the work of Synge, Joyce, and Yeats: "The hero is betrayed or expelled by a community (which has itself conspired to create the idea of heroism as a means to its own salvation)."[33] The expelled Nora in *In the Shadow of the Glen* is also one of these heroes, but Deane describes the Revival's major figures as male despite Molly Bloom, Cathleen ni Houlihan, and the Countess Cathleen, among others. At the end of the essay, Deane briefly mentions "heroines," but Pegeen Mike barely gets a word. Though Deane notes that Christy's language turns him into a hero, he neglects Pegeen Mike's role both in creating Christy and in reinventing herself. Pegeen Mike's reading of Christy allows him to become a hero and splits the role of hero between two characters, one male and one female. Pegeen's decision not to leave with Christy does not simply consign her to the daily concerns of the cottage and

---

[31] Ibid., 39.   [32] Ibid., 39.
[33] Deane, "Synge and Heroism," *Celtic Revivals*, 51–62.

small town, while Christy travels off as a heroic, eloquent loner. The mythic element of the play does not disappear with Christy's final exit. Pegeen remains in the town, not as a typical member of the community, but as a troubling presence, caustic but linguistically gifted. Pegeen will not become like Shaun simply because, with few other choices, she has agreed to marry him. Her final famous, cry, "Oh, my grief, I've lost him surely. I've lost the only playboy of the western world" not only gives the play its grand title but also shows that Pegeen will cling to linguistic luxury, the same kind of language that allowed her to create herself and Christy as the play's protagonists.[34] Like the Widow Quin, Pegeen stays in the community as a provocateur. The play begins with Pegeen alone and ends with her final cry, and the changes in her character are at least as important as Christy's transformation.

A close look at the creation of the play and its language shows that the play is about a collaborative artistic relationship, about two artists caught in a societal structure that limits them both. James Kilroy's plot summary spends two paragraphs before even mentioning Pegeen. When Pegeen mentions "his small, aristocratic feet," according to Kilroy, "this is the beginning of Christy's discovery of himself."[35] This moment actually asks the audience to focus on Pegeen's role in the collaborative creation of two artists, and Kilroy points out that, "Pegeen notes the power of that speech." Pegeen's recognition, her identifying Christy as an artist, then, should be an argument for focusing on her character as well, one that casts the two as co-creators of art and language. Pegeen is not a passive stand-in for the audience; instead, she is the actress, the love interest, the co-writer, all the women who had helped Synge imagine inaccessible lives and language culminating in his work with Molly Allgood and her specific influence on the part. And due to that influence and that relationship, the play has evolved to treat the two characters as artists. Only with Molly Allgood could Synge have created these characters and language, and only with Pegeen could Christy create himself as a poet with her as collaborating co-author of their own new identities.

When he met Molly and began to write *The Playboy* for her in 1906, Synge was creating the play from diverse material including the stories he

---

[34] Synge, *Playboy*, 111.

[35] James F. Kilroy joins the chorus of critics who argue that the play is about Christy becoming a poet, defending the "purple" language in *The Playboy* because it emphasizes Christy's transformation. See Kilroy, *The "Playboy" Riots* (Oxford: Oxford University Press, 1971).

had heard in the West from the "little hostess" discussed above who originally inspired Pegeen Mike. Writing Christy gave him the most trouble while he drafted the play; creating Pegeen's character came more easily because she was based on Molly, and he had their constant correspondence to guide him.[36] In *The Playboy*, Christy Mahon and Pegeen imagine a separate existence outside of the restrictions of cottage and community. When Mahon's presence reveals the falsity of Christy's original tale, Pegeen uses her fantastic language both to banish him and to mourn his passing. Synge's mother raised him with the advice, paraphrasing Corinthians, "Be ye in the world but separate from the world," and he created a play with hero and heroine both alienated from and included in the community.[37] His letters to Molly show that he saw the two of them in an analogous position, distinguished from others because of their creativity. At the end of February 1907, about a month after their work together on *The Playboy* ended in the riotous premier, Synge wrote to Molly, "I, and some other people of genius I have known, in my youth nearly always got a wild impulse to tramp the world in the spring or autumn, the time the birds migrate, so as you're a genius too it's right and proper that you should have the impulse."[38] He designated himself and Molly as part of an intellectual elite, unbound by the rules of human society. At the time, many of his letters struggled to imagine the two of them settled and married, able to bring their relationship into the public domain. Molly remembered both the professional and personal aspects of their relationship in a 1949 interview a few years before her death in 1952: "What is there I cannot say about John? To me he was everything, in his work and personality."[39] Synge and Molly's position, both as part of the Abbey and as separate in their time alone together, contributed to Synge's negotiation of Pegeen's and Christy's places in the community.

Synge had ample opportunity to become engaged to women of his own class, but his choice of Molly, a verbally adept fighter who had to sustain a family in poverty, shows that he hoped in both his relationships and in his art to try and give voice in an anti-romantic way to the real work and language of women who struggle. He both admired and feared her

---

[36] Often Synge wrote of his frustrations writing Christy to Molly: "Now for the Play Boy – God confound him!" (*LM*, 75).

[37] John Millington Synge, *Collected Letters of J. M. Synge, Vols 1 and 2*, ed. Ann Saddlemyer (Oxford: Clarendon Press, vol. 1, 1983, vol. 2, 1984) (hereafter JMSCL).

[38] *LM*, 98.

[39] Qtd. in E. H. Mikhail, *The Abbey Theatre: Interviews and Recollections* (Rowman & Littlefield Publishers, 1988).

outspokenness in a dynamic that will be familiar to those who know Pegeen Mike's role in *The Playboy*. Tensions about her norm-busting behavior run through their correspondence. In July 1906, Synge expressed concerns about her whereabouts and decorum; across the top, Molly wrote, "Idiotic." The next letter shows her insistence on her own rules for courtship: "I got your card this morning forwarded to Lady Gregory's before I left. I asked you not to send me postcards to avoid gossip please don't do so next time."[40] By turns inspired and annoyed by Molly's refusal to play by the tenets of their shared moment, Synge wrote her flouting of societal decorum into Pegeen Mike. One can imagine that Molly's penchant for testing social boundaries might have contributed to Synge's decision to burn her part of their correspondence.

Synge's letters to Molly show his dependence on her for ideas and language for the play. When an artist named Kusek was visiting the Abbey from Eastern Europe, Synge writes to Molly and awkwardly requests that Molly and Sara show up and act out a kind of Irishness that was inaccessible to him without their presence. He asks that they perform a keen and model Aran clothing and provide food: Synge requests that they make tea and cakes "*at my expense*" (emphasis in original), explaining that "if it's a bother don't mind and we'll let him starve, if it isn't perhaps you might tell Mrs. Martin we're coming so that she might have clean cups!" He needs both women to enact a female Irishness that he cannot access and to stage manage the small performance, though his discomfort with the class divisions and with his own dependence shows in phrases like "perhaps you might."[41] This kind of correspondence is a function of class, showing Synge's need for the Allgood sisters to demonstrate to his visitor the parts of Irish performance that, due to the constraints of his gender and class, he cannot demonstrate or embody. And, of course, these city actresses would be acting the roles of Aran women in this teatime performance for the foreign visitors in one of the many examples of Abbey dramatics beyond the boundaries of the stage.

While Synge was drafting *The Playboy*, Molly wrote to him much about "lonesomeness," a feeling he would make central to the experience of Pegeen Mike. To Molly, he writes in exasperation, "I am glad to hear you are lonesome its very good for you." Synge at this point was overcome with jealousy after reports that Allgood was walking arm in arm with Dossie Wright: "you must see Dossie hanged before you take his arm again."[42]

[40] *LM*, 2.   [41] *LM*, 8.   [42] *LM*, 6.

From Synge's letters it is easy to see that Molly Allgood did not take these admonishments from Synge well and was looking for distraction and release from a busy, work-filled life in a society with specific rules for girls like her; her outlook echoes in Pegeen Mike.

Because Synge associated Molly with nature, he created a romance between Christy and Pegeen based on images of the land. Molly and Synge also conducted much of their relationship out of doors in the country out of necessity since the claustrophobic class and gender roles at the Abbey would have made public personal interaction difficult. This aspect of the play came out of the fabric of Synge's letters to Molly, and the correspondence, both before and after the premier, describes Molly and Synge as separate from the pressures of society. Christy's description of "you and me ... pacing Neifin in the dews of the night, the times sweet smells do be rising ... " sounds like the scraps of paper Synge wrote to Molly while outdoors on bicycle rides through Kelly in 1907. Pegeen builds on Christy's imagery ("in the sides of Neifin, when the night is down"),[43] collaborating with him to create a place apart through language. The excerpt below, typical of Synge's many letters to Molly, uses the language of Pegeen and Christy: "I can hear the sea birds clapping their wings in the cliff under me. The air is full of the smell of honey from the heather, and there is a seal sneezing and blowing in the sea just under me. It is all wonderful and if only I had my little changling with me!"[44] Pegeen imagines life outside of the confines of the cottage and surrounding community: "Yourself and me would shelter easy in a narrow bush."[45] Soon after the *Playboy* premier a year and half earlier, he had written: "The mountains looked lovely today. I can not tell you how much I longed to be away among them with my Pegeen Mike."[46] Indeed, only in correspondence and on outdoor walks were the two able to speak privately; though they worked together at the theater, they could rarely speak alone at rehearsals. Synge relied on their walks for inspiration, and his July 1907 trip to Wicklow was filled with memories of Molly. He suggests that she use thoughts of their time outdoors as an escape: "think over all the beautiful things you've seen out here and in our other walks and make a little fair land in your skull for you to live your changling's life when Mary Street is not tolerable."[47] This is one of the places where we get a hint of what Molly's letters and discussions covered. Clearly, she had expressed frustration with the crowded, poverty-stricken life of her large family, headed by a single parent, in tenement

---

[43] Synge, *Playboy*, 103.   [44] *LM*, 16.   [45] Synge, *Playboy*, 91.   [46] *LM*, 90.
[47] *LM*, 162.

Dublin. Synge filled his letters both with the anticipation of future walks and with memories of past times outdoors, especially when he was ill: "I have been thinking often of those late evenings we had up on the mountain road in Glen Cree, and feeling to you as I felt to you then in that wonderful solemnity and calm."[48] Synge would develop this association between Molly and nature in *Deirdre of the Sorrows*, writing a version of the mythic character linked to the land of her birth; in *The Playboy*, he dramatizes days outdoors with Molly in Pegeen and Christy's ideas of a future life outside of the community.

Synge wrote to Molly after one of their frequent squabbles: "we both have such strong wills,"[49] and Pegeen certainly matches Christy in energy and verbal ability. When Christy describes himself "spearing salmons" with Pegeen as "an angel's lamp to me from this day out,"[50] she answers by including herself in his activities: "if I was your wife I'd be along with you those nights." The character of Pegeen reflects the way that Synge saw Molly Allgood not as an idealized, absent figure, but as a missed and challenging presence to be called out to in lyrical letters. Consequently, his Pegeen matches Christy in verbal ability, refusing to be simply a "lamp" and joining him in his imaginary adventures. Pegeen prides herself on her way with words: "I was a great hand at coaxing the bailiffs, or coining funny nicknames for the stars of the night."[51] Ahead of his time, Synge hoped that his fiancée would continue her creative work after their marriage: "You have real talent I think and real talent of any kind is a priceless thing so I would be sorry to see you give up the stage unless you could use your talent in some other way—Suppose you and I write a play together! Wouldn't that be great!"[52] He jokes, "you can write all the men's parts—I know you like men—and I'll write all the female"; this jest hints at Synge's interest in continuing to write female characters and his jealousy of the men Molly worked with in the company as well as the ways that their relationship challenged both traditional gender roles and class structures. These images of a collaborative future built around creative projects appear again and again in the letters until Synge's health deteriorated quickly in 1908. Synge encouraged Molly to write a play based on her grandmother:

> I've a new idea. Do you think you could write a little comedy to play in yourself; say about your life in the convent school? ... The one thing needful is to get hold of some little centre of life that you know thoroughly,

[48] *LM*, 176–7.   [49] *LM*, 52.   [50] Synge, *Playboy*, 91.   [51] Ibid.
[52] *LM*, 180.

and that is not quite familiar to every one. I'm sure your old grandmother would be a lovely character in a play. Think about it, little heart, and when you're acting notice how the scenes etc. are worked out, one into the other.[53]

These are experiences and relationships that, through Molly's telling, helped Synge imagine the characters of *The Playboy*, but that he ultimately cannot access except through her. The "centre(s) of life" he wants her to write about are all-female, convent schools and relationships with grandmothers, areas of Irish female working-class life that would always be foreign to Synge. In his advice to think about theater "when you're acting," Synge expresses his conception of their relationship in terms of two artists, two creators of theater. In Molly he found a way into some of that language and imagery, but he counseled her to write her own plays because she was closer to that experience.

In the patronizing tone that comes into some of his letters, he counsels her in September of 1907: "I want you to get a Note Book and write down everything you read... in a few years you'll be the best educated actress in Europe, and I want you to take pride and pleasure in your progress."[54] Though Synge adopted this high-handed attitude with Molly in some of his letters, addressing her as a protégé or student, he usually did so while suggesting ways she develop her already considerable artistic talents. She bristled at this tone, and he often apologized for sending her "a Sermon!"[55] (Here, again, a reader must be adept at noticing from Synge's response what is missing in Allgood's part of the correspondence.) His visions for their future are wrapped up in his aspirations for both of their careers: "I have been building castles in the air this morning no end," he writes in November 1907, and he goes on to describe a fantasy of the Abbey "coming to grief"; "in about ten years I saw us starting a Dublin company of our own with you as leading lady of course and first Stage Manager! Then by that time Dublin will be better educated and I saw big houses coming in, and a real Irish Drama getting on its legs at least thanks to the enthusiasm of the extraordinary gifted and subtle actress Mrs. J. M. Tramp!"[56] Synge and Molly not only courted and prepared for marriage in their letters, but he also saw her as a promising young colleague and admired the skills she had that he lacked. His hopes for their future happiness had as much to do with artistic work

---

[53] *LM*, 159.   [54] *LM*, 40.   [55] *LM*, 101.   [56] *LM*, 218.

together as they did romance, and about Dublin changing and becoming a place where they could thrive.

Synge critiqued her acting, and she advised him on drafts of his work. A fortnight before the January 1907 premier of *The Playboy*, he watched a rehearsal, but Molly had stayed home because of problems with her eye. Frustrated at missing her in the role, he wrote, "the first act anyhow goes swimmingly. I am longing to hear you in Pegeen Mike with the others. If your eye doesn't get better soon I'll have to go and teach you your part myself, so as not to tire you by my reading it."[57] In June 1907, he called her performance as Pegeen in a revival of *The Playboy* "CAPITAL," and a few months later, praised her acting in Lady Gregory's Devorgilla: "You are a genius after your Mona and that's no lie."[58] In April 1907, he sent her some poetry, asking for her opinion. He responded to her corrections a few days later: "I have written the verses again; your criticism is useful!"[59] In a few months, he asked for her advice on his work again, "Tell me what you think of my Wicklow article," and two weeks later, he agreed with her criticism and asked for more: "Tell me by and by what you thought dull as I want the opinions of competent people—or changelings—before I begin knocking them into a book."[60] In December, he wrote of *The Tinker's Wedding* "I wish I had you here to advise me about it."[61] Their letters are a form of workshop where they go over drafts of each other's work. Synge remarks on sessions when they worked on these plays together, moments critics cannot recapture but that we can see in the evidence of the plays themselves, texts that reflect conversations that we can recover through close reading.

The letters were vital to Synge from the start of their friendship. He often wrote lines like "What are those few lines for a starving man? I wanted to hear how you got home, and how you supped, and how everybody's temper is, and what you did yesterday, and what you read or didn't read, and God knows what, and yet you're too lazy to tell me!"[62] Words are also central to the relationship between Pegeen Mike and Christy; he says, "with rapture," "I'll have your words from this day filling my ears, and that look is come upon you meeting my two eyes, and I watching you loafing around in the warm sun, or rinsing your ankles when the night has come."[63] Pegeen's speech creates Christy anew, and at times Synge credited his letters to Molly with keeping him alive. Ill in bed in November 1906, he wrote to Molly, "write to me every day. I lie here listening for the postman's knock."[64]

---

[57] *LM*, 85.   [58] *LM*, 154, 210.   [59] *LM*, 123.   [60] *LM*, 160, 169.
[61] *LM*, 227.   [62] *LM*, 11.   [63] Synge, *Playboy*, 59.   [64] *LM*, 92.

Language acts as a lifeline in *The Playboy* as well: Christy's story gains him entry and prowess in the town, while Pegeen remakes him and herself through language.

Synge began the play in September 1904, and in these early drafts, the action revolves solely around Christy Mahon; after Synge began to work with Molly, the focus changed. The early titles (The Murderer (A Farce), Murder Will Out, The Fool of the Family, The Fool of Farnham, and Christy Mahon) highlight Christy's prominence and the importance of the murder, which was to begin the play and take place onstage. The final title, after Molly helped bring Pegeen's character to prominence, comes from Pegeen's name for Christy, stressing the importance of her role in his development as an artist. Synge began to imagine vague "love affairs, etc." for Christy in the months after beginning the play in the autumn of 1904.[65] He also based the play, according to an interview in *The Freeman's Journal* after the infamous January 26, 1907 performance, on the case of James Lynchehaun, a man who had assaulted a woman on Achill Island.[66] In the first drafts, though, he removed these women from the story; only after associating his memories of the "little hostess" of The Great Blaskets with Molly Allgood did he develop the female characters. On Inishmaan in 1899, "the oldest man on the island" told Synge another story he would rework into *The Playboy*. The initial tale, of a Connemara man "who killed his father with the blow of a spade when he was in a passion and then fled to the island," features no female characters.[67] The islanders who protected the criminal came into the story as "they," and Synge had not yet begun to write about the women who would receive the murderer. In the version Synge heard, the criminal waited, hidden, in Dun Conor, one of Synge's favorite haunts, while the police searched for him, "and he could hear their boots grinding the stones over his head."[68] Synge often sat in Dun Conor while the islanders attended Mass: "It is Holy Day, and I have come up to sit on the Dun while the people are at Mass."[69] Waiting alone for Mass to end, he describes the solitary silence of the morning and must have associated these isolated moments, apart from the community, with the criminal who hid in the same spot many years ago. By the time he had finished the play, Pegeen Mike—and the Widow Quin—had taken on as much importance as Christy, with Pegeen's rich language

[65] J. M. Synge, *Collected Works: Vols 3 and 4, Plays*, ed. Ann Saddlemyer (London: Oxford University Press, 1962–8), 295.

[66] Greene and Stephens, *J. M. Synge*, 260.   [67] Synge, *Collected Works: Vol. 2, Prose*, 95.

[68] Ibid., 95.   [69] Ibid., 82.

beginning the play: "Six yards of stuff for to make a yellow gown. A pair of lace boots with lengthy heels on them and brassy eyes."[70] Synge decided on the idea of a trousseau and the list only in his later drafts, after he knew Molly and during the years that they began to discuss marriage. As Synge and Molly worked together to create a new kind of Irish heroine, Synge wrote major changes into the role, reflecting the concerns from the letters they exchanged. Her input caused him to heighten the importance both of Pegeen's character and of her status as a woman limited by a society that did not appreciate her genius.

The same year that Synge saw Molly in a walk-on part in *The Well of the Saints*, he began writing *The Playboy*. By early December of that year, 1905, Molly had taken on her stage name, Maire O'Neill, and had gained the role of Cathleen in *Riders to the Sea*. The next year, her courtship with Synge well underway, he helped her replace her sister Sara as Nora in *The Shadow of the Glen*. Though he wrote that part before meeting Molly, he began to identify her with the role, and he developed Nora's independence in Pegeen.[71] In fact, the female characters became increasingly independent, chafing at their social roles, as his relationship with Molly grew and he heard from her about her own frustrations as a creative person. Their courtship began that year, in 1906, while Molly rehearsed the part of Nora with Synge. He would sign hundreds of letters he wrote to her with the role of the man who succeeds with Nora, "Your Old Tramp." According to Ann Saddlemyer, the "first use of 'Old Tramp' follows naturally from their private rehearsals of *The Shadow of the Glen* early in 1906," as Synge took on the persona of the man Nora joins to escape her oppressive existence in the cottage.[72] These "private rehearsals" would repeat in the hospital room writing/acting of Deirdre that I discuss in Chapter 4. During this intense first year of their courtship, he wrote *The Playboy*, developing the character of Pegeen as he knew Molly better and discussed the play with her. 1906 was also the year when Synge began to mediate between the actors and directors. He finished the play at

---

[70] Synge, *Playboy*, 9.

[71] Though Synge signed his letters "Your Old Tramp," identifying with the man who wins Nora Burke at the end of *Shadow*, in a letter dated July 20, 1906 he jokingly gives himself both roles, signing off with "Your old tramp alias Dan Burke!" (*LM*, 4) He would begin to identify more with the infatuated elderly suitor in drafts of *Deirdre of the Sorrows*, written during his illness. In November 1907, he remembered her acting in the part of Nora while missing her: "Do you remember your first show of Nora at the Midland? And how you sent me a message that you wanted to see me after it, and beamed with delight when I praised you for it? It is unfortunate that our life separates us so much" (*LM*, 220).

[72] *LM*, xxi.

the end of the year, but revised right up to performance in January 1907, when Molly played Pegeen at the famous first production.

Like Pegeen, who describes herself as "the fright of seven townlands for me biting tongue," Molly was quick to anger and adept with powerful words.[73] Synge often wrote lines like, "Your note…cut me like a knife. It brings tears into my throat when I see you trying to pick a quarrel."[74] Some of Molly's later letters to friends survive and add to the verbally irreverent, forceful person that comes through in Synge's responses to her. In her 1930 letters to a friend in New York, Ria Mooney, she offers her opinion of theater and is actively involved in revising plays. She discusses plans to do a play of *Wuthering Heights* and ends her letters with lines like, "Listen, hussy, when are we going to come to you?" or "I want to see you again and often, so that we can have a real gossip."[75] After playing Christy Mahon in an Australian production starring Molly as Pegeen Mike, Arthur Shields remembered, "She lifted you on a wave that carried you with her and brought you successfully to shore. Often she fought like a wildcat in the wings with you. But once she was on stage, only her art counted."[76] Drama critic James Douglas was impressed by Molly's power in a 1910 revival of *The Playboy*, writing in *The Leader*, "Miss O'Neill unconsciously dominates the men she acts with. She has race in her. She holds her head up and walks and uses the gestures of a conquerer [*sic*]. As Pegeen, she is swift, protean, a ruler of men, and yet as simple and fresh as a wild strawberry."[77] There is a problematic element of Arnoldian Celtic praise here that comes up in discussions of Molly onstage, but her power in performance shows up in contemporary accounts.

Molly often acted against Synge's wishes, and he would respond with letters describing his misery. In September 1906, she stayed on in Stephens Green though Synge disapproved of these arrangements: "You agreed not to stay there as I did not like it for you. Now at the LAST moment you tell me that you are going back on your definite word."[78] He angrily, intemperately ends his letter with "You have finally ruined my holiday." Molly responded to the tirade by not writing him back, and Synge wrote again, typically, with

[73] Synge, *Playboy*, 92.   [74] *LM*, 73.

[75] This correspondence can be found in the Ria Mooney papers, National Library of Ireland, http://catalogue.nli.ie/Collection/vtls000570039.

[76] Qtd. in Mikhail, *W. B. Yeats*, 135.

[77] Qtd. in E. Coxhead, *Daughters of Erin: Five Women of the Irish Renaissance* (London: Smythe, 1979), 196.

[78] *LM*, 24.

complaints about his health. In October, he wrote about his wish to avoid visiting her mother, probably to discuss marriage. In one of the few places where we have her actual part of the correspondence, she wrote in pencil on the letter:

> you may stop if you like, I don't care if I never heard from you or saw you again so there! & please don't let thoughts of me come into your head when you are writing your play. It would be dreadful if your speeches were upset I don't care a 'rap' for the theatre or anyone in it the pantomime season is on and I can easily get a shop; in fact I shall go out this afternoon & apply for one. M. Allgood.[79]

The threat to "get a shop" is thrown in to bait Synge with class difference; Molly is conjuring for Synge ideas of her acting in socially questionable drama, highlighting her tough risk-taking personality and the class gulf between them. These were all triggers for Synge in other letters, and they hit their mark. This correspondence dates from mid-October 1906, and, a couple of weeks later, Synge wrote to Molly, "I had a dreadful turn of despair over the Playboy last night—it seemed helpless–";[80] he struggled with the play most when misunderstandings arose with Molly, and his difficulty was always with Christy. Basing Pegeen on as irreverent and verbally dexterous a person as Molly whose letters gave him plenty to work with was easier than creating the male part of the couple. She claimed that her emotional nature helped her act: "An actor must have that capacity to feel the character he plays. It's that kind of expression and feeling I tried to put into my part of Pegeen Mike as I speak to my lover Christy Mahon in Playboy."[81] Synge wrote the role of Pegeen Mike, also irreverent and easily angered, during his correspondence; Pegeen responds to Shawn's concern about the church, "Stop tormenting me with Father Reilly,"[82] and goes on to imitate his squeamishness. What we know of Molly's letters is that she often mocked and tormented Synge's more upper-class ideas about proper behavior, and he found her challenging language both frustrating and fascinating, especially as her writing found its way into Pegeen Mike.

In the Allgood family, Molly was known as "the wild one," and Synge's letters show that she never feared him, an older man of a higher social

---

[79] *LM*, 38.   [80] *LM*, 44.   [81] Qtd. in Mikhail, *W. B. Yeats*, 82.
[82] Synge, *Playboy*, 12.

class.[83] A few months after her sister Sara Allgood joined the Abbey, Molly became part of the company in 1905. The sisters maintained a competitiveness,[84] and Synge's emphasis on Pegeen's role in *The Playboy* while toning down Sally's Widow Quin must have had much to do with creating the larger part for Molly. Sara gave her sister a backhanded compliment in her memoirs: "She could turn her head to anything without trouble... she was, and still is, amazingly quick with her tongue, always ready with the witty answer, and full of fun and laughter... I have never seen her study a part, when she learned them I do not know."[85] Synge was impressed by Molly's natural quickness and aptitude. She was not an easy person to control; Sara remembered attempting to get the company in order as a stage manager in 1908: "the Company had become too difficult to manage, the biggest offenders were Arthur Sinclair, my sister, Maire O'Neill, and Michael Dolan."[86] Lennox Robinson tried to take over from Sara, but "he too was unable to cope with them, and after a few months he resigned." Synge chose as a partner a woman who was difficult to control and whose voice comes through, even from lost letters, in a role that he revised with her to heighten the importance of a frustrated and linguistically gifted young Pegeen Mike.

Synge's letters show that Molly told him stories of her hardscrabble childhood and adolescence, and Pegeen Mike owes her self-reliance to Molly. Like Pegeen, Molly had to fend for herself from an early age and developed a determined, competitive personality as a result. Molly and Sara Allgood grew up with an "anti-Catholic" Protestant father and a Catholic mother. Their mother worked with priests to get her children secret Catholic religious education without the father's knowledge. The girls learned early the importance of playing roles. As Sara describes the isolation of their childhood: "we always felt that there was something 'different' about us, a family, we... never really mingled."[87] Like Synge, who wrote of his family, "It is funny how I am sort of an 'outsider' with them all,"[88] Sara and Molly, between two cultures, lived a childhood set apart from others. Their father died in 1896, leaving their mother with eight children between the ages of

---

[83] Sara Allgood, "Memories," unpublished manuscript, Berg Collection, New York Public Library, 17.

[84] Molly's memory of her decision to take the name Maire O'Neill reveals how much she wanted to differentiate herself from her sister: "I wanted to be different to Sara, of course, who kept the family name of Allgood. You know the dreams and ambitions of a young actress: she wants to be independent and different from everyone. I wanted to be different from Sara, and to be on my own, to make my own fame and name, so I chose to be Maire O'Neill... and here I am" (qtd. in Mikhail, *W. B. Yeats*, 81).

[85] *LM*, 18.   [86] Allgood, "Memories," 9.   [87] *LM*, 186.   [88] *LM*, 186.

5 months and 15 years and very little money. His last words to their mother voiced a lifelong obsession: "Educate them. Educate them. Put a dictionary under my feet."[89] Both Molly and Sara went to work in local Dublin shops after their father's death; both brought their money home to the family; and they continued to support their family throughout their theatrical careers. Most of their siblings worked at the Abbey: a sister handed out and designed programs and a brother worked on scenery. Their mother read novels to them in the evening, endeavoring to further their education, and allowed Sara to go work at the Abbey only when Lady Gregory promised to look after her as if she were her own daughter. Molly chose her grandmother's name for the stage, telling her sister, "otherwise the whole damn family will be in the programme."[90]

Like most of the iconic female roles at the Abbey, Pegeen's ending in *The Playboy* changed after rehearsal and discussion with the lead actress. Roger McHugh, in his Preface to *J. M. Synge Centenary Papers*, argues that Synge changed the final scene after watching Molly in rehearsals and revisiting the play's evolution with her. Synge changed the draft from one that reads that Pegeen Mike rushes out to make sure that she hasn't lost Christy to one where she "throws her shawl over her head and wails that she has lost him. It is much better so."[91] By crediting this role to "happy chance," McHugh occludes Molly's role in that change, a revision that gives us the title and the most powerful moment in the play. Through watching Molly perform and developing the character with her, Synge shifts the focus to Pegeen Mike at the end—the other hero who gets the last word. McHugh goes on to argue that what made Synge's plays capture "the individuality of a nation" are "the people of Aran and of Cois Fhairrge." In fact, through his knowledge of Molly and his work with her, he was able to write complex women and an Ireland that challenges "the saga people."[92]

Without Synge's knowledge of Molly, Pegeen Mike would have been a more generic, less controversial figure. What set the critics and audience off was her specificity. The Fays had hoped for a more stereotypical, shallow and sweet version of Irish womanhood. As W. G. Fay remembers, "Frank and I begged with (Synge) to make Pegeen a decent likeable country girl,

---

[89] Allgood, "Memories," 9.   [90] Ibid., 48.

[91] J. M. Synge, *Centenary Papers 1971*, ed. Maurice Harman (Dublin: Dolmen Press, 1971), xii.

[92] Synge, as I discuss in Chapter 5, derided "the saga people" in his creation of a new Deirdre. See J. M. Synge, *The Collected Letters of J. M. Synge, 1907-1909*, 2 vols, ed. Ann Saddlemyer (Oxford: Clarendon Press, 1984), ii, 56.

which she might easily have been without injury to the play," but Synge insisted on creating a more complicated and controversial female lead based on Molly's challenging personality.[93] Synge refused to change language he believed important to the play: W. G. Fay remembers pleading with Synge to remove the violent scenes in *The Playboy*: "to take out the scene in the last ask when the peasants burn Christy." The restrictions and possibilities of the stage, however, cause the play to remain fluid up to and during its production. Lady Gregory remembered the effect of the stage on Synge's drafts of *The Playboy*, a play that, like most of the Abbey texts, was a work in progress during performance:

> He worked very hard at The Playboy, altering it a good deal as he went on. He had first planned the opening act in the ploughed field, where the quarrel between Christy and his father took place. But when he thought of the actual stage he could not see any possible side wings for the 'wide, windy corner of high distant hills.' He had also talked of the return of the father being at the very door of the chapel where Christy was to wed Pegeen; but in the end all took place within the one cottage room. We all tried at that time for as little scene-shifting as might be, for the economy of scenery and stage-hands.[94]

Gregory brings up what distinguishes writing for theatrical production: Synge changed his earlier drafts in part because of the limitations and possibilities of the Abbey set and theater workers. Heidi Holder traces the way that actions became storytelling in the drafts of *The Playboy*, most notably in the onstage violence that turns into story as Synge reworked the play for performance.[95] Máire Nic Shiubhlaigh corroborates Gregory's memory that Synge had started the play outdoors but "subsequently rewrote parts of the play for the interior when it was pointed out that the presentation of the original scene was impossible."[96] Lady Gregory regretted that cuts Synge had allowed her to make had not reached the performers for the *Playboy* premier: "He gave me leave to do this (cut some language). I am

---

[93] William George Fay and Catherine MacFarlane Carswell, *The Fays of the Abbey Theatre: An Autobiographical Record* (London: Rich and Cowan, 1935), 213.

[94] Lady Augusta Gregory, *Our Irish Theatre* (London: Putnam, 1913), 79–80.

[95] Heidi Holder, "Between Fiction and Reality: Synge's *Playboy* and Its Audience," *Journal of Modern Literature*, 14:4 (Spring 1988): 530.

[96] Máire Nic Shiubhlaigh, *The Splendid Years* (Dublin: James Duffy, 2016 [1955]), 80.

sorry that they were not taken out before it had been played at all."[97] These statements show how authorial and textual fixity in the world of the Abbey are elusive and stress the importance of examining how the plays came to be through observation of stagecraft and performance as well as input from the actresses playing the leads.

Though Molly played Pegeen Mike exclusively for years, the role of Christy Mahon went from Willie Fay to Fred O'Donovan after Synge's death. While Fay's interpretation of Christy was "a little sardonic," O'Donovan gave the role "more charm and gaiety," and there was "no trouble with the audience."[98] Máire Nic Shiubhlaigh preferred Fay's Christy: "His love scene with Pegeen, played exquisitely by Maire O'Neill, was one of the most beautiful pieces of acting I have ever seen," but he troubled the line between tragedy and comedy in the play, and the audience would be more comfortable with O'Donovan's approach.[99] The play, then, comes out of the letters as a love story, in Molly Allgood's stage interpretation, a retelling of her relationship with Synge that explores the tensions between two artists who hope to escape from an unappreciative and stultifying society.

On that night, January 26, 1907, the curtain raiser was Synge's earlier drama *Riders to the Sea*, a tragedy about a woman and her two daughters and the loss of the men in her family to the sea. The response from the audience to this particularly maternal, stoic, and loving picture of tragic Irish womanhood was "long and appreciative applause."[100] What was different about womanhood in *The Playboy*? While the women in *Riders* engage in lament, Pegeen searches for joy, and that emotion and its artistic freedom set off the audience. There was something about Molly playing her particular brand of exhilaration in language that triggered a response, even in the newspaper reviews after the performance.

In performance, the play was still in flux; like most theater, as I discussed in the Introduction, it was still being written before and after reaching the stage. Lady Gregory had tried to change some of the more offensive language, she claimed, with Synge's permission, but the changes did not reach the players in the chaos of the first nights. Fay, as Christy, altered the lines that sent the crowds into riot, "what'd I care if you brought me a drift of chosen females standing in their shifts itself, maybe, from this place to the

[97] Gregory, *Our Irish Theatre*, 80–1.
[98] Padraig Colum, *The Road Round Ireland* (New York, Macmillan, 1930), 268–9.
[99] Nic Shiubhlaigh, *The Splendid Years*, 82.   [100] Synge, *Centenary Papers 1971*, 75.

Eastern world?" to "a drift of Mayo girls," making the offense more personal and specific. According to Máire Nic Shiubhlaigh, the play "was played seriously almost somberly, as though each character had been studied and its nastiness made apparent."

Synge writes to Molly the next day "exhilarated." The pronouns he uses are important:

> It is better any day to have the row we had last night, than to have your play fizzling out in half-hearted applause. Now we'll be talked about. We're an event in the history of the Irish stage.[101]

The "we" he refers to here is their twosome, their work together bringing the play into text and performance. And he wants them noticed, talked about— this is a rebuke to the traditional idea of their relationship.[102]

The riots were an urban and suburban community's horror at what they saw as a misrepresentation of the female, rural West, an ideal source of feminine Irishness. During the January 26, 1907 premier, "A smartly clad gentleman in the stalls protested against the Widow Quin's poverty."[103] Women are the flashpoint in this moment that reveals the relationship between gender and questions of poverty and class; had Synge kept to the early, pre-Molly drafts that only concerned Christy, the response would have been different. That night, the line between the stage and the audience broke down—the realism of the set and the suggestion that "some of the policemen might be best occupied arresting Christie" led to confusion about that boundary. Yeats himself played the role of his class, gender, and theater privilege, as noted by the *Herald*: "Yeats, like Poe's raven, upon a privileged staircase at the side of the stage." He played a version of himself here, an icon of privilege and access. After the curtain, the performance of songs protesting the play with some actual fisticuffs went to the street. On the third night, "not more than six consecutive lines had been audible." If the audience was only hearing parts of the play, then what were they responding to? Not the actual play, but the realism of the set and characters. In Padraic Colum's memory, the problem started with Christy Mahon's entry: "The scene was

---

[101] *LM*, 88.

[102] Paige Reynolds, in *Modernism, Drama, and the Audience for Irish Spectacle* (Cambridge: Cambridge University Press, 2007), like many critics, quotes this same passage and, like others, she does not discuss the "we'll" or the "we're" that signal's Synge's sense that the play belonged to them both.

[103] Synge, *Centenary Papers 1971*, 81.

too representational. There stood a man with a horrible bloodied bandage upon his head, making a figure that took the whole thing out of the atmosphere of high comedy."[104] And this has much to do with how the Abbey audience had been trained to view gauzy myths of Ireland, of Gods and Fighting men.[105] The Abbey taught the audience to expect one thing; tensions of class and religion mounted, and then this challenging performance erupted.

The response to *The Playboy* had everything to do with the young woman performing the lead role onstage. She had brought to the writing, revision, and performance of the role her signature attitude of challenge, and the audience responded. The comments by University College, Dublin librarian D. J. O'Donoghue and architect MacNamara illustrate the fact that the men in the audience lived in a world of gender roles that was regressive and reactionary.[106] With shifts in society, the roles of women are tightened and policed. O'Donoghue and MacNamara, after the play, "agreed fervently that it was a good thing they had their wives at home."[107] The idea that women needed to be protected from offending images of femininity onstage shows strange fears about infection, as if the performance of an actress that offends gender roles could somehow contagiously affect women in the audience. The language above about the wives is better suited to children, but not uncommon in the Dublin of 1907. *The Freeman's Journal* writes about the play, "as for his women, it is not possible, even if it were desirable, to class them." The writer for the *Journal*, then, loses language in the face of what he sees as the unutterable, an Irish woman expressing dissatisfaction with her life and the hope of joy with a young man who, through language, offers a possible way out that they can work towards together. This is what is unspeakable—the mention of unhappiness and the hope for escape. Pegeen's agency, limited as it is, and her hope for more possibility through a relationship with a fellow would-be artist, constitute an extreme threat for the audience and the writer of the review. Critics add their voice to the

---

[104] Colum, *The Road Round Ireland*, 76.

[105] Colum and the audience respond here to the contrast, one Synge and Molly were at pains to highlight, between their interpretation of stagecraft and Irishness onstage and that of AE and his ethereal 1902 *Deirdre*.

[106] *Engendering Ireland: New Reflections on Modern History and Literature*, edited by Laura Kelly, Sarah-Ann Buckley, and Rebecca-Anne Barr (Cambridge Scholars Publishing, 2015) traces the development of gendered spaces in the Irish public sphere. *Performance Ireland Special Issue: Gender, Sexuality, and the City*, edited by Cormac O'Brien and Shonagh Hill also helpfully maps the gender dynamics in the Irish public sphere.

[107] Synge, *Centenary Papers 1971*, 77.

critiques of Pegeen Mike's femininity even as late as the mid-1990s: "Pegeen Mike is more circumspect. Of course, this would be in keeping with a maidenly demeanor."[108] "Maidenly demeanor" seems inappropriate for Pegeen and misses the tone of the play, and phrases such as this one continue the *Playboy* riot tendency to police women's bodies. Pegeen Mike, built out of Synge's norm-busting relationship with Molly, continues to throw off critics and challenge viewers.

Pegeen directs the production as Synge imagined Molly eventually stage managing and directing Dublin theater projects they would produce together. She knows from the start where everyone is and begins the play ordering props. The setting is not a tidy cottage but a messy pub, a place of work like the Abbey. Once Christy Mahon shows up, Pegeen directs him, decides on his family and his past, and interrupts him to redirect his conversation, "wisht your talking of girls."[109] Christy entertains ideas of belonging to a higher class after Pegeen suggests he might be from an aristocratic background; anything goes in this new setting for Christy at first, and Pegeen is willing to re-imagine his identity and her own as well, managing the identities onstage.

Though portrayals of femininity got the vocal responses during the premier, the play's depiction of Irish masculinity was a source of real anguish for the audience, and the more vocal concerns about the women onstage protested too much, occluding the fear of how the men behaved in the play. From the first scene, Shawn is an anti-tramp, one with "little will to be walking off to wakes and weddings in the darkness of the night," and Pegeen's summation of the sacred Irish village community of the West is a "queer lot"—those unable to function in physical or mental health. Pegeen has no use for the clergy, and when Shawn expresses fear at staying with her alone, she retorts, "stop tormenting me with Father Reilly." Shawn astutely notes the similarity between Pegeen and Christy: "She wouldn't suit you, and she with the divil's own temper the way you'd be strangling one another in a score of days;"[110] this description is an apt assessment of many of the Synge/Allgood letters. In his vanity as he continues to flip gender roles, Christy likes trying on Shawn's clothes, has done little to no work, and wants Pegeen to see him in his new outfit. Ever the businesswoman, Widow Quin tries to get Shawn to pay her with farm items and livestock to marry Christy and keep him from Pegeen. Shawn is game. The sea remains the locus of

---

[108] Daniel Casey, ed., *Critical Essays on J. M. Synge* (Boston, MA: n.p., 1994), 131.
[109] Synge, *Playboy*, 54.   [110] Ibid., 11.

Pegeen's and the Widow Quin's fantasies; Pegeen is tempted to sail away and "marry a Jew-man."[111] Abby Bender's *Israelites in Erin* argues that Irish and Jewish people "understood their nationalisms in complex, even incongruous ways" leading to "paradoxical analogies" in Revival images of Exodus.[112] In this evocation of Judaism, Pegeen casts the "Jew-man" as an exotic stranger on the seas, but the line is also freighted with the suggestions of diaspora and landlessness in the connections between Jewish and Irish identities that Bender describes. The island village's proximity, as Widow Quin reminds us watching the boats go by, to the ocean pathways of trade and the non-Irish on those boats, tantalizes those onshore. The villagers, the women in particular, are looking for an imaginative way out, an Exodus of the mind from the limitations of their circumscribed lives. The male characters represent fear, and the two women redefine identities and challenge nationalist icons. The women here experience desire, expressing a sexuality that reflects Synge's fears of Molly's relationships with other men in the letters.

While Synge worked on *The Playboy*, he brought Molly into existing parts for revival performances of his earlier plays. He wrote to Lady Gregory on March 10, 1906, "I have just performed the delicate operation of getting Sara Allgood out of Nora Burke's part—where she was impossible—and getting Molly Allgood in. Molly A's voice is too young for the part but she feels it, and has some expression."[113] As Edward Stephens, Synge's nephew and biographer, argues: "From Molly he was creating an image of the woman to whom he could relate himself in adult life, and was gradually to unite it with his earlier imaginings to form the composite conception of woman dramatized in his closing works."[114] Stephens hints here at a part of my argument: Synge's vision of Molly and his use of her language and performance to create Pegeen Mike build on his earlier observations of women, but in the case of their relationship, he has access to her language through letters and more extensive conversation. This closeness allows him to write a new kind of heroine, one that threatens nationalist orthodoxy.

In John Butler Yeats's sketch "Synge at Rehearsal," Synge, looking up from below the stage, watches the 1907 preparations for *The Playboy* with focus and amusement (Figure 3.3).[115] Yeats and Gregory both emphasized

---

[111] Ibid., 92.

[112] Abby Bender, *Israelites in Erin* (Syracuse, NY: Syracuse University Press, 2015), 2.

[113] *LM*, xix.   [114] Greene and Stephens, *J. M. Synge*, 178.

[115] May Craig remembers, "Offstage in those days, Máire wore glasses. You could see that Synge was very taken with her. I used to see him as he had been drawn by J. B. Yeats . . . in that

Figure 3.3 "Synge at Rehearsal," by J. B. Yeats
Source: Courtesy of the Abbey Theatre Archive.

Synge's reserved nature in their memoirs. Yeats describes him as "a drifting, silent man, full of hidden passion," and Gregory comments on his "complete absorption in his own dream"[116] These misreadings are strategic: Yeats and Gregory imagined Synge as an example of the Ascendancy loner, separate from the drama of the stage. Synge was, however, involved with theatrical productions as well as politics at the Abbey; Sara Allgood's description of Synge reminds us of his position as liaison between actors and directors. Unlike Yeats, Gregory, and Annie Horniman, he was clearly at ease with the players: according to Allgood, "we would never take a liberty with her or W. B. Yeats or laugh and chatter with them as we did with J. M. Synge."[117]

pencil sketch 'Synge at Rehearsal' leaning forward and looking adoringly at Máire" (qtd. in Mikhail, *W. B. Yeats*, 78–9).

    [116] W. B. Yeats, *Memoirs: An Autobiography—First Draft, Journal*, ed. Denis Donoghue (New York: Macmillan, 1974), 203; Gregory, *Our Irish Theatre*, 76.

    [117] Allgood, "Memories," 44.

Her memory of him counters his reputation as a distant artist: "I remember him so well, in the Green Room with us he would play his fiddle, or tell us stories of his travels abroad, and his living on the Aran Islands, and his great love for the Islanders. He was a very nervous, very high strung man and extremely shy, but not with us."[118] To the actors, Synge showed a different side of his persona—one that allowed for more casual collaboration.

After collaborating on *The Playboy*, Synge and Molly went on to work as actress and director on theatrical productions at the Abbey. A year after the premier of *The Playboy*, Synge directed Molly Allgood in Hermann Sudermann's *Teja*, a play about a husband and wife, as he and Molly began to realize their hopes of a future working together as creative artists. *Teja*, the first of Lady Gregory's translated plays to be directed by Synge, starred Molly Allgood in the lead role of Bathlida. The translation is an example of Gregory's efforts to produce famous foreign plays in "Kiltartan" dialect; she translated Sudermann's *Teja* from German. The March 1908 production garnered accolades from *The Freeman's Journal*: J. M. Kerrigan and Maire O'Neill "were the most admirable."[119] How the reviewer knew how a woman in a "Gothic camp" might act is beside the point; he found Molly's performance persuasive. The play tells the story of "the effect of woman upon warrior," as the Allgood character teaches her bloodthirsty soldier husband humanity. As Christy responds to Pegeen's attentions by growing more expansive in his language and idea of himself, Allgood's character in *Teja* transforms her husband.

In April 1908, Synge again directed Molly in another play translated into "Kiltartanese" by Lady Gregory, Moliere's *The Rogueries of Scapin*. The Fays had departed from the company in January, leaving Synge and Yeats in control of the daily work of the theater, with Sara Allgood as stage manager. This increased involvement in the Abbey for Synge, as well as hopes of setting up house for his planned marriage to Molly, precipitated his move from his mother's house to Rathmines in February. Gregory wrote Synge in March 1907 to say that she was "translating 'Scapin' as hard as I can for Easter Monday," but the play would not be produced for another year.[120] Synge was proud of Molly's accomplishment and their work together on this play, writing to Lady Gregory a few months before the premier, on January 3

[118] Ibid., 49.
[119] Qtd. in R. Hogan and J. Kilroy, *Modern Irish Drama: A Documentary History, Vol. 3, The Abbey Theatre: The Years of Synge, 1905–1909* (Dolmen Press, 1978), 218.
[120] Qtd. in *Lady Gregory: Fifty Years After*, ed. Ann Saddlemyer and Colin Smythe (Gerard's Cross, 1987), 283.

1909: "I have spoken very strongly to (Henderson) about this exaggerated starring of Miss Allgood. He is quite infatuated. He says Scapin did not go in Belfast—because Scapin is nothing without Miss Allgood!"[121] His praise both of Allgood's work in Scapin and of her effect on Henderson end the letter on a gleeful note, slighting Gregory's *Rogueries*. Molly had been discussing rehearsals of Gregory's translation of Moliere's *The Miser* with Synge. That play, also starring Molly Allgood and Fred O'Donovan, would open on January 21, 1909. The letter also shows Synge's argument that a play necessitates certain performers to be effective.

As I discuss in detail in Chapter Five, Synge and Molly would collaborate on his last, unfinished play, *Deirdre of the Sorrows*, another characterization of a woman who does not fit into nationalist iconography. After the famous production of the *The Playboy* in late January 1907, an offended anonymous writer for *The Freeman's Journal* objected to Molly Allgood's mention of "shifts" in the play: a word "which the lady would probably never utter in ordinary circumstances, even to herself."[122] Signing off as "a Western girl," this writer defends Molly against the words in the play as if Molly were somehow a captive of the script and not complicit in its production. In fact, Molly's provocative, creative personality allowed Synge to imagine a Pegeen Mike with a gift for language. Her words allow her to re-imagine herself and Christy Mahon as artists who work together under trapped social circumstances, like the couple who created the play. Molly would name her daughter Pegeen, and one remembers Synge's early comments on creation of children and art. The play's role was their creation, and Molly signaled that when she decided on a name for her own child.

[121] J. M. Synge, *Some Letters of John M. Synge to Lady Gregory and W.B. Yeats*, ed. Ann Saddlemyer (Dublin: Cuala Press, 1971), 84.

[122] Qtd. in Jonathan Saville, ed., *From Script to Production* (Ann Arbor: University of Michigan Press, 1975), 237.

4

A "Brutal" Deirdre

Molly Allgood's Body and *Deirdre of the Sorrows*

This chapter contrasts Yeats's queens with the physicality of women's bodies on the stages of Synge's plays. The contrast in the way that these two writers imagined both women and nation is due to the contributions of the women who inspired, performed, and revised their plays. In the case of Molly Allgood and Synge's *Deirdre of the Sorrows*, Molly, at Synge's deathbed instruction, completed the play with Yeats and Lady Gregory, and then, in a collaborative moment that brought together issues of class, gender, and authorship, Molly performed the premier. Yeats himself diagnosed what made Synge's writing different from his own in *The Death of Synge*: "He loves all that has edge, all that is salt in the mouth, all that is rough to the hand, all that heightens the emotions by contest, all that stings into life the sense of tragedy."[1] The link between Synge and the gritty lives of his central female characters was Molly Allgood's language and body. To Ann Saddlemyer, *Deirdre of the Sorrows* was a form of "the man speaking" to Molly, Synge expressing himself to her; in this chapter I investigate the ways that Molly Allgood herself, not just Synge's efforts to reach her, affect the play as it was conceived, written, posthumously completed, and performed.

This chapter investigates the specific ways that Synge's fiancée, Abbey actress Molly Allgood, guided revision of Revival tropes through her language and physical performance, influencing Synge's ideas of nation and the body.[2] Their relationship was different from any other collaboration between writers and actresses in the Revival; Synge and Molly were engaged to be married and had daily conversation in person and in writing about the play that they were creating together. The depth of their relationship while they worked on the play and Molly's work completing the draft after Synge's

---

[1] W. B. Yeats, "The Death of Synge," *Essays and Introductions* (New York: Macmillan, 1962), 326–7.
[2] Declan Kiberd writes that Synge "built" his revision of an ethereal Deirdre "into the very structure and style of *Deirdre of the Sorrows*" in *The Cambridge Companion to J. M. Synge*, ed. P. J. Mathews, (Cambridge: Cambridge University Press), 66.

Gender, Performance, and Authorship at the Abbey Theatre. Elizabeth Brewer Redwine, Oxford University Press (2021). © Elizabeth Brewer Redwine. DOI: 10.1093/oso/9780192896346.003.0004

death led to a Deirdre that challenges accepted Revival ideas of femininity and nation.

Molly Allgood died in 1952 at the age of 67, from burns due to a fall into her fireplace at her small London apartment. This chapter will end with a more extensive discussion of that moment, but it is worth keeping Allgood's destitute end in mind and considering the real consequences of who gets credit for the major texts of the Abbey and how being written out of the story affects the lives of performers, especially if they are Irish, female, and working class. The Deirdre myth was, as we shall see in the next two chapters, a flashpoint for writers of the Revival. Molly Allgood guided Synge in his re-imagining of Deirdre, and their Deirdre presented new ways of thinking about nation, women, myth, and history, grounding the revered symbol of female Ireland in physicality and the real.

In December 1906, a few weeks after Florence Darragh's premier performance as Yeats's *Deirdre*, J. M. Synge began to carry out his plans to write a play with Molly Allgood stripping the myth of "saga" and making it "human" and "brutal." Asking her to collaborate with him on the project, he was characteristically pragmatic about his own health problems: "If I don't kick the bucket I ought to be able to do good work and plenty of it. You must help me and keep me up to it."[3] Synge disliked both Darragh's interpretation of Yeats's play and George Russell's ethereal *Deirdre* (1902), and set out to create a new take on the myth with Molly, one that performed their shared interest in the bodily grotesque and in Ireland as an actual physical place. This chapter ends with a discussion of how, after Synge's death, Molly Allgood, with Yeats and Lady Gregory, completed the unfinished text of the play for the stage. Allgood's contributions both during Synge's creation of the role and after his death, lost to criticism, show that the play's unorthodox approach to performance, nation, and the body are thanks to her.

Writing *Deirdre of the Sorrows*, Synge and Molly Allgood have a clear agenda: they hope to replace Yeatsian queens onstage with a specific woman's body, a particular role written with the aid of the woman performer.[4]

---

[3] J. M. Synge and Maire O'Neill, *Letters to Molly: John Millington Synge to Maire O'Neill, 1906–1909*, ed. Ann Saddlemyer (Cambridge, MA: Belknap Press of Harvard University Press, 1971), 68.

[4] Mary Burke, "Killing the Queen: Yeats, McDonagh, and Punk," *Gender, Sex, and Sexuality.* Critical Insights Series. Ed. Margaret Breen (Ipswich, MA: Salem Press, 2014); Eavann Boland's *Object Lessons: The Life of the Woman and the Poet in Our Time* (New York: W. W. Norton, 1998) provides further discussion of the effect of Yeatsian queen imagery on contemporary poetry.

The questions that Molly Allgood and Synge raised about what it means to be a "queen," how female power figures onstage and in song embody power, continue to bedevil Irish writers and critics in interesting ways. Allgood and Synge's challenge of Irish queen hagiography predates a future move in the punk movement, introducing grit into what was previously symbolic. In "Killing the Queen: Yeats, McDonagh, and Punk," Mary Burke brings the discussion of Yeats's queens across the ocean to British theater and the "reduced queen" of McDonagh's "Beauty Queen of Leenanne" and the London Irish Sex Pistols' "Killing the Queen." In their punk inversions, McDonagh, Johnny Rotten, and Synge react not only to *Cathleen ni Houlihan*, but to the series of queens created by Yeats, Lady Gregory, and the actresses I will discuss in Chapter 5. In 1910, eight years after *Cathleen ni Houlihan* brought the tableaux queens of Inghinidhe to the Abbey stage, Molly Allgood challenged ideas about women, history, and power in her embodiment of a script she had helped write.

The contrast between Synge's image of Deirdre and Yeats's had everything to do with the very different women who helped them create theatrical texts. Yeats wrote many of his plays for unattainable, Pre-Raphaelite women like Laura Armstrong and Maud Gonne, imagining them as idealized sacrificial figures removed from everyday life. "Yeats's early poetry," as Elizabeth Butler Cullingford points out, "consistently deploys the traditional romance structure of elevation and debasement: the mistress is above and the lover is at her feet," and his 1906 *Deirdre* continues this pattern, as I discuss in the following chapter.[5] With his last, unfinished play, *Deirdre of the Sorrows*, J. M. Synge countered both the iconography of Yeats's 1890s poetry and drama and Yeats's take on Deirdre with a part written for Molly Allgood. Synge's nephew Edward Stephens remembered a conversation with his uncle about the project: "I said, 'Won't you be accused of copying George Russell and Yeats? Haven't they written plays about Deirdre?' He said, 'Oh no—there isn't any danger of that. People are entitled to use those old stories in any way they wish. My treatment of the story wouldn't be like either of theirs.'"[6] While Yeats wrote for inaccessible women, Synge created the major parts in his plays for Molly Allgood, his close companion and fiancée; the disparity between the writers' relationships with female performers led

---

[5] Elizabeth Butler Cullingford, *Gender and History in Yeats's Love Poetry* (Cambridge: Cambridge University Press, 1993), 25.

[6] David H. Greene and Edward M. Stephens, *J. M. Synge: 1871–1909* (New York: New York University Press, 1989), 301.

them to create contrasting Deirdres. And in writing a new Deirdre, Synge also countered Revival images of what Marjorie Howes calls the "complex... intersections between nationality, gender, and class,"[7] tying these concepts, so often ethereal in the work of other Abbey playwrights, to his particular knowledge of his fiancée.

Molly Allgood's working-class background differed from that of the upper- and upper-middle-class women who collaborated with Yeats. Molly's upbringing helped Synge imagine a new kind of female heroism. Unlike the wealthy Anglo-Irish or British women who played the leads in Yeats's plays, Molly Allgood, as I discussed in Chapter 3, was raised in tenement Dublin by a Catholic mother and a Protestant father and had to work from a young age to support her family and dissemble to practice Catholicism. Onstage, Molly developed a naturalistic approach to acting, and, in contrast to the tall beauties who inspired Yeats's otherworldly heroines, she was short and petite. Her irreverent personality, a survival tool during her upbringing, also inspired Synge to write a new Deirdre in contrast to the stately, blank-verse speaking role Yeats created for Gonne, Florence Farr, Florence Darragh, and Mrs. Patrick Campbell. Synge hoped that his play, as he explained to the Irish American journalist Frederick J. Gregg on September 12, 1907, would offer an alternative to Yeats's and AE's views of both legend and Ireland: "A play on Deirdre—it would be amusing to compare it with Yeats and Russell (AE)—but I am a little afraid that the 'Saga' people might loosen my grip on reality."[8] Molly Allgood's matter-of-fact attitude towards life and performance helped Synge to ground the play in "ordinary life."[9] Yeats's struggle to find the perfect Deirdre for the stage, and his quest for the right actress, also contrasts with Synge, who wrote for one woman he knew well and left the play with instructions for her to revise when he died.

Because of Molly Allgood's intense involvement with her family and the social life of the Abbey and Dublin, Synge wrote a Deirdre defined by her relationship with others. Synge was an isolated man who wrote about community, and Molly Allgood was his link to that experience. Yeats's Deirdre begins the play in isolation and distances herself from all other characters but her lover by the final scene, while Synge's Deirdre lives and

---

[7] Marjorie Howes, *Yeats's Nations: Gender, Class, and Irishness* (Cambridge: Cambridge University Press, 1996), 10.

[8] J. M. Synge, *The Collected Letters of J. M. Synge, 1907–1909, Vol. 2*, ed. Ann Saddlemyer (Oxford: Clarendon Press, 1984), 56.

[9] J. M. Synge, *The Complete Works of J. M. Synge: Plays, Prose, and Poetry*, ed. Aidan Arrowsmith (Ware: Wordsworth Editions, 2008), 433.

dies in a web of relationships. Chapter 5 details how Yeats helped to write a new kind of "passionate and solitary" Deirdre based on the performance he sought from Darragh and Campbell; he wrote the part originally in an effort to imagine Maud Gonne as separate from the scandal of divorce and modernity.[10] While Yeats begins his play with Deirdre's and Naoise's arrival in Emain on the day of their lonely deaths, Synge builds a community around Deirdre for two acts, constructing, in the first act, a life with her caretakers, Lavarcham and the Old Woman, in her childhood home of Slieve Fuadh. Synge called Molly Allgood a changeling, misspelled "changling"; after her father's death, as I discuss in Chapter 3, economic problems had landed her in an orphanage.[11] She quickly escaped the children's home and returned to her mother's house to join her seven brothers and sisters in their work to support the family. Molly took a job in a shop until she followed her sister to the Abbey. In Synge's play, Deirdre is an orphan, but, like Molly, she is nevertheless the center of a network of familial and community ties.

Molly's large family was unconventional and financially troubled; the children all found work after their father's death, most of them at the Abbey. And for the Allgood family, the Abbey was not simply a place for artistic and political expression but also the location of their employment. This family needed the paychecks, and Yeats, Synge, and Gregory often missed the importance of salaries to a family in financial need.[12] The group was closely knit, and the Allgood sisters fostered familial relationships in the Abbey as well. While Yeats removed figures original to the legend who had personal relationships with Deirdre, Synge recovered these characters and made them central to his retelling of the myth. Synge wrote Molly's connections into the play: Lavarcham, the Old Woman, and the Sons of Usnach, absent from Yeats's *Deirdre*, maintain familial ties with Deirdre and Naisi in Synge's version in relationships that are important to survival. Indeed, Naisi and Deirdre exchange harsh words before his death because he chooses to go fight with his brothers who are crying out for him, emphasizing the importance of family and community to Synge's idea of heroism. Survival in

[10] W. B. Yeats, *Explorations* (New York: Macmillan, 1962), 416.

[11] For a feminist discussion of the changeling in Irish literature, see M. Sihra, ed., *Women in Irish Drama: A Century of Authorship and Representation* (Basingstoke: Palgrave Macmillan, 2007), 181.

[12] Adrian Frazier provides an invaluable summary of the class issues and questions of salary at the Abbey in *Behind the Scenes: Yeats, Horniman, and the Struggle for the Abbey Theatre* (Berkeley: University of California Press, 1990).

Synge's and Molly's formulation has everything to do with one's relationship to others.

By including the outdoors as part of her community, the Deirdre created by Synge and Molly possesses a strong connection to nature, and not the fairy world of poems like Yeats's *The Stolen Child*, but a specific exterior landscape. Unlike Yeats and Russell, Synge did not imagine Deirdre as a link to an ideal Irish past; land in his play is not imaginary but as tactile as dirt, an important prop in the last act. He created a female character connected not to an ideal nation but to the specific mountainous landscape of her birth. Ireland, in this play, is not an abstract idea but a collection of particular, local, known places. In Russell's version of the myth, on the other hand, Ireland exists on a grand scale; Russell's Ainle says to Deirdre in exile, "Dear sister, it is the land which gave us birth; which ever like a mother whispered to us, and its whisper is sweeter than the promise of beloved lips."[13] Russell lands the audience squarely in the world of a nation figured as a mother. Conceiving of national allegiance and Deirdre's power as equally majestic, Russell's take on the myth blames Deirdre for distracting the Sons of Usnach from their duty to a grandly imagined, fairy Ireland, or "Mother Dana who breathed up love through the dim earth to my heart."[14] Naisi admonishes Deirdre in Russell's play: "Deirdre! Deirdre! It is not right for you, beautiful woman, to come between a thousand exiles and their own land." There is nothing "dim" in the descriptions of Ireland that Synge and Molly Allgood created in his last play; all is particular.

In Synge's interpretation, Ireland resembles neither mother nor lover, and Deirdre's attachment to the mountain of her birth lacks the symbolic quality of Cathleen ni Houlihan's role as a representation of an imagined Ireland. Lavarcham admonishes Conchubar for his efforts to separate Deirdre from the mountains of her youth. In exile, this Deirdre longs not for an ideal Ireland, but for the place of her childhood: "I'm wishing to set my foot on Slieve Fuadh, where I was running one time and leaping the streams."[15] Synge's Deirdre, more at home outdoors than in a palace, begins the play "without a thought but for her beauty and to be straying in the hills."[16] The older women, Deirdre's caretakers, know her better than any of the other characters and associate her with the animals in the mountains: "she's little call to mind an old woman when she has the birds to school her . . . I'd do as well speaking to a lamb of ten weeks out racing the hills."[17] The letters show

---

[13] George Russell, *Imaginations and Reveries* (Frankfurt: Outlook, 2018), 160.
[14] Ibid., 164.   [15] Synge, *Complete Works*, 171.   [16] Ibid., 147.   [17] Ibid., 150.

that Synge imagined a less idealized Deirdre based on his knowledge of Molly; he rejected Revival icons of woman as a symbol of nationhood, preferring to include the land that Deirdre knew as part of her community.

Chapter 3 explained how Synge's association between Molly and nature contributed to the language of *The Playboy*. In the last years of his life, his letters to Molly show that his creativity as a writer, his sense of loss as an ailing man, and his concept of her as a Deirdre of the open air came from his memories of walking with her outdoors. (As I discuss in the previous chapter, Molly's side of the correspondence is lost. Synge likely destroyed it to protect her reputation, so readers must carefully reconstruct her perspective from his responses.) On November 1, 1907, he wrote a hopeful letter to her about his progress on the play: "I worked hard and I think well on Deirdre this morning. If I go on like this I may have it done for the season if only I escape illness."[18] This confident update on Deirdre precedes a description of a recent walk with Molly and details the local landscape. Synge succeeded at *Deirdre of the Sorrows* when he was happy with Molly, and, as he wrote in September 1908, they were happiest outside: "However in a few days with the help of God we'll be out in the glens again and then we won't be in danger of getting at cross purposes as we are in these accursed letters."[19] When they did clash on these walks, the disagreements helped him write of the "hard word(s)" between Naisi, Deirdre, and Conchubar.[20] In August 1908, in the midst of his work on *Deirdre of the Sorrows*, he wrote to Molly: "I wasn't at the worse I think for our great little walk on Saturday... I've been working at Deirdre this morning."[21] During the more painful days of his illness, he pined most for these walks: "my God if we could only be well again and out in the hills for one long summer day what heaven it would be. I feel ready to cry I am getting better so slowly."[22] This wish made its way into his vision of Deirdre as a girl of the outdoors. Like Synge approaching his own death, Deirdre remembers walks outside as she prepares to die, and says to Naisi: "I'll turn my thoughts back from this night, that's pitiful for want of pity, to the time it was your rods and cloaks made a little tent for me... "[23] Both in the play and in Synge's letters, walks outdoors continue in memory after they are no longer possible. In the final lines of the play, Lavarcham's lament for Deirdre's death both claims the importance of

[18] J. M. Synge and M. O'Neill, *Letters to Molly: John Millington Synge to Maire O'Neill, 1906–1909*, ed. Ann Saddlemyer (Cambridge, MA: Belknap Press of Harvard University Press, 1971), 209.

[19] Ibid., 275.   [20] Synge, *Complete Works*, 179 (hereafter *P & P*).

[21] Ibid., 269–70.   [22] Ibid., 269–70.   [23] Ibid., 213.

Deirdre's relationship to her caretaker and emphasizes her link to the natural world as one of the many familial ties: "Deirdre is dead, and Naisi is dead, and if the oaks and stars could die for sorrow, it's a dark sky and a hard and naked earth we'd have this night in Emain."[24] In Lavarcham's keen, nature senses Deirdre's departure and feels sympathy for her, and, in the play's closing image, Ireland is again local, evoked by the specific landscape of Emain.

If earlier versions of the woman-as-nation trope tend to efface the individuality of the symbolic actress, linking the heroine with an idealized nation, Synge's work on *Deirdre of the Sorrows* demonstrates his appreciation for Molly as a unique individual. As he hoped to bring "personality" into his poetry, he also preferred performance styles that emphasized the individuality of the actor. Molly's approach to theater influenced Synge; Lennox Robinson contrasted her style of acting with her sister Sara's: "Sally's tragedy was grandiose, Molly's was intimate and personal."[25] Synge's December 1906 reaction to the established British actresses Yeats brought into the company reveals Synge's problems with what he saw as a "readymade style" in contrast to Molly's more realistic, human performance:

> Looking back from here with the sort of perspective that distance gives I greatly dislike the impression that Yeats's Deirdre or rather Mrs. Darragh left on me. Emotion—if it cannot be given with some trace of distinction or nobility—is best left to the imagination of the audience. Did not Cleopatra, and Lady Macbeth, and Miranda make more impression when they were played by small boys than when they are done by Mrs. Pat Campbell... I would rather go on trying with our own people for ten years, than bring in this readymade style that is so likely to destroy the sort of distinction everyone recognises in our own company.[26]

Soon after the premier of Yeats's *Deirdre*, starring the British actress Florence Darragh, Synge responded with frustration to the kind of performance given by Yeats's lead actresses. Synge's problem with a "readymade style" reveals the importance of Molly's particular personality and distinct acting technique to his concept of *Deirdre of the Sorrows*. He regrets what he sees as

[24] Ibid., 217.
[25] Qtd. in E. H. Mikhail, *The Abbey Theatre: Interviews and Recollections* (Rowman & Littlefield Publishers, 1988).
[26] Qtd. in Synge, *Complete Works*, xxi–xii.

the lack of "distinction or nobility" in the work of the actresses who collaborated with Yeats and defines the best acting as opposed to pretension. Deploying that word, "nobility," Synge throws down a gauntlet to Yeats who was always sensitive to issues of class and performance, as Marjorie Howes has argued.[27]

Synge wrote this preference for "distinction" into *Deirdre of the Sorrows*. Lavarcham explains Deirdre's particular appeal: "I'll be sailing back and forward on the seas to be looking on your face and the little ways you have that none can equal." Deirdre's willfulness, a trait she shares with Molly, distinguishes her from the other characters as well. Lavarcham complains, again and again, about her inability to control Deirdre: "When all is said, it's her like will be the master till the end of time," she says, and "with all my talking it's willfuller she's growing these two months or three."[28] "I couldn't keep her," the Old Woman attests, "I've no hold on her." Synge took this language straight from his letters to Molly. In July 1908, he begged her not to become involved in Abbey politics: "For my sake have no rows, it would kill me." She would often refuse to write Synge back immediately when he attempted to guide her; his next letter to her after the above warning begins "I think you are treating me very badly."[29] Synge revised these letters for his play, writing Molly's strong-mindedness into his idea of Deirdre not as an idealized version of his fiancée but as a representative of his knowledge of Molly's specific personality. While the Deirdres of Yeats and Russell are heroic and inaccessible like the iconic women who played in their productions, Synge's title character is based on Molly's style of acting and lacks the grandiosity of previous interpretations of the heroine.

Writing about Molly, Synge further challenged Revival ideas of femininity by describing the grotesque physical effects of death on the female body. While Yeats painstakingly wrote his female characters into immortality in his plays and imagined them outlasting the ravages of time and modernity in his early poetry, Synge refused to exalt the bodies of queens, concentrating instead on the physical in describing their dead bodies as "eaten of fleas and vermin."[30] In the poem "Queens," too earthy in its original form for the Cuala Press, Synge writes of now-dead queens (including Deirdre) idealized by earlier writers.[31] Of the queen's names, only "wormy sheepskin" remains,

---

[27] Howes, *Yeats's Nations*, 46.   [28] *P & P*, 185, 179.   [29] *LM*, 255.

[30] *P & P*, 225.

[31] For a discussion of Lolly Yeats's issues with some of the language in Synge's poems, see Ann Saddlemyer, "The Poetizing of Synge," in *Synge and his Influences: Centenary Essays from the Synge Summer School*, ed. Patrick Lonergan (Dublin: Carysfort, 2011). Saddlemyer describes

echoing Synge's Preface: "there is no (poetic) timber that has not strong roots among the clay and worms."[32] The poem ends with Molly as an ironic, prosaic queen, only reigning because she is alive in the moment[33] of the poem with death awaiting her:

> Yet these are rotten—I ask their pardon—
> And we've the sun on rock and garden;
> These are rotten, so you're the Queen
> Of all are living, or have been.[34]

Repeating the word "rotten," Synge opposed Yeats's bodiless female figures with a relentless image of physical death. While Revival poets like Yeats had focused on the moon, Synge turns to the sun, the force that both warms and rots. Synge's images of death contrast with the final stanza of Yeats's "The Rose of the World" (1892):

> Bow down, archangels, in your dim abode:
> Before you were, or any hearts to beat,
> Weary and kind one lingered by His seat;
> He made the world to be a grassy road
> Before her wandering feet.[35]

While Synge's poem describes a specific afternoon with Molly and the actual state of the buried bodies of the dead, Yeats situates his lines in an unearthly "dim abode," describing a female figure and deity that exist beyond time, before the creation of angels. That "dim" light, echoed in Russell's *Deirdre*, contrasts with the harsh realities that Synge tried to bring to his treatment of legend. Based on Yeats's fantasy of the unreachable Maud Gonne, this "one" occupies a non-physical space between life and death outside of measurable time and is only coded by her feet; the rest of her remains mysterious. Synge, however, not only imagines Molly, like his Deirdre, as mortal, but focuses on the impact of this mortality on the bodies of the female dead, distancing his

Lolly Yeats's concerns about the reception of some of Synge's more ribald and controversial poems in the 1909 Cuala edition of Synge's *Poems and Translations*.

[32] Ibid., 222.

[33] J. M. Synge, *Collected Works: Vol. 1, Poems*, ed. Robin Skelton (London: Oxford University Press, 1962), 57.

[34] Ibid., 225.   [35] Ibid., 57.

concept of death from both the language of Yeats's poems and his ideal of the mythical Deirdre figure.

Russell's Deirdre wills herself to death with no awareness of physical mortality. She describes death not as a physical state but as a far-off place for herself and Naisi: "we shall go hand in hand through the Country of Immortal Youth."[36] Russell's characters reach death through spells and druid magic; Naisi hallucinates surrounding waves as he leaves life, and Deirdre tells him, "the spell of the Druid and his terrible chant have made a mist around your eyes." Before writing Deirdre, Synge had already roundly critiqued Russell's treatment of heroic figures. His poem, "The Passing of the Shee," subtitled "After looking at one of AE's pictures," begins with mockery and challenge, imitating the language of the Celtic Twilight only to insert jarringly anti-Revival phrases like "yet skinny." The phrase stands out, forcing the unflatteringly physical into the ethereal world of Irish myth and suggesting that these characters of "feeble blood" lack strength and substance:

> Adieu sweet Angus, Maeve, and Fand
> Ye plumed yet skinny Shee
> That poets plays with hand in hand
> To learn their ecstasy.[37]

The poem could not more clearly or irreverently establish Synge's position against the Celtic Twilight ideal of a mythic past, putting readers on notice that he heralded a new way of writing about Ireland and warning of the dangers of over-identification with figures of folklore. That "skinny" brings the body, again, into the ethereal conversation about mythic Irish fairy femininity. Yeats's "The Stolen Child" is also skewered in this farewell to fairies with "hand in hand."[38] Russell included ornate language and imagery of the "Shee" in his Deirdre as well as his visual arts. In his treatment of the myth, the heroine interacts with otherworldly beings: "Last night in a dream I saw the blessed Shee upon the mountains, and they looked at me with eyes of love." After beginning with the above parodic farewell, Synge offers an

---

[36] *P & P*, 52.   [37] Ibid., 232.

[38] Readers of Yeats poetry would remember the fairies "hand in hand" with the child who leaves cottage life to live in the fairy world in Yeats's 1889 poem "The Stolen Child." In mocking this sacred poem of the Revival, Synge suggests that the male poets eager to escape reality with fairies are avoiding reality.

alternative image made up of his own take on grotesque Irishness and humanity:

> We'll stretch in Red Dan Sally's ditch,
> And drink in the Tubber fair,
> Or poach with Red Dan Philly's bitch
> The badger and the hare.[39]

The final lines of the poem land us in the bawdy world of *The Tinker's Wedding*, a play that begins with a ditch onstage. (As I discuss later on, dirt and graves are also important parts of stage design in the final act of *Deirdre of the Sorrows*.) The imaginary men and women of the first stanza, much-written-of mythic figures (though Deirdre is conspicuously absent) comprised the "saga people('s)" efforts to imagine a nation. Early Revival plays like Russell's *Deirdre* used the mythic figures from the Irish oral tradition and offered a distant, pre-English past as both a model for the present and an imaginative return to an unsullied peasant life. Icons like Maeve, Fand, and the women of the Sidhe are pushed offstage in Synge's merciless critique of this tradition, only to be replaced by a ditch owner and a dog. The poaching characters in the poem also upend Yeats's lifelong obsession with "horsemen" and "ancient hounds" as class-coded references to Ascendancy hunting. Those cherished symbols are replaced here with drunken poachers, celebrated for stealing the food they hunt and using someone else's dog to do so. And the name of the dog owner, "Red Dan," pushes back against Yeats's idyllic stories and poems of Red Hanrahan from the 1890s and early 1900s.

While the characters in Yeats's *Deirdre* speak a Shakespearean blank verse befitting their haughty nobility, those in Synge's version converse not only in his peasant form of dialect, but also in the grotesque language of his correspondence with Molly. The physical sexuality of Synge's Deirdre contrasts with the bodiless sensuality of Yeats's and Russell's interpretations of the heroine. Naisi, in Russell's interpretation, speaks a formal language to a retiring Deirdre, "Poor timid dove, I had forgotten thy weakness" (31). In *Deirdre of the Sorrows*, on the other hand, Lavarcham describes Deirdre as nakedly physical, "bathing in the sun ... with her white skin, and her red lips, and the blue water and the ferns about her."[40] In their letters, Synge and

---

[39] *P & P*, 232.   [40] Ibid., 179.

Molly discussed menstruation, gas, and other bodily processes absent from Yeats's more formal letters to women, and this grotesque language animates *Deirdre of the Sorrows*. It is hard to imagine Yeats ever writing to Maud Gonne with one of Synge's questions to Molly: "I hope the gooseberry didn't disagree?"[41] On September 9, 1908, Synge wrote to his fiancée, " I was very much tickled by your story about Sally and the curse" (*LM*, 276). Synge brings this physical element into the poem "In May." He remembers a comment to Molly while they watched two birds: "Such... Are I and you, / When you've kissed me black and blue."[42] Yeats wrote in his Preface to the Cuala edition of *Deirdre of the Sorrows*: "[Synge] felt that this story, as he had told it, required a grotesque element mixed into its lyrical melancholy to give contrast and create an impression of solidity, and had begun this mixing with the character of Owen."[43] Owen, consumed by eating, jealousy, and his impossible desire for Deirdre, expresses a skewed, physical view of life: "The full moon, I'm thinking, is squeezing the crack in my skull. Was there ever a man crossed nine waves after a fool's wife and he not away in his head?" Synge argued that "before a verse can be human again it must learn to be brutal," and he insisted on this harsh language for the characters in *Deirdre of the Sorrows*, writing to Molly in early December 1906, "I finished... the 7th revision of Act III yesterday. It 'goes' now all through—the Act III I mean—but it wants a good deal of strengthening, of 'making it personal' still before it will satisfy me."[44] Lavarcham speaks of the body with startling, physical language: "Naisi, is it? I didn't care if the crows were stripping his thigh-bones at the dawn of day."[45] To Synge, "making personal" meant including coarse descriptions of bodily states, mixing, as he wrote in the Preface to his poems, the "ordinary" with the "exalted."[46] Synge praised poets who "used the whole of their personal life in their material" and brought the language of his letters to Molly into his last play; he tended to avoid these topics with other correspondents. Molly and Synge routinely wrote honest letters not simply about health, but about their physical states, and his conversation with her helped him to write both a sexual Deirdre and grotesque language for the play's male and female characters.

---

[41] John Millington Synge, *Collected Letters of J. M. Synge, Vols 1 and 2*, ed. Ann Saddlemyer (Oxford: Clarendon Press, vol. 1, 1983, vol. 2, 1984), ii, 165.

[42] *P & P*, 236.

[43] J. M. Synge, *Collected Works: Vols 3 and 4, Plays*, ed. Ann Saddlemyer (London: Oxford University Press, 1962), iv, 179.

[44] *P & P*, 222; *LM*, 223.   [45] *P & P*, 193.   [46] Ibid., 222.

In Yeats's *Deirdre*, as in his early poetry for Gonne, dying into immortality releases the title character, who remains always young and beautiful. Though Deirdre has not begun to age in Synge's play, physical change looms in the background of each scene. As Owen points out to Deirdre in *Deirdre of the Sorrows*, "With a sad cry that brings dignity to his voice," "Queens get old, Deirdre, with their white and long arms going from them, and their backs hooping. I tell you it's a poor thing to see a queen's nose reaching down to scrape her chin."[47] When she knows of her own impending death, Deirdre comes to regret missing the changes of the future: "It is I who am desolate; I, Deirdre, that will not live till I am old."[48] In Act II, fear of the effects of the passage of time guides Deidre and Naisi's decision to return to Ireland and Conchubar's court. Deirdre reveals this dread to Lavarcham:

> It's lonesome this place having happiness like ours, till I'm asking each day will this day match yesterday, and will to-morrow take a good place beside the same day in the year that's gone and wondering all times is it a game worth playing, living on till you're dried and old, and our joy is gone forever.[49]

Change awaits offstage for Deirdre and Naisi in Synge's play, tainting happiness with foreboding. Naisi expresses a similar fear, admitting he worries "I'd weary of her voice and Deirdre'd see I'd wearied."[50] As Synge's death and separation from Molly waited inevitably in the wings while he drafted the play, Deirdre's mortality looms behind the action. Synge's memory of his mother, who died while he was writing the play in October 1908, caused him to write lovingly of old age; Lavarcham says to Deirdre, "I tell you there's little hurt in getting old, though young girls and poets do be storming at the shapes of age."[51] Some of Mrs. Synge's practicality and acceptance survive in these lines from Lavarcham, as does Synge's own regret at missing aging in an early death. In Russell's play, the characters are barely mortal and death changes little: "We are immortals, and it does not become us to grieve."[52] While in Yeats's play, death is a noble escape from treachery into a timeless state, in Synge's version, "death is a poor untidy thing though it's a queen that dies."[53]

Synge's own illness and impending death, expressed in his letters to Molly, had much to do with his attitude towards mortality as "poor and

---

[47] Ibid., 196.   [48] Ibid., 212.   [49] Ibid., 193–4.   [50] Ibid., 198.
[51] Ibid., 194.   [52] Russell, *Imaginations and Reveries*, 31.   [53] *P & P*, 203.

untidy" and his refusal to glorify death in *Deirdre of the Sorrows*.[54] He wrote the play between severe, often touch and go, bouts of illness up until his 1909 death in hospital of Hodgkin's lymphoma. In the spring of 1908, he revised the first act of *Deirdre of the Sorrows* until he had an operation in early April. That summer, in Scotland, he struggled with the second act, the part of the play that gave him the most trouble. His mother's October death and his own failing health then forced him to stop work until November. By January 1909, he worked daily, but his symptoms prevented him from writing for more than short periods at a time. A letter to Molly during a particularly painful week typically avoids pity or histrionics and refuses to romanticize his condition: "Remember if anyone asks you how I am doing you are to say I'm alright. I don't want people condoling with me."[55] Intensely private about his health problems, he confided to her about his discomfort, fears, and frustrations, though no-nonsense Molly occasionally chastised him for his "selfpitiful" letters.[56] He wrote a farewell note in May 1908 before a risky operation; he survived, and she received the last letter ten months later when he died in March 1909. The tone is typically rational and honest, avoiding the dramatic:

> This is a mere line for you, my poor child, in case anything goes wrong with me tomorrow to bid you good-bye and ask you to be brave and good, and not to forget the good times we've had and the beautiful things we've seen together. Your old Friend.[57]

Because Synge lived with illness for so many years, his approach to death and change remained matter-of-fact. Rather than presenting Deirdre as a character destined for eternal youth in an ethereal early death, his play is full of description of the changes that will bring her closer to death should she live; eventual mortality is inevitable even if she does not choose to die with Naisi. In his letters to Molly, Synge developed an attitude towards the daily effects of time and mortality that opposed the concept of death as an otherworldly realm expressed in the Deirdre plays of Yeats and George Russell.

Yeats's Deirdre, distant from the choices she must face from the play's start, dissembles perfectly to trick Conchubar in the final scenes. Synge's *Deirdre of the Sorrows*, however, forces the physicality of death on the

---

[54] Ibid., 203.   [55] *LM*, 134.   [56] Ibid., 309.   [57] Ibid., 317.

audience through both stagecraft and dialogue. In the third act of Synge's play, after Naisi has left Deirdre to face death with his brothers, she discovers him and the Sons of Usnach in a grave onstage. For the rest of the act, the grave awaits with three dead bodies. In contrast to this realism, AE's Deirdre was "presented under a gauze upon which Fay played a green arc, giving the stage a ghostly, mist-like appearance... The characters had the appearance of figures rising out of the mist."[58] While Russell used a fabric to create a blurry, supernatural visual effect, Synge and Molly brought actual dirt and clay onto the stage. Deirdre joins the dead in the play's final moments after throwing clay on the bodies, and this action forces the physical mortality of the bodies in the grave on the audience. Synge's Deirdre eventually achieves a "high and quiet tone," but her initial response to Naisi's departure and death is more immediate than the haughtiness of Yeats's heroine, and she struggles before achieving quietness.[59] After Naisi's death, "bewildered and terrified," she tells Conchubar, "It is not I will be a queen." She achieves the restraint necessary to fool Conchubar only after responding more and "more wildly" to his plan.[60] Synge's Deirdre eventually achieves a "tone that stops" Conchubar with its power before she chooses her own death. She does so, however, only after reacting with panic and fear before joining the other dead in the grave onstage.

This scene raises questions about the physical bodies, playing alive and dead, on the Irish stage. Both Allgood sisters came from the traditions of Inghinidhe na hÉireann, a street theater I discuss in the previous chapters, developed before the Abbey and dedicated to performance of Irish history and myth through magic lantern shows and tableaux. The nationalist theaters brought in actresses from this movement, and the use of tableaux impacted both the Abbey and the political risings and protests to follow. Photographs of Constance Markievicz and Maud Gonne speaking to crowds show the influence of tableaux, and the graves on the stage in Synge's play are precursors to the bodies of the "dead men" buried in lime after the Rising in 1916.[61] As I discuss in the final chapter, Synge's own graveside was the site of an impromptu performance when Sara Allgood, Molly's sister, at Yeats's

[58] Máire Nic Shiubhlaigh, *The Splendid Years* (Dublin: James Duffy, 2016 [1955]), 19.

[59] *P & P*, 216.   [60] Ibid., 211.

[61] For a description of how the execution and burial of the men of the Rising affected the community and the women in their lives in particular, see Lucy McDiarmid, *At Home in the Revolution: What Women Said and Did in 1916* (Dublin: Royal Irish Academy, 2015), ch. 6, "The Kilmainham Farewell," 141–64.

request, recited the lines she made famous in *Riders to the Sea* by his grave: "We can't all be living forever, and we must be satisfied."

Both Yeats's and Russell's interpretations of Deirdre were revived and performed while Synge wrote *Deirdre of the Sorrows*, and he and Molly responded to these performances with an ever-stronger desire to define their play against the earlier treatments of the story. In a letter dated November 1908, Synge wrote to Molly, consigning the ownership of the 1908 *Deirdre* production not to Yeats, but to Mrs. Patrick Campbell, one of the women who made the role famous. Crediting the actress with the production was common for Synge:

> [Joseph] Hone saw Mrs. P[at]'s Deirdre in London. He says it was not so well done as in the Abbey, but that it was very well put on and the men were tall and fine-looking. I think I have got the first scene in A. II right now—so the Act may be nearly finished when you come back.[62]

The letter is typical; news about Yeats's play for "Mrs. P" often preceded updates on his own work on *Deirdre of the Sorrows*. Synge collaborated with Molly on his version to create a part that would demand a different kind of performance than the ethereal acting favored by Yeats and Russell, and the nuts and bolts tone of the letters he sent her while writing reveals the way that they imagined the play together. In October 1907, he wrote Molly before going to see Mrs. Pat in *Hedda Gabler* and Suderman's *Magda*, "I'm sure I won't like her at all—from what I have heard and seen of her."[63] His friend Agnes Tobin told him of the 1908 London production of Yeats's *Deirdre*, as he reported to Molly: "Mrs. P had some lovely moments but was spoiled by bad company and poor mise-en-scene."[64] Molly and Synge followed these reports closely while working on their own version of Deirdre, one that was to counter Mrs. Patrick Campbell's take on the character in her successful 1908 revival of Yeats's play. While writing *Deirdre of the Sorrows* in mid-December 1907, Synge complained to Molly: "Yes I see they are doing AE's *Deirdre* at the Abbey tonight. Madame M. is Lavarcham I think. There was an absurd 'puff' about the play in the I. Times today written evidently by one of themselves. They should have more sense."[65] By "themselves" and "they" Synge meant the "saga people" at the Abbey involved in the revival of Russell's *Deirdre*, and "Madame M"

---

[62] *LM*, 304.   [63] Ibid., 208.   [64] JMSCL, ii, 235.   [65] Ibid., 104.

refs to Constance Markievicz. (Yeats had, in fact, had quiet doubts about AE's interpretation of the myth as well, as I discuss in Chapter 5.) Synge's disdain both for the play and the Abbey's promotion of the revival production reveals his impatience with iconic, distant versions of the title character. Like Maud Gonne in Yeats's *Cathleen ni Houlihan*, Markievicz, a rising star of the Republican movement, would blur nationalism with theater, playing the "druidess" Lavarcham. Nicholas Allen claims that of the starring actors in the 1902 premiere of Russell's play, Máire Nic Shiubhlaigh, Constance Markievicz, and Seamus O'Sullivan, "all three had impeccable nationalist credentials," and the 1907 revival would follow suit.[66] While other writers chose well-known theater stars or nationalist icons to play Deirdre, Synge built his character around the younger, less-established Molly, known as an Abbey actress.

Molly's experience at the Abbey gave Synge a valuable perspective on performance; her advice to him on the productions she had performed or watched affected his writing and revisions. On November 24, 1908, three years after the premier of *The Well of the Saints*, a letter that Synge wrote to Molly explains the importance of performance to his revision of plays even years after they first premiered:

> I have very nearly got a full version now of the second act of Deirdre. I wish I could see a show of *The Well of the Saints*. The third act used to go so well, and I thought I had improved it, but now you say it drags.[67]

Molly's interpretations of the plays performed at the Abbey helped Synge decide how to rework his older plays, and her readings of parts and advice while he composed a play for the first time helped him write and rewrite new characters and scenes: "[*Deirdre of the Sorrows*] is delicate work a scene is so easily spoiled. I am anxious to hear you read it to me."[68] In December 1907, he hoped that she would develop a more traditional literary background to further hone her ability to critique and revise his work:

> I wish you'd read a lot of the best things—G(olden) Treasury, Shakespeare, and so on—I'll have to rely a good deal on your criticism . . . Anyone with a quick intelligence—and you have them ten times over—who reads and

---

[66] Nicholas Allen, *George Russell (AE) and the New Ireland, 1905–1930* (Dublin: Four Courts Press, 2003), 36.
[67] *LM*, 302.   [68] Ibid., 309.

knows the masterpieces can very soon tell if some new work is rubbish or a masterpiece too.[69]

He often asked about her own projects, writing about her part in *The Country Dressmaker* by William Poel: "I am anxious to hear all about it."[70] Considering himself and Molly to be fellow artists and collaborators, he joked about renting a place for free "because after we have lived there and written verses about it, [it] will become so famous that they'll be able to sell it to an American art collector for £50,000."[71] The "we" here is indicative of how Synge and Molly Allgood viewed their working relationship and their engagement; the description of themselves as dramatists creating texts together is typical. He took an active interest in Molly's work and demanded the same involvement from her. While he followed her acting career and counseled her on parts to take or reject, she helped him with interpretations of performances as well as plays in progress.

Molly and Synge did not just collaborate on the theatrical aspects of *Deirdre of the Sorrows*. On this project in particular, he relied on her critical judgment, and his letters to her often sound like a writer's journal. He told her of his doubts about revising four acts into three in November 1907: "As it is, I am not sure that the plan I have is a good one. Ideas seem so admirable when they occur to you, and then they get so doubtful when you have thought them over for a while."[72] Only to Molly did he reveal both these anxieties and the specific stresses and decisions of creating the play, not only because she was closest to him but also because he saw the project as one involving them both. In some letters, he directly solicited her input on a problem with the play, asking on December 3, 1906 after they had repeatedly gone through drafts of *Deirdre of the Sorrows*: "How do you like my Deirdre now that you have seen it so often?"[73] Deirdre's part came more easily than Naisi's; on the question of doing away with Act Two, Synge demanded Molly's advice on August 24, 1908: "It will be useful...as Naisi's part was so weak in the last Act. Now what do you say to me?"[74] The two met regularly to discuss his revisions, as Synge wrote on November 11, 1907: "I want to show you my Deirdre some day soon perhaps I can on Sunday"[75] Her letters gave him fresh ideas, and he joked that she may "beat me at letter writing, and that wouldn't do, would it?"[76] Finally, Synge wrote to

[69] Ibid., 223.   [70] JMSCL, ii, 166.   [71] Ibid., 205.   [72] *LM*, 211.
[73] Ibid., 68.   [74] Ibid., 270.   [75] Ibid., 213.   [76] Ibid., 254.

Molly that his work on Deirdre was indistinguishable from his love for her: "I am pouring my heart out to you in Deirdre all day long."[77] Synge requested help and advice from Molly throughout their work on *Deirdre of the Sorrows*, and this collaboration only continued through his final illness and after his death.

Molly had been taking dictation from Synge for the play since September, and the two probably made more changes during those typing sessions. While in the hospital, he discussed the unfinished project with her during her frequent visits to Elpis Nursing Home. Yeats recorded Molly's memories of helping Synge write the play in the last months of his illness: "Sometimes he would get very despondent, thinking he could not finish it, and then she would act it for him in his room and he would write a little more, and then he would despond again, and then the acting would begin again."[78] This kind of collaboration is central to my argument: Synge getting stuck writing due to physical pain and exhaustion, Molly's performance right there in the hospital, and then his writing, and their discussion throughout the composition of the text build the play. The portrayal of the body as grotesque and of death as physically real should not surprise us considering the way the play was composed: what could be farther from a romantic ideal of ethereal Ireland than an institutional hospital deathbed?

Molly saw him at the hospital every day except for a seven-day tour with the Abbey in February. A week after entering the hospital, he made out a will leaving her a lifetime annuity of £80, £52 if she married.[79] He died on March 24, 1909, leaving a note on the back of one of the thousands of manuscript pages of *Deirdre of the Sorrows* requesting that Yeats look after the project. After Synge's death, Yeats received a letter written in May 1908, before an earlier operation, asking Yeats to try to preserve parts of *Deirdre of the Sorrows* as well as the Kerry and Wicklow articles. The letter ends with Synge's characteristic reticence: "Do what you can. Good luck. J. M. Synge."[80] Molly had told Synge in October 1908 that she would not attend the funeral, and he had turned the conversation into a poem, "A Question," beginning, "I asked if I got sick and died would you / With my black funeral go walking to" (*P&P* 233). Molly's response completes the poem:

[77] Ibid., 214.
[78] W. B. Yeats, *Memoirs: An Autobiography—First Draft, Journal*, ed. Denis Donoghue (New York: Macmillan, 1974), 208.
[79] Greene and Stephens, *J. M. Synge*, 330.   [80] JMSCL, ii, 155.

> And No, you said, for if you saw a crew
> Of living idiots pressing around that new
> Oak coffin—they alive, I dead beneath
> That board—you'd rave and rend them with your teeth.[81]

Synge delighted in Molly's honesty and quick anger, and they collaborated on this poem six months before his death during an intense period of work on *Deirdre of the Sorrows*. The poem, with the physical dead body next to the beloved, retells the end of their play by imagining her response to his death. He wrote to her after showing Yeats the poem: "I did one new poem—that is partly *your* work—that he says is *M a g n I f I c e n t*."[82] His version of the creation of the poem suggests that he transcribed her language, raising questions about authorship in this poem and others. Molly Allgood should get credit for helping with the poems and finishing the final play. Synge wrote Molly's take on the physicality of death and his own dead body into both poems and play.

In the summer of 1909, a few months after Synge's death, Yeats, Lady Gregory, and Molly Allgood, after difficulties obtaining drafts from Synge's family, attempted to revise the *Deirdre of the Sorrows* manuscript. Ann Saddlemyer believes that Molly knew Synge's final intentions for the play from helping him and reading his passages aloud in November and December 1908.[83] During that summer of 1909, Yeats, Molly, and Lady Gregory were "ignorant of the notebook materials" for *Deirdre of the Sorrows* beyond the manuscript begrudgingly given to them by Synge's relatives.[84] Yeats and Lady Gregory, as Yeats explains in the Preface to *Deirdre of the Sorrows*, decided to publish the version that Synge had left without any changes. Some alterations to Deirdre's speeches remain in the manuscript, however, and were incorporated into the play. Saddlemyer believes these to be in Molly's hand:

> Although notes to the present edition suggest that alterations have been made by an unknown hand, especially to Deirdre's final speeches, it is conceivable that these were written in by Molly during Synge's frantic final revisions. The only definite allocations that can be made to others occur in minor stage directions, and here again they were probably determined by Molly, who directed the first production.[85]

---

[81] *P & P*, 233. [82] *LM*, 283. [83] Synge, *Complete Works*, iv, xxix.
[84] Ibid., xxx. [85] Ibid., xxx.

Molly, then, might have made not only alterations during the last days of Synge's illness, but also the only changes to Synge's final version of *Deirdre of the Sorrows* from those months of work in the summer of 1909. Her decision to modify the stage directions continues her history of working with Synge not as muse but as a collaborator. Though he notes elsewhere that Molly helped with the manuscript, in some versions, Yeats only remembered working with Gregory. This mis-remembering shows how, as a male, upper middle-class writer, though he understood, on some level, the importance of performance, he was unable to see the extent of Molly's influence. In his Preface to the play he wrote:

> Synge asked that either I or Lady Gregory should write some few words to make this possible [the presence of the knife in the final scene], but after writing in a passage we were little satisfied and thought it better to have the play performed, as it is printed here, with no word of ours.[86]

Yeats did, however, understand the importance of Molly's role in preparing the production. He wrote to John Quinn about working on *Deirdre of the Sorrows*: "I think it would be impossible in any company except ours. I can't imagine anybody getting his peculiar rhythm without being personally instructed in it" and praised Molly as the Abbey's best dialogue actress.[87]

Deirdre of the Sorrows finally reached the stage at the Abbey Theatre on January 13, 1910, ten months after Synge's death. Molly Allgood both directed the production and played the lead character (Figures 4.1 and 4.2). Performers close to her played the community of characters she and Synge had created around Deirdre: her sister Sara played Lavarcham, and her future husband Arthur Sinclair played Conchubar. The production received mixed reviews. Most objected to the use of peasant speech for such revered mythical characters and found the play slow but praised Molly Allgood in the lead role. Joseph Holloway, never a fan of Synge's plays, with the exception of *Riders to the Sea*, disliked the use of rural speech for the iconic legendary figures:

> When the play was over and done, Seumas O'Sullivan said, as many of us chattered in the vestibule, that "There was nothing incomplete about it.

---

[86] Ibid., 179.

[87] W. B. Yeats, *The Letters of W. B. Yeats*, ed. Allan Wade (London: R. Hard-Davis, 1954), 510.

Figure 4.1 Molly Allgood in the 1910 premier of *Deirdre of the Sorrows*; note the "presence of the knife" that Yeats describes

Source: Courtesy of the Abbey Theatre Archive.

The people in the play were human beings at all events and not merely inanimate Kings and Queens!" I grant that the loftiness of the theme was trailed in the mud if that's what he meant by "human beings," but the treatment took the grandeur and poetry out of the tale.[88]

Synge and Molly, then, had succeeded in rewriting the Deirdre saga as a human drama, though, as Yeats pointed out in the Preface, Synge was unable to bring as many "grotesque elements" into the final manuscript as he would have liked. The reviews echo Synge's hopes for creating a Deirdre to be played by Molly with a natural, personal "distinction." Holloway, despite his quarrel with Synge's handling of saga material, appreciated Molly's

---

[88] Joseph Holloway, *Joseph Holloway's Abbey Theatre: A Selection from His Unpublished Journal: "Impressions of a Dublin Play-Goer,"* ed. Robert Hogan and Michael J. O'Neill (Carbondale: Southern Illinois University Press; London: Feffer & Simmons, 1967), 134.

Figure 4.2 Ben Bay's drawing of Molly Allgood (Maire O'Neill) as the title
character in *Deirdre of the Sorrows* in 1910, the play she created with Synge
Source: Image courtesy of The National Library of Ireland.

interpretation of the main role: "Maire O'Neill was a distinct success as
'Deirdre'...Her acting was always sincere and restrained."[89] Firin, a
reviewer for *The Irish Times*, wrote of Molly: "Her grit was restrained but
forceful. As the young girl her passions were poetic and touching. Hers was
the chief part of the tragedy; hers the principal triumph of the evening."[90]
That "grit" reminds us how Molly and Synge insisted on dirt onstage in the
final scene and bodies performing that reminded the audience of physical
mortality. A. H. of *The Daily Mail* found in Molly's performance the natural
approach to acting that Lennox Robinson has praised as well: "It is a
pleasure to see her walk, erect, supple, natural, like a woman of the soil,
accustomed to carrying a pitcher on her head."[91] Again "soil," like "grit"

---

[89] Ibid.   [90] Nesta Jones, *File on Synge* (London: Bloomsbury, 1994), 87.
[91] Ibid., 88.

suggests that Molly Allgood succeeded in tethering this legend to the ground. This description shows how differently the actresses who collaborated with Yeats interpreted the role; they performed Deirdre, as I discuss in Chapter 5, as a distant and aristocratic character. Ann Saddlemyer wrote of the late changes Synge made to the play: "Although he retained a hint of mysticism until very late drafts, eventually he rejected all dependence of prophesy or premonition; similarly the Sons of Usnach meet their death not through druidic incantations but because they are tricked and outnumbered."[92] Synge decided to eschew any unrealistic elements, choosing to tell, instead, a story of believable characters, not supernatural "saga people," and Molly's interpretation of the role brought this change in Deirdre to the stage.

Two years after Synge's death, Molly married George Mair, critic at *The Manchester Guardian*, and had two children with him, Pegeen and John, the first named for the character she helped create and the second, possibly, for Synge. Her son was a writer who published the thriller, now a radio play, *Never Come Back*, in 1941, and *The Fourth Forger*, a historical take on eighteenth-century Shakespearian forgery, in 1942. A member of the Royal Air Force, John died in World War II. Pegeen became a lyric writer. In 1926, Molly Allgood's husband Mair died, and she soon married Abbey actor Arthur Sinclair whom she subsequently divorced. Until her death in 1952, she continued to act both in films and onstage. She always felt a claim on the roles Synge had written for and with her, and in a 1949 interview with *The Irish Press*, she said:

> What is there I cannot say about John? To me he was everything, in his work and personality . . . But perhaps his greatness to me is wound up with the fact that for me he wrote his most famous plays, "The Playboy of the Western World" and "Deirdre of the Sorrows" when I was only eighteen.[93]

Molly Allgood felt ownership of these roles, and her interest was not simply artistic. Playing bit parts to keep herself alive as an older woman, she needed the money from the roles that she had helped create and made famous. (And she probably shaved a few years off her age in the memory of Synge and

---

[92] Ann Saddlemyer, *J. M. Synge, Four Plays, a Casebook*, ed. Ronald Ayling (Basingstoke: Macmillan, 1992), 168. The language of this review exoticized Allgood, who, as noted throughout, was not from the far west of Ireland but a Dublin tenement not far from the Abbey Theatre.
[93] Qtd. in Mikhail, *W. B. Yeats*, 81–2.

Deirdre of the Sorrows above to preserve her ability to perform younger roles.) When she, along with Yeats and Lady Gregory, struggled to convince the Synge family to allow her to perform both *Deirdre of the Sorrows* and *The Playboy of the Western World*, she brought her sense of ownership of the plays into the discussion. Yeats recalled her saying to Edward Stephens, "If you forbid us to play Deirdre and Playboy, you ruin my life. They were written for me, and their performance in London is my only chance of making a career."[94] As her ingénue looks began to fade, Molly Allgood had few ways of making money. Shortly after she appealed to the family, Yeats records, the Synges promised them the manuscript of *Deirdre of the Sorrows*.

Yeats's criticism of Molly Allgood's premier performance in *Deirdre of the Sorrows* reveals how much his ideas of female performance and heroism differed from Synge's:

> [Fred] Donovan and Miss O'Neill were as passionless as the rest. Miss O'Neill had personal charm, pathos, distinction even, fancy, beauty, but never passion—never intensity, nothing came out of a brooding mind. All was but observation, curiosity, desire to please. Her foot never touched the unchanging rock, the secret place beyond life; her talent showed itself, like that of all the others, social, modern, a faculty of comedy. Pathos she has, the nearest to tragedy the comedian can come as a rule, for that is conscious of our presence and would have our pity. Passion she has not, for that looks beyond mankind and asks no pity, not even of God. It realizes, substantiates, attains, scorns, governs, and is most mighty when it passes from our sight.[95]

Yeats's critique of Molly here is steeped in the coded classist language of his letters to Gregory lamenting "Catholic actresses" and their "lack of passion." The Deirdre plays are a flashpoint for issues that Marjorie Howes lays out in her *Yeats's Nations: Gender, Class, and Irishness*, questions about class, gender, ownership, and nationalism, and this selection from Yeats's *Memoirs* employs, in a polite and occluded way, the fears about Catholic women and performance that are more hysterical in his letters.[96] Yeats had hoped, too, for a removed performance, one that would "touch the secret

---

[94] Yeats, *Memoirs*, 218.   [95] Ibid., 239.

[96] Yeats used the word "hysterical" for women who, in his mind, became overly emotional about politics, especially in "I have heard the hysterical women say" in the first line to "Lapis Lazuli." Ironically, that word is apt for his panicked reaction to Catholic bodies onstage.

place beyond life," and Allgood's failure to meet Yeats's standards tells us much more about the differences between Synge's and Yeats's preferred acting styles and dramaturgy than the merits of her performance. Synge's letters to Molly make clear that he disdained the "mighty" and scornful attitudes of the stars of the theater who had played Yeats's *Deirdre*, preferring the "personal charm" at the root of Molly's take on the character. Reviewers called her interpretation of the part "restrained," and Synge had hoped for a "quiet" performance; she acted, even Yeats admits, with "distinction," as Synge had wished.[97] Synge disliked the mishandling of "emotion" he saw in the women who played Yeats's heroines, and many have approved of Molly's "passionless" Deirdre since she developed that style of performing the part with him until his last days. Synge certainly wrote a Deirdre of the real and shifting earth, not of a Yeatsian realm "beyond mankind," touching an imagined "unchanging rock." Yeats changed his judgment of Molly during the second performance: "Last night Miss O'Neill had so improved her performance that I began to think she may have some real tragic power."[98] She and Synge, however, treated the Deirdre myth in a way that opposed Yeats's exalted view of heroism and performance.

I will end this chapter where it started: Molly died in 1952 aged 67 in London from burns sustained when she fell into a fire in her apartment. It was a cold and wet November, and she was struggling both financially and with her addiction to alcoholism; her drinking had worsened after her son's death in World War II ten years before. The previous year, she had appeared with one line as an ailing woman in the 1951 film *A Christmas Carol*, and she was scheduled to do a radio version of O'Casey's *The Silver Tassie*. She continued to act not just because she loved the craft but also because she had no choice and had to generate income. No longer what Lennox Robinson called "deliciously impish," Allgood was forced to take what bit parts she could get.[99] Molly Allgood had been obliged to negotiate with Synge's estate and with Abbey directors even to be allowed to perform the plays she so influenced and helped to create. The end of her life shows that despite her success at the Abbey and on film, she was unable to escape a cycle of poverty that had started with a childhood stay in an orphanage and ended with her eking out a living in a small apartment. Nothing is just about Molly Allgood's end; without her, Synge's greatest drama would never have existed. Let us follow the advice of Synge's and Molly's *Deirdre of the Sorrows*

[97] Synge, *Complete Works*, iv, xxi–xxii.   [98] Yeats, *Memoirs*, 240.
[99] "Maire O'Neill," in *The Irish Times* (obituary), November 3–4, 1952.

and force ourselves to look at the grotesque, the unpleasant, and the rotten dead. What happened to Molly Allgood's body gives the lie to Revival fantasies about disembodied women living in a realm separate from the real impact of class and power. The actual moment of her 1952 fall in that London apartment is unseen, but we know that she was in exile alone, that she was in dire financial straits, and that she had lost two brothers to World War I, a fiancé to Hodgkin's lymphoma, a son to World War II, and a husband to a long illness in 1926. We also know that a reconsideration of her work on both *The Playboy of the Western World* and *Deirdre of the Sorrows* is long overdue.

5

Collaboration and Yeats's *Deirdre*

"passionate and solitary"
or "the voice of the crowd"?

Deirdre is a play about the death of a woman, continuing an obsession that animated Yeats's work from his earliest collaboration with Laura Armstrong in the 1880s. Because this play shows a woman's death onstage, it is worth taking a moment to consider the actual end of these players' lives as part of my argument for remembering and reading theatrical texts differently. Who wins and who loses in the way we accredit performance and writing? The final days of these women's stories gives a clear answer, one I will read more specifically in my section on the afterlives of Abbey actresses on film. Power dynamics show up when we examine the legacy and last days of each of these women and the male writers: Yeats with a Nobel Prize, Gonne "a dark tomb haunter" attending funerals, Gregory dying quietly of breast cancer at Coole, Farr surrendering to cancer in Ceylon (a death as traumatic to Yeats as the loss of Synge), Allgood in Hollywood after years of playing the Irish maid for Twentieth Century Fox, and Mrs. Patrick Campbell, isolated at the advent of World War II in France, penniless after trying to make a go as a character actress in Hollywood.[1] Synge, an upper-class Anglo Irishman, died young, but never had to worry about finances, and Chapter 4 details the end of Molly Allgood's life. Credit for this *Deirdre* went to Yeats, and the contributions of the women remain unknown; the three actresses, Farr, Sara Allgood, and Campbell, lived the end of their days in exile because they needed to work for money to live on until their deaths. Allgood and Campbell accepted any available parts for older women in Hollywood to make ends meet until their last days. The layered story of *Deirdre*'s journey to the stage is an

---

[1] George Bernard Shaw had to pay for her funeral expenses, tacitly acknowledging their history and the fact that even in penury she honored their agreement not to sell their correspondence, as a review of a sale of her letters in 2002 explains: see https://www.independ ent.co.uk/news/uk/home-news/shaws-love-for-real-life-eliza-doolittle-174588.html.

Gender, Performance, and Authorship at the Abbey Theatre. Elizabeth Brewer Redwine, Oxford University Press (2021). © Elizabeth Brewer Redwine. DOI: 10.1093/oso/9780192896346.003.0005

argument for Yeats's need for female performers and writers to achieve his work and a stark reminder about how authorship affected people's lives.

The writing of this play rests on the dramatized death of a sexual woman, and the importance of that woman's body runs through all the fraught arguments about the way the play reached the stage. The story of Yeats's composition and revision of *Deirdre* reflects his early mis-readings of Maud Gonne,[2] his reliance on Lady Gregory for both source material and contributions to texts, his attempts to control the Abbey Theatre, and his anxieties about dependence on women, writ large in the way he collaborated with actresses on this text. The tensions around casting and the seven-year arc of composition, performance, and revision of *Deirdre* trace changes in Yeats's earliest images of Ireland as a woman from 1902 to his tortured attempts to find the right actress for the lead role to his final revisions after working extensively on the script with Mrs. Patrick Campbell in 1909. This chapter investigates why Yeats compulsively rewrote this play about the sexuality and death of a powerful woman for thousands of pages over seven years. The need to rewrite after female performance reflects his relationships with women who had a stake in the text and performance and proves that the connections between gender, nation, and, increasingly, class posed thorny questions for him steeped in issues of ownership and representation. This chapter starts with April 1902, a month that shows the confluence of theatrical work and inspiration from various members of Inghinidhe na hÉireann. Chapter 2 discussed the way that Gonne, the Allgood sisters, AE, and Máire Nic Shiubhlaigh's collaborative *Deirdre* reached the stage that month with the premier of Yeats's and Gregory's *Cathleen ni Houlihan*. That production would, along with Lady Gregory's textual contributions from her folktale *Cuchulain of Muirthmene*, to use Yeats's own formulation, "set (him) writing."[3]

Yeats's *Deirdre* began as a response to AE's 1902 *Deirdre*, a performance that spoke to collaborative ideas of gender and nation and set up the dangers of female Irishness. Inghinidhe na hÉireann produced AE's *Deirdre* on a double bill with *Cathleen ni Houlihan* on April 2, 1902. In a high-stakes

---

[2] As I discuss in Chapter 2, Yeats met Maud Gonne in 1889 and began turning his idea of her into poetry and plays, a project that would be an engine for his creativity for the rest of his life. Unlike Yeats, who advocated cultural nationalism and had a fraught relationship with nationalist groups, Gonne was a violent proponent of Irish nationalism. The two never married and maintained a friendship. Gonne married John MacBride in 1903 to Yeats's horror.

[3] Qtd. in R. F. Foster *W. B. Yeats: A Life, I. The Apprentice Mage* (Oxford: Oxford University Press, 1997), 34.

literary game of tag, AE wrote his *Deirdre* in response to his frustrations over the fraught writing of *Diarmuid and Grania*, a collaborative play by Yeats and George Moore and produced, controversially, with English actors in 1901. Irishwoman Máire Nic Shiubhlaigh, with bona fide nationalist credentials, played Lavarcham and fellow Inghinidhe member and nationalist Máire T. Quinn played the title role; AE produced his play with Inghinidhe and strategically stocked the cast with nationalist Dublin women as a critique of *Diarmuid and Grania*'s all-British cast and production the year before.

Careful reading of casting and performance in the years leading up to 1907 show how controversy about women onstage had been boiling since the earliest years of the Revival and that in writing a Deirdre, Yeats was inserting himself into that debate. Who would play Deirdre remained central to the ongoing argument. That April evening in 1902 has been discussed and mined for insights into the dramatic and revolutionary years to come, mostly privileging Yeats's play (written, of course, with Gregory), but it is worth returning to that night and AE's play in particular for two reasons, to reveal both the influence of *Deirdre* on further incarnations of the myth and the way that the two plays worked together to further ideas of gender and nation.[4] The women of Inghinidhe thought that the double bill was paramount, that two partnered versions of Irish legendary womanhood needed to reach the stage together in crucial ways. I discuss Cathleen elsewhere in this book, and scholarship on that play is vast and influential, but AE's *Deirdre* is underrepresented in critical and literary histories; close reading bears out this conversation between the two plays, one that set off the competing Deirdres of the Revival as sisters of Cathleen to any theater-goer or newspaper reader of the time.

Most important for my argument about these sources of Yeats's *Deirdre* is that the earlier version by AE, published in 1901 and performed privately at a birthday party before reaching the public in 1902, came to the stage as a collaborative performance by Inghinidhe na hÉireann. AE played the Druid, casting himself as part of a theatrical movement performing a mystical version of ancient Ireland. AE's play is most concerned with Deirdre's visions and relationships with the Sidhe, reflecting the collaborative history of Inghinidhe, a group of Irish nationalist women who were inspired by Irish myth and history to perform tableaux, short plays, and magic lantern shows

---

[4] For more on the critical reception of the *Deirdre* plays at the Abbey, see W. M. Wickstrom, *The Deirdre Plays of AE, Yeats, and Synge: Patterns of Irish Exile* (Stanford, CA: Stanford University Press, 1968).

around Dublin. At the start of AE's play, Lavarcham is a Druidess, linked with the female knowledge of the fairy world. In Act I, Conchubar is only concerned with thwarting the violent prediction of the Druid at Deirdre's birth, and Naisi sees Deirdre first as an immortal, an "enchantress."[5] AE's mystical bent and Inghinidhe's fascination with Irish female mythic figures created a play and performance, behind a scrim of gauze, that cast the audience into a female-dominated world of Irish myth. Inghinidhe had performed tableaux of mythic figures on street corners in Dublin leading up to this performance, and, as Frazier argues, the idea that these productions are owned by authors would have been anathema to the way the performances were run in 1902; the production gave evidence of the collaborative nature of the play.

AE's *Deirdre* is about tension between the actual woman and the idealized beauty who will go down in myth; this tension parallels the experience of the actresses embodying mythical roles. The woman herself, and the actress, has a body and the possibility of motherhood. Like Cathleen, though, AE's Deirdre is "half of their world," connected to the women of the Sidhe. While the men in *Cathleen ni Houlihan* are peripheral, second even to the women of the house in importance, AE's Naisi and Conchubar contribute important ideas to the play. AE created a more complex Conchubar, and sympathized with this "wise king, though moody and passionate at times, for he was cursed in his youth for some crime against the Sidhe." In a tension with Cathleen ni Houlihan as a problematic mother figure, Joyce's "old sow that eats her farrow,"[6] Eri, or Ireland, in AE's play is figured as heartbreakingly maternal: "it is the land which gave us birth, and its whisper is sweeter than the promise of beloved lips. Though we are kings here in Alba, we are exiles, and the heart is far from its home. (A distant shout is heard.)"[7] This "distant shout" echoes in the sound "like cheering" Cathleen; in that play, we hear the noise of the invasion from the cottage as incoherent, violent speech intrudes upon the domestic.[8] Deirdre asks Naisi, "Beloved, am I become so little to you that your heart is empty and sighs for Eri?"[9] Here Deirdre echoes

---

[5]   George Russell [AE], *Deirdre* (Chicago, IL: DePaul University Press, 1970), 14.

[6]   James Joyce, *Ulysses* (London: Faber, 1930), 171.   [7]   Russell, *Deirdre*, 19.

[8]   W. B. Yeats and Lady Gregory, *Cathleen ni Houlihan*, *The Collected Works of W. B. Yeats*, Vol. II, *The Plays* (New York: Scribner, 2011), 83. Theater-goers of 1902 would experience this nostalgia as well, a nostalgia for an idealized past Ireland ready to fight in 1798, and the offstage shout functioned in the early nationalist theater as a reminder of the thin line between the theater and nationalist tensions in Dublin, a preview to 1916.

[9]   Russell, *Deirdre*, 19.

the women in the cottage in *Cathleen ni Houlihan*, women trying to keep a man from sacrifice to a maternal, luring, and deadly Ireland.

A program from the Abbey archive bears out the argument for collective community ownership of these plays and shows that womanhood and Irishness on stage were contested ground. Program, play, and production are here issued by Inghinidhe na hÉireann, and AE's *Deirdre* has top billing followed by *Cathleen ni Houlihan*. The program also includes an advertisement for the actress who played Lavarcham, Máire Nic Shiubhlaigh's father's printing press and for magic lantern shows, reminding the reader that the nascent Irish dramatic movement was at this point a family affair. No one involved came without siblings and parents as part of the movement, including the Yeats and Gregory families who would contribute the artistic help of Robert Gregory and Jack B. Yeats. Finally, Inghinidhe uses the program as a recruiting tool. After explaining that the *United Irishman* is the only nationalist paper of Ireland, the program includes promotional materials for Inghinidhe na hÉireann:

1. To encourage the study of Gaelic, of Irish Literature, Music, and Art, especially amongst the young, by the organising and teaching of classes for the above subjects. 2. To support and popularise Irish manufactures. 3. To discourage the reading and circulation of low English literature, the singing of English songs, the attending of vulgar English entertainments at theatres and music-halls, and to combat in every way English influence, which is doing so much injury to the artistic taste and refinement of the Irish people.

Rules of the organization are also listed including that "each member must adopt a Gaelic name by which she shall be known in the Association" and that "each member shall pledge herself to support Irish manufacture by using as far as possible Irish-made goods in her household and dress." Membership is open to those "of Irish birth or descent, and must accept the principle of Independent Nationality for Ireland. Candidates must be proposed and seconded by two members of the Association, a week to elapse between nomination and election. Election by ballot."[10]

Here the society wrestles with the same question that animates the Citizen in Joyce's *Ulysses* and goes back to Shakespeare's MacDuff: "What ish my

---

[10] *Programme for Deirdre and Cathleen* [sic] *Ni Houlihan*, Abbey Theatre Archives, 1902.

nation?"[11] By the parameters set out above, Gonne herself, director of Inghinidhe, would be ineligible due to her complicated Irish and British identity and background. She was Irish neither by birth nor descent, and the theater would also have been reeling from the controversy surrounding British actors performing Yeats's and George Moore's *Diarmuid and Grania* in 1901, the previous year. The "election by ballot" also argues for a democratic concept of theater and speech, one Yeats would attempt to rein in both as his autocratic ideas of theater came to fruition and as he worked, to an extent, at the will of Annie Horniman.[12] The entire performance of AE's 1902 play, from gauze curtain to costumes to casting, reflected Inghinidhe's forms of theater. Finally, words like "vulgar" show Inghinidhe deploying the same class markers that Yeats would use against the Irish middle classes, as contentious ideas of a "pure" Irishness percolated under the surface of Revival performance. This class- and gender-fraught question of who gets to be Irish and who gets credit for writing and performance would haunt the casting of Deirdre in the years to come.In choosing to compose a Deirdre play, Yeats put himself squarely into the fray; his hope to write a version of the myth was an effort to express his own views with a vehicle familiar to Dublin and the other writers of the Revival. Of AE's version, he wrote in 1904 during the planning stages of his own text: "(Russell's) *Deirdre* is by a dear friend and a charming writer, but I do not consider it a good play," continuing an argument about representation that would drive the two apart and that comes out in their contrasting presentations of the myth. In *Dramatic Personae*, Yeats shows how these plays responded to each other in the argument about myth: "A. E. gave his *Deirdre*, a protest against *Diarmuid and Grania* because the play had made mere men out of heroes... all its male characters resembled Lord Tennyson's King Arthur."[13] "Men" is misleading; the most controversial figures onstage would always be female, and Yeats's strategic comparison to the impeccably British Tennyson and English hero King Arthur troubles the Irishness of AE's play.

---

[11] For a discussion of MacDuff and Irish characters in Shakespeare, see Mark Thornton Burnett and Ramona Way, eds, *Shakespeare and Ireland: History, Politics, Culture* (New York: St. Martin's Press, 1997).

[12] Adrian Frazier, in *Behind the Scenes: Yeats, Horniman, and the Struggle for the Abbey Theatre* (Berkeley: University of California Press, 1990), argues that class issues undergirded the tension that led to the Abbey Theatre split in 1905 when most of the actors left the theater over professionalization and treatment by the directors. Máire Nic Shiubhlaigh provides a first-person account of this exit in *The Splendid Years: Memoirs of an Abbey Actress and 1916 Rebel* (Dublin: James Duffy, 2016 [1955]).

[13] W. B. Yeats, *The Collected Works of W. B. Yeats, III, Autobiographies*, ed. William H. O'Donnell and Douglas N. Archibald (New York: Palgrave Macmillan, 1999), 331.

Both plays in the 1902 production, *Cathleen ni Houlihan* and AE's *Deirdre*, feature Ireland as a devouring mother tempting young men away from their human beloved. AE's *Deirdre* envisions a future not of violent sacrifice, but of oral history mourning loss, a commentary on Cathleen as maternal threat: "I know the gift we will give to the Gael will be a memory to pity and sigh over, and I shall be the priestess of tears." Deirdre is enacting memory on the stage, while Cathleen, that incendiary figure of Maud Gonne walking through the audience, embodies the threatening female Ireland that cost Deirdre Naisi: "Beloved," Deirdre says in AE's version, "am I become so little to you that your heart is empty, and sighs for Eri?"[14] Like the women in the cottage in Yeats's *Cathleen ni Houlihan*, Deirdre competes with the power of a deadly, feminized nation. Naisi and his brothers compliment her, but they do not listen to her. What AE and Inghinidhe emphasize in this version is the brothers' and Conchubar's inability to hear Deirdre, a tension that Yeats would re-enact in his own version. She admonishes them, "O let me speak"—she is complimented for her beauty but constantly unheard and interrupted. Naisi responds with anger to her attempts to explain her version of events, her premonition, her sense of their place in myth and history: "I shall not accuse him (Fergus) on the foolish fancy of a woman." Male comradery and male language win out over Deirdre's feminine language. AE's *Deirdre* dies and loses in the play, but the play ends up reifying her knowledge and version of the myth. Though they agreed on little, AE and Yeats both romanticized and fetishized a kind of female knowledge that they worked into those two performances, and their suspicion that the male figures misread and need female revision played out in how they wrote the plays. Ardan's dismissal of Deirdre, "The darkness is in your mind alone, poor sister. Great is our joy to hear the message of Fergus" shows a suspicion on the part of the playwrights that their versions of the plays are dependent on female performance and language. Deirdre's speech towards the end of the play acts as advice on drafting manuscripts and hearing the advice of women: "Why did you not take my counsel, Naisi? For now it is too late— too late."[15] In Yeats's drafting of his version of the Deirdre myth, however, it was never too late; he would bring in counsel, language, and blocking from female collaborators for ten years in his efforts to work out female mythic Irishness for the stage. This tension between what the Deirdres of the Abbey saw as male and female language reveals a gender bending aspect to Yeats's

---

[14] Russell, *Deirdre*, 19.   [15] Ibid., 27.

and Gonne's fraught relationship. As Yeats begins to draft Deirdre in part as a response to Gonne's choices, he identifies with the Revival language of Ireland as mythical and social while the male language of violence comes out of Gonne's letters justifying her decisions.

James Pethica has explained the complicated "economies of indebtedness" that undergird the friendship and collaborations between Yeats and Lady Gregory, a different but related dynamic to Yeats's interactions in writing texts and producing plays with Gonne.[16] The earliest drafts of Deirdre bear not only the stamp of AE's earlier version and Gonne's seminal 1902 performance as Cathleen, but also reveal Gregory's contributions. Gregory, then, not only co-authored, as Pethica has proven, Cathleen ni Houlihan; she also gave Yeats the translated text he used as a basis for his first drafts of Deirdre. Further complicating notions of authorship, Lady Gregory then wrote parts of his early drafts of the play. When Gregory, later on in this story, expresses rage at Florence Darragh's interpretation of the title role, she is not just a reviewer, but both writer of source material and co-author who feels that an agreement has been breached between herself and a collaborating writer, one wrapped up with high stakes ideas of nationhood and gender. Gregory worked on Cuchulain, she claimed, to create a "storehouse for poets," and in response to a 1900 dream of Yeats cautioning her, "It's not your business to write – Your business is to make an atmosphere."[17] (Yeats would advise his readers, "In dreams begin responsibility,"[18] so dreams were a way for these co-authors to discuss what was unsayable in waking hours.) And perhaps to her, in some ways, collecting the stories and co-writing with Yeats while providing him with the refuge of Coole was creating an "atmosphere," but by any definition, she was also a co-author. She began Cuchulain because Yeats refused to translate the Ulster Cycle himself. Her Cuchulain of Muirthmene came out in April 1902, shortly following the cathartic Deirdre/Cathleen ni Houlihan double bill. During October 1906, a month that Yeats spent composing Deirdre, he would write to Synge: "Lady Gregory has helped me very much with the scenario and it is

---

[16] James Pethica, "Patronage and Creative Exchange: Yeats, Lady Gregory, and the Economy of Indebtedness," in Deirdre Toomey, ed., Yeats and Women (New York: Palgrave Macmillan, 1997), 168.

[17] Qtd. in Colm Toibin, Lady Gregory's Toothbrush (Madison: University of Wisconsin Press, 2002), 37.

[18] W. B. Yeats, The Collected Works of W. B. Yeats, Vol. 1, the Poems, ed. Richard J. Finneran (New York: Scribner, 1997), 100.

necessary to have the play performed at a season when she can see it."[19] And in *Our Irish Theatre*, Gregory writes, "I worked as well at the plot and construction of some of the poetic plays, especially *The King's Threshold* and *Deirdre*."[20] Gregory's response to her work with Yeats is its own complicated story, one Pethica tells well; she both effaces her contribution and then claims her own role, revealing inner conflicts about her voice in playwriting with Yeats. Dorothea West remembered Yeats explaining to her that Gregory "wrote my Deirdre in fundamental mass."[21] Before she co-authored those early drafts, however, Gregory's *Cuchulain of Muirthmene* gave Yeats the framework for the play, and a close look at her version of the myth bears this out.

From the beginning of her version of this story, Gregory addresses a lack, responding to how the myth has or has not survived, to a misremembering and a neglect. Like any good introduction, then, hers to *Cuchulain of Muirthmene* strategically sets out a new project against an old one and claims an audience. She writes "to the people of Kiltartan"—"there is very little of the history of Cuchulain left in the memory of the people, but only that they were brave men and good fighters, and that Deirdre was beautiful."[22] The ever-present issue of representation, of "real" Irishness rears its head here. Addressing "the people of Kiltartan," her dedication reads as a personal note, beginning, "My dear friends," in an odd claim to connection to a place and a people that carries a whiff of appropriation. She explains that, ironically, the Irish is too old and archaic for these people to understand so she is rewriting it, translating the best parts, to return the stories to them. In a move familiar to anyone who has read the introductions and prefaces of the Revival and their claims to authenticity as an effort to both occlude and congratulate the Anglo-Irish author-as-conduit, she claims that she "put nothing of my own that could be helped." With her nurse from childhood, Mary Sheridan, as a model, she vows to tell the story in "plain and simple words." Sheridan joins the crowd of servants to the Anglo-Irish claimed as sources, cousin to Synge's "servant girls in the

[19] W. B. Yeats, *The Collected Letters of W. B. Yeats, V, 1905–1907*, ed. Eric Domville, (Oxford: Oxford University Press, 2005), 509.

[20] Lady Gregory, *Our Irish Theatre* (London: Putnam, 1913), 83.

[21] W. B. Yeats, *Deirdre, Manuscript Materials* (Ithaca, NY: Cornell University Press, 2004), xxxv.

[22] Lady Gregory, *Cuchulain of Muirthemme: The Story of the Men of the Red Branch of Ulster* (London: John Murray, 1902), v.

kitchen."[23] Their version of events is lost, though it would be interesting to hear how the perspectives of these women servants line up with these authors' efforts to speak for them.

The entire Introduction shows what Lucy MacDiarmid has called Lady Gregory's "tactical brilliance" in her subtle and coded argument for a series of stories from the people, the folk, or the crowd, depending on who is speaking of this amorphous, fictional idea of a group without language, an Irish version of Spivak's "subaltern."[24] In this account, Gregory is the hard-working lady of a country house, opposed to the male, academic Dublin world:

> And indeed if there were more respect for Irish things among the learned men that live in the college at Dublin where so many of these writings are stored, this work would not have been left to a woman of the house that has to be minding the place, and listening to complaints, and dividing her share of food.[25]

Admonishing male Dublin academic culture as not "Irish" enough in their supposed spurning of Irish subjects, Gregory also manages to cast herself as "a woman of the house" who spends her time feeding her community, keeping the peace, and maintaining her home; an older and less proselytizing sister to Yeats's controversial Countess Cathleen. What appealed to Yeats from this version that mixed the Deirdre myth and Irish identity was the way that Gregory rooted the language and the text in a source material that was far from the urban middle class that increasingly incited fear in Yeats. Her old nurse and "the people of Kiltartan" embodied, for Yeats, a country peasant Irish identity that he wanted to tap for mythic material; without Gregory, he had access to neither the "noble" nor the "beggar man." This Deirdre replicated the class structure of Coole in ways that appealed to Yeats as close readings of his letters show, and the ensuing battles over casting were infused with these class tensions. Setting herself up as opposed to the literary elite in Dublin, though as a future director of the

---

[23] J. M. Synge claimed to have composed "*The Shadow of the Glen* by eavesdropping on 'the servant girls in the kitchen.'" "Preface," *The Playboy of the Western World: A Comedy in Three Acts* (Dublin: n.p., 1907), vi.

[24] Giyatri Spivak, "Can the Subaltern Speak? Revised edition," *Can the Subaltern Speak: Reflections on the History of an Idea*, ed. Rosalind C. Morris (New York: Columbia University Press, 2010), 21.

[25] Gregory, *Cuchulain*, vi.

Abbey and published writer she would occupy that urban space, Gregory falls back on her identity as landed countrywoman, deploying tropes around food and home central to both her class and her gender.

Yeats was, of course, accused of "log rolling" in his Preface to "the best book to have come out of Ireland in my time," but it is worth examining how his use of Gregory's Cuchulain book is part of a Yeatsian pattern of both collaborating with women who shadow the final text and claiming a certain kind of Irishness.[26] Textual collaboration here retains traces of performance; these were originally oral stories in a dialect familiar to Gregory from tales from her nurse and her "Kiltartan friends." In 1902, as Dublin reeled from the April double bill, Yeats set out to write a Deirdre as a way of revising earlier versions of Ireland as a woman from AE and his own *Cathleen ni Houlihan*, though his take on the story would retain the imprints of both of these earlier plays. He was seeking a new vehicle for his image of Gonne as one in need of separation from modernity. Gregory's *Deirdre* tale provided him with the materials for that new role. Even Gregory's *Deirdre* is the result of years of untold authors; Yeats writes of Gregory's *Deirdre* that "a dozen manuscripts have to give their best before the beads are ready for the necklace," and he argues for the "beautiful speech of those who speak in Irish" as its own dialect of English.[27] This version of composition prefigures Yeats's playwriting especially in the case of his *Deirdre*, and it treads a fine line between taking credit for a new version of the myth and claiming that the story is ancient and author-less. This tension between contending that the myth is his own while asserting an ancient authenticity rooted in an Irish identity animates the drafting and performance of this play.

Yeats ends this Preface by expounding on Gregory's "Kiltartan friends," by creating his own idea of an "Irish country people" formed by these stories and by this way of speaking, a mystical, mythical "people" with "quick intelligence," "abundant imagination," and "courtly manners." Coole and Gregory were a way in for Yeats to an idealized nation reflecting a secret life of Ireland that, however fictional, Yeats sought to reveal. There is an odd Orientalizing of his own country here; the idea of the West as a place apart but emblematic of the best of the "people" gives Yeats ballast against the ensuing "filthy modern tide."[28] Using Gregory's version of the story is its

---

[26] W. B. Yeats, "Preface," in Gregory, *Cuchulain*, vii. The accusation of "logrolling" comes from *The New Ireland Review* on p. 253.

[27] Yeats, "Preface," in Gregory, *Cuchulain*, vii.

[28] Joseph Lennon's *Irish Orientalism: A Literary and Intellectual History* (Syracuse, NY: Syracuse University Press, 2008) uncovers archival material to trace the sources of Ireland's

own kind of eavesdropping. Yeats responded to this version of the myth as a perfect way to separate his equally mythical version of Maud Gonne, in his theater, from the choices that she was making to align herself with violent nationalism, John MacBride, and what Yeats saw, in his increasingly class-obsessed years, as Catholic middle-class culture.[29] The Preface to Gregory's collection describes this Arnoldian "Irish" character—"his mind constantly escaped out of daily circumstance ... his imagination was always running off to Tir-nan-ogue, to the land of promise, which is as near to country-people of today as it was to Cuchulain and his companions." What clues can this Preface give us to Yeats's *Deirdre*, already fermenting in his mind? She "might be some mild modern housewife but for her prophetic wisdom"— he classes Deirdre and Emer with Helen and Brunhilde because this is a claim for an ancient culture with threads to the Ireland of his time, and Gonne, always linked with Helen in his mind, would have been animating his idea of an ancient Deirdre. His later Gonne poems bear the marks of his early turn to Deirdre, spurred by her decisions, as well. She is increasingly fated in these evolving ideas of her; questions like "How could I blame her?"[30] suggest that, like Helen and Deirdre, Gonne was playing out a scripted future that she could not control. Her beauty compels this, taking her agency, and allowing Yeats to write her future even when it is anathema to his vision of her.

At the end of this Preface, Yeats conjures a memory from his Sligo childhood, and here he is lamenting the fact that he was not told these stories; he also manages to link his merchant seamen ancestors of Sligo to this tale:

Orientalism and, in a second part, argues for the Orientalism in the Revival tropes and images of both Ireland and a mysterious, nebulous "East."

[29] Gonne's marriage to John MacBride in 1903 was traumatizing to Yeats. When he had met her and built his poetic and theatrical apparatus of inspiration around her, Maud Gonne was already secretly involved with French revolutionary Lucien Millevoye. She gave birth to a child, Georges, who died in infancy and then had a second daughter named Iseult with Millevoye; Yeats believed Iseult to be a ward. Yeats's castle in the air about Maud as a single and otherworldly muse fell apart when she married MacBride, a violent nationalist and abusive husband. Yeats wrote a devastated letter begging her to reconsider, but she married MacBride in 1903, and he was abusive to her and Iseult. After years of estrangement that fractured her nationalist support, MacBride died in the Easter Rising of 1916. For a book-length discussion of Gonne and Millevoye's relationship, see Adrian Frazier's excellent *The Adulterous Muse: Maud Gonne, Lucien Millevoye, and W. B. Yeats* (Dublin: Lilliput, 2016).

[30] W. B. Yeats, *The Collected Works of W. B. Yeats, Vol. 1, the Poems*, ed. Richard J. Finneran (New York: Scribner, 1997), 89.

When I was a child I had only to climb the hill behind the house to see long, blue, ragged hills flowing along the Southern horizon. What beauty was lost to me, what depth of emotion is still perhaps lacking in me, because nobody told me, not even the merchant captains who knew everything, that Cruachan of the Enchantment lay beneath those long, blue, ragged hills![31]

This Preface reads Gregory's collection as a reflection of an Ireland and a "country people" that is as mythical as Deirdre and as close to Yeats's heart. In his habit of telling Irish country inhabitants about themselves, Yeats lays on thick his interpretation of this community and uses this ideal as a way to think about a new verse play, one that would lead his vision of Gonne away from the violence that attracted her, the violence she had pushed him to include in *Cathleen ni Houlihan*. Also, he makes an assumption that his sea captain relatives "knew everything," though in his family lore those Pollexfens were the silent keepers of all folk stories. John Butler Yeats said that in marrying Susan Pollexfen he had "given tongue to the sea cliffs."[32] As Deirdre Toomey argues, Yeats's fascination with Gonne is rooted in his loss of his mother and a link to those silent Pollexfens as an authentic Irish identity.[33] He published this Preface a month before the April 1902 performance of *Deirdre* and *Cathleen*; his childhood memories of Sligo, his fascination with the class divisions at Coole, and his obsessive imaginings of Gonne and Gregory's writing started him thinking of this new version of the Deirdre myth as he watched AE's interpretation with his incendiary *Cathleen ni Houlihan*, a text also written with Gregory.

What did Yeats take from Gregory's version? His growing ideal of Gonne as "an Irish Helen"[34] found a parallel in his reading of Gregory's Deirdre; Lavarcham foretells: "for I see by Druid signs that it is on account of a daughter belonging to you, that more blood will be shed than ever was shed in Ireland since time and race began."[35] The young woman is responsible for

---

[31] W. B. Yeats, *The Cutting of an Agate* (New York: Macmillan, 1912), 11.

[32] Qtd. in Norman Jeffares, *The Circus Animals: Essays on W. B. Yeats* (London: Macmillan, 1970), 121.

[33] Deirdre Toomey's "Away" brilliantly traces Yeats's fascination with a certain type of woman (and Maud Gonne is only one example of many) to the loss of his mother first to wordless, motionless depression and then to death. She links his interest in fairy lore and Sligo to that early loss. See Deirdre Toomey, ed., *Yeats and Women* (New York: Palgrave Macmillan, 1997), 135–67.

[34] In *Yeats's Verse-Plays: The Revisions, 1900–1910* (London: Oxford University Press, 1965), Suheil Bushrui reads the Helenization of Gonne in the play on p. 120.

[35] Gregory, *Cuchulain*, 104.

the bloodshed due to the kind of power that Yeats would later call, speaking of Gonne, "burdensome beauty." Familiar language like "for your sake"[36] and the sense of helpless, fated beauty come through in Gregory's text: "Let Deirdre be her name; harm will come through her," Gregory writes, and "there will be trouble on Ulster for your sake."[37] Gregory's text of *Deirdre* gave Yeats a way to write about the danger of beauty, the desire to hide that power, and the fear of that influence. This tension would reverberate in his play and in his poetry into old age, from *A Prayer for my Daughter*'s fantasy of a woman lovely but not dangerously beautiful, motionless, "rooted in some dear, perpetual place,"[38] *Broken Dreams*, and his last poems like *Politics*. The "grave apart" for Deirdre in Gregory's text fed Yeats's desire for Gonne to live away from the strife that he saw due to her beauty, though, in reality, Gonne sought this kind of violence and used her extravagant height and beauty as a tool to raise money and galvanize crowds; we see this in her provocative entrance through the audience in 1902. Her deployment of these theatrical, performative ways of convincing the audience at the Abbey in *Cathleen ni Houlihan* grew, as I discussed in Chapter 2, out of her street theater performances in Inghinidhe na hÉireann. In response, Yeats created a Deirdre, as opposed to AE's and, later, Synge's, who lived with Lavarcham "in the lonely place among the hills without the knowledge or the notice of any strange person, until Deirdre was fourteen years of age."[39] What Yeats removed from his drafts was Lavarcham teaching Deirdre folk knowledge; as he watched performances on the Abbey stage and reacted to his loss of Gonne, his Deirdre became increasingly isolated in revision.

The irony of this period of Yeats's life is his obsession with class-based individuality and his simultaneous dependence on a series of women for the crafting of his play. According to Foster, back in Coole in 1905 as he drafts with Gregory in earnest, Yeats is "beginning a play on the theme of the tragic heroine Deirdre which preoccupied him throughout the summer. The subject was resonant; already treated by Russell and Rolleston, WBY was apparently anxious to put his mark on the story of 'Ireland's Helen,' or, as Dublin would have it, 'The Second Mrs. Conchobar.'"[40] The Dublin quip shows an effort to humanize Deirdre, to blame her for her sexual experience

---

[36] "Burdensome beauty" and "For your sole sake" are from "Broken Dreams," in W. B. Yeats, *Poems* (London: Fisher Unwin, 1899), 153.
[37] Gregory, *Cuchulain*, 105.   [38] Yeats, *Poems*, 188.   [39] Gregory, *Cuchulain*, 106.
[40] Foster, *The Apprentice Mage*, 321.

with two men, and to demythologize mythic heroines; one senses from that witticism of the Dublin street that there was some exhaustion with the male authors of the Abbey's constant vying to tell this female-dominated Irish myth. These tensions around class, religion, and female representation onstage would erupt, of course, in 1907 in the *Playboy* riots. The idea of Yeats putting any kind of individualist stamp on the story, one he published far and wide as he wrote, is intentionally misleading on Yeats's part. He depended on Gregory not only during this summer and fall for lodging, food, and the time and space to write, but also for a connection to a landed class that he admired with the tenacity of the town child, the outsider, and the artist's son who many years ago felt "too penniless a suitor" for the Gore Booth daughters at the Sligo big house that towered over his childhood, Lissadel.[41] Gregory also gave him access not only to her version of the story but also to her knowledge of Irish, of the local landscape and history, and of the techniques of playwriting so important to his efforts to make a success of "his" version of Deirdre. Foster acknowledges that during this early drafting period, "Gregory's influence is vital":

> WBY spent all summer and much of autumn 1904 at Coole; their collabo-
> ration became even closer. His eyes were especially troublesome, and she
> typed most of his letters; her own voice sounds through them, in the archness
> of the language and modulation of tone for different correspondents.[42]

How this "voice sounds through" is part of my argument for foregrounding the more complex and occluded forms of collaboration as opposed to those that privilege traditionally male ways of claiming authorship in the Irish context of the Revival at the expense of the women who influenced, per-formed, and revised the texts. Gregory also managed the "theatre business, management of men"[43] during this controversial period; without that help, Yeats would have had no time and space to write.

All evidence points to Yeats's deep affinity for class division, one that is linked to gender stereotypes and an important part of his revisions of *Deirdre*. While he began to write *Deirdre* in 1904, Yeats wrote to Fay, "We must grope our way towards a new yet ancient perfection . . . Our movements

---

[41] W. B. Yeats, *Memoirs: An Autobiography—First Draft, Journal*, ed. Denis Donoghue (New York: Macmillan, 1974), 78.
[42] Foster, *The Apprentice Mage*, 321.
[43] Yeats, "The Fascination of What's Difficult," *Poems*, 92.

are clumsy for we are children, but we are a devil of a long way from our coffins."[44] Yeats had characterized the work that came out of his collaborations with both Gonne and Gregory as their children, and there are hints of his eugenicist future in the idea of this progeny. This advice to Fay also suggests how new this turn to ancient source material still felt to the writers of the Abbey and how many were trying to make their own stamp on ancient versions of Ireland. Gonne would soon produce *Dawn*, a nationalist play of female mythic power built from her work on *Cathleen ni Houlihan* and as director of Inghinidhe na hÉireann. In a letter to Ricketts during the summer when he was composing *Deirdre* at Coole, Yeats wrote that the plays were "a cry for more abundant and more intense life" and "tragic exultation."[45] This form of life would be increasingly coded in classist language and opposed to the life of the towns and middle classes, especially as Yeats read Nietzsche. His January 1906 letter to Russell stands as an attempt to recast the theater in class terms. With knowledge of Yeats's dependence on the many to realize his texts, it is impossible not to marvel at his attempt to argue for individualism in his writing to Russell: "Neither your character nor the character of any of us need defense. We should not discuss such things with any but our equals."[46] And by "us" here, Yeats means the Anglo-Irish directors; Foster points out that Yeats's "increased consciousness of class difference at this time also reflected the social nature of the acting profession, still regarded in many circles as 'unsuitable.'" Yeats's choice of actresses came out of his efforts to redefine Ireland in this class- and gender-based way. He chafed against, but ultimately had to accept, his dependence on the actresses for performance and revision. As actresses interpreted the role of Deirdre, arguments over casting and interpretation laid bare questions of national identity and class structure, always more extreme around questions of femininity and Irish performance.

Questions of class were central to Yeats's argument with much of Dublin over Lane's effort to set up a permanent art collection for the city. Yeats, in Moore's recollection,

began to thunder like Ben Tillett himself against the middle classes, stamping his feet, working himself into a great passion, and all because the middle classes did not dip their hands into their pockets and give Lane the money he wanted for his exhibition. It is impossible to imagine the hatred that came into his voice when he spoke the words 'the middle

[44] Yeats, *The Collected Letters of W. B. Yeats, V, 1905–1907*, 440.   [45] Ibid., 436.
[46] Ibid., 466.

classes'; one would have thought he was speaking against a personal foe...
he could hardly have gathered in the United States the ridiculous idea that
none but titled and carriage-folk can appreciate pictures. And we asked
ourselves why Willie Yeats should feel himself called upon to denounce the
class to which he himself belonged essentially; on one side excellent mercantile millers and shipowners and on the other a portrait painter of rare
talent.[47]

First, we must remember that Yeats is writing against AE's *Deirdre* at this
point while also quietly using that play as a model. As the actresses and
actors left his theatrical enterprise, in a story well-chronicled by Adrian
Frazier, the company divided along the lines of individualism and dependence on Horniman's capital.[48] Yeats's casting choices and drafting of *Deirdre*
and his extreme reaction to Gonne's political and personal moves had
everything to do with his anathema to a Catholic middle class that must
have touched his anxieties as Yeats was, AE reminds us, a member of a
Protestant middle class not far from the group he so vocally hated. In
response, during those seven years as he battled over who was to play
Deirdre, Yeats narrowed the focus of his play to emphasize upper-class
characters.

Despite all of his discussion of a "theatre for the few,"[49] Yeats's response
to the opening of the theater in the last week of 1904 tells of a man quietly
focused on appreciative audiences and a "packed house," as he wrote to
Gregory. His concern with the size of the audience throughout the Deirdre
story shows how much popular success meant to him despite his arguments
to the contrary. He hoped that his plays would be widely appreciated and
also needed the revenue from audiences so that the Abbey could function
and remain viable. The theater opened on December 27, 1904, with *On
Baile's Strand*, *Spreading the News*, and Máire Nic Shiubhlaigh, the actress
who first played Lavarcham in AE's *Deirdre*, now the lead in *Cathleen ni
Houlihan*, further linking the two plays of April 1902. Both of those performances from 1902 would have shadowed Máire onstage and Yeats's claim to
writing a new version of the Deirdre myth signaled both a connection with
these performances of the past and something new. Yeats was in charge

---

[47] George Moore, "Vale," *Yeats's Poetry, Drama, and Prose* (New York: W. W. Norton,
2000), 325.
[48] Adrian Frazier explains the intricacies of the Abbey at this time in his *Behind the Scenes*.
[49] W. B. Yeats, *Beltaine (Routledge Revivals): The Organ of the Irish Literary Theatre*
(London: Routledge, 1970), 20.

(Lady Gregory was home sick) and announced that Deirdre was in the works and would be onstage soon. His telegram after the performances to Gregory lauding the size of the audience for all plays and hers as an "immense success" suggests that this kind of accolade was still important to a man raised in economic insecurity between homes in Sligo, Howth, and London, attempting to financially sustain a theater in Dublin.

In May 1906, Yeats writes in a Preface his own idea of collaboration mixed with his increasing obsession with class, the "noble and the beggar-man" and, as a town boy himself, though he would rather the reader forget that, his distaste for the town. First, here is his definition of the language of the "folk"—of course, this is his interpretation through Gregory:

> The extravagance, the joyous irony, the far-flying phantasy, the aristocratic gaiety, the resounding and rushing words of the comedy of the country-side, of the folk as we say, is akin to the elevation of poetry, which can but shrink even to the world's edge from the harsh, cunning, traditionless humor of the towns.[50]

And here is his nod to the authorial question, an acknowledgment about the way he composed his plays, though the writers, most especially Gregory, get recognition here, not the actresses:

> we have talked over one another's work so many times, that when a play of mine comes in to my memory I cannot always tell how much even of the radical structure I may not owe to the writers of "The Lost Saint" or of "The Shadow of the Glen," or more than all, to the writer of 'Hyacinth Halvey'; or that I would have written at all in so heady a mood if I did not know that one or the other were at hand to throw a bushel of laughter into the common basket.[51]

And yet, the "common basket" is, on the contrary, a legacy of printed material, of texts attributed to specific authors. Following Pethica, we need to examine not only how the writings of Gregory and Moore transformed Yeats's work, but the influence of actresses as well. In July 1906, while he is working on *Deirdre*, his Preface explains that "Perhaps one can explain in

[50] W. B. Yeats, *The Variorum Edition of the Poems of W. B. Yeats*, ed. Peter Alt and Russell K. Alspach (New York: Macmillan, 1957), 1293.
[51] Ibid., 1293.

plays, where one has much more room than in songs and ballads, even those intricate thoughts, or elaborate emotions, that are one's self."[52] Those thoughts and emotions are what are revealed onstage and seeing the performances of women allowed Yeats to revise and create the inner lives of the characters.

To Foster, "the old esprit de corps of Inghinidhe na hÉireann or Sinn Fein...as far as posterity was concerned...were irretrievably swept aside into subordinate roles by WBY's increasingly powerful sense of his own history."[53] And yet, we need not accept Yeats's version of events, and it is incumbent on us to recover those "subordinate roles" in acknowledging that nothing was possible for Yeats in theater without the contributions of a cast of women, and his search for an actress shows his efforts to find a way to get to the stage this new idea of art, Irishness, class, and gender. He would not at first succeed; the line of actresses and Gregory's help pushed him to re-imagine Deirdre, itself a re-imagining of early Deirdres and of the long line of mythic female characters before it. So the play tries to both tie this new version to the continuum of mythic female characters of the revival and to one-up those who came before. Yeats tries in *Deirdre* to make a statement about a new kind of Irish heroine that has grown out of earlier versions with a difference, embodying new ideas of class and tradition. This is why, as we will see, he needed to claim an Irishness for the British actress Florence Darragh and to initially import talent, but the bumps in the road ending in Mrs. Patrick Campbell's later success show that he still needed the old collaborative model.

One of the best footnotes in Yeats criticism is Deirdre Toomey's, when she writes, in *Yeats and Women*, "I have not considered the case against Maud Gonne, as this has been thoroughly rehearsed in the last forty years of Yeats criticism."[54] Toomey chronicles the shock of Gonne's status as a mother on Yeats in December of 1898.[55] And life with Gonne as a friend continued to be a series of shocks and quarrels, and that controversy surrounding Gonne "spurred (him) into song." The initial composition of *Deirdre* deals with a second shock, a shock reverberating from the first, when Maud Gonne married MacBride. Toomey's "Away," as I discuss in Chapter 1, argues for Yeats's depressed, silent, "fairy" mother as the root of his obsession with Gonne and his need to write women as part of another world. Interestingly, Deirdre is not a mother; Lavarcam, the foster mother,

---

[52] Ibid., 851.   [53] Foster, *The Apprentice Mage*, 328.
[54] Toomey, *Yeats and Women*, 31.   [55] Ibid., 6.

disappears as Yeats revises; Cathleen is only a mythic mother, and the Bridget characters of mothers in cottages, written by Gregory into *Cathleen ni Houlihan*, disappear from Yeats's *Deirdre* and subsequent verse plays: maternity gets written out along with female community except for the singing women at the start who maintain that link. Heiresses of Florence Farr, the musicians frame the story and explain the link to myth and previous Deirdres, and they also showcase the history of the Abbey from Inghinidhe (the Allgood sisters, Sara and Molly, were members) and the first productions to the ensuing verse experiments. The musicians' version of events retains some of that tension between male and female speech in the play.

Why did Yeats write maternity, even foster motherhood, out of his version of *Deirdre* and ensuing verse dramas? Why did his text of the play increasingly isolate female characters? Toomey argues that "to be presented with Maud Gonne as a mother was to have a bizarre psychic structure threatened, if not dismantled."[56] While Yeats was drafting *Deirdre*, to be presented with Gonne as a wife to a "drunken, vainglorious lout"[57] spoiled her consecrated persona—one conflated for Yeats with class, gender, and Irishness and in need of rescue in the writing of *Deirdre*. Maternity is an important part of this story: "This remarkable hiatus in Yeats's poetic career is evidence of the collapse of an imaginative world built upon an erroneous conception of Maud Gonne."[58] Toomey reads this explosion as debilitating to his poetry for two years. Though he did stop writing poetry during those years, he continued to try and read and ultimately misread Gonne in his writing for theater.

Yeats conceived the idea for the play out of his increasingly fraught discussion of nationalism with Maud Gonne, one I have discussed in Chapter 2 on the two Cathleen plays that he wrote for her. AE's *Deirdre*, performed with *Cathleen ni Houlihan*, stayed in Yeats's mind like a challenge, and as his relationship with Gonne became more fraught when she tried to turn their work together to support her version of nationalism, Yeats returned to the Deirdre myth—a story about the power of a woman's beauty—as a way to wrestle with his desire for Gonne as a woman beyond daily politics. This ongoing conversation began when they first met in 1884 and is shot through with the gender and class issues central to their relationship. Yeats cast Gonne in his poetry as a recalcitrant muse, and the

---

[56] Ibid., 7.   [57] Yeats, "Easter 1916," *Poems*, 182.
[58] Toomey, Yeats and Women, 9.

reputation stuck, but the real story is her influence on the language and imagery in his plays as a nationalist, correspondent, and performer, both onstage and in the political arena.

In 1903, a year after playing *Cathleen ni Houlihan*, Maud Gonne converted to Catholicism and married John MacBride. These two acts clashed with Yeats's image of her as an untouchable icon; in response, he removed characters based on her, in his poems and plays, from politics, violence, and community. When she revealed to him her plans for marriage and conversion in late January 1903, he wrote her a desperate, incoherent letter arguing that the marriage would bring "down your soul to a lower order of faith [*sic*] is thrusting you down socially, is thrusting you down to the people."[59] He defined their work together as a project to train "a few strong aristocratic spirits" to "uplift the nation," exposing his increasingly individualistic and class-based idea of nationalism.[60] At the end of the letter, he pleads with her to "come back to yourself" and "take up again the proud solitary haughty life which made [you] seem like one of the Golden Gods." Maud Gonne responded by reminding him that he misread her in seeing her as a beauty separate from the people, and that the *Cathleen ni Houlihan* she identified with was one who created community: "You say I leave the few to mix myself with the crowd while Willie I have always told you I am the voice, the soul of the *crowd*."[61] In 1905, her marriage to MacBride ended with a humiliating public separation. With *Deirdre*, Yeats responded to Gonne's public and private problems as well as to her more militant nationalism by writing a new and solitary heroine, untouched by politics and sacrificing herself for love. The early versions of the play chart Deirdre's course from life as a mortal caught in a web of political intrigue to her chosen death with her lover Naoise, contrasting the epic language of the heroine's love for Naoise with the false words of the court. Yeats's new heroine, in direct opposition to the violent, communal nationalism of Gonne's vision of *Cathleen ni Houlihan*, would choose the love of one man and poetic language over politics.

Though Yeats and Gonne both imagined an inherent Irishness of the soul, dependent on neither birth nor residence, they interpreted the meaning of nation differently. Questions about definitions of nation are at the heart of the ideas that engendered *Deirdre*, and his disagreement with Gonne

[59] Maud Gonne, *The Gonne–Yeats Letters: 1893–1938*, ed. Anna MacBride White and A. Norman Jeffares (New York: Norton, 1993), 165.
[60] Ibid., 165.   [61] Ibid., 166.

fostered that growing idea of nation, for Yeats, as essentially artistic. A complaint she wrote to Yeats about *Cathleen ni Houlihan* reveals that Gonne's distaste for Yeats's revision of that play came from a belief in an essential Ireland that speaks through artists: "You get a purely Irish conception of a play, & as you work it out, it becomes less and less Irish – I have noticed this more than once in a work of yours that you have read to me in various staged of development."[62] Because the play, to Gonne, came from the pure spirit of a nation, she saw *Cathleen ni Houlihan* as "more national than anything Hyde has written, but it was written rapidly as it came to you directly from the life forces of Ireland";[63] of course, Gonne's version of events here excluded Lady Gregory's contribution to that play. The many women who worked with Yeats would often deny each other's influence, and questions of ownership vex the history of this play in particular. Working on *Cathleen ni Houlihan*, Yeats and Gonne began to realize that their views of nationalism were developing in opposite directions. In a common complaint, Gonne wrote to defend herself against a charge of changing her policies in February 1904: "I think you have ALTERED your views in National art you think I have in some ways changed mine . . . still I believe we shall be able to work together for Ireland just the same as in the past."[64] These letters bear out Gonne's frustration with Yeats's misreading of her as a muse, an ideal, "Helenized" figure, dangerous, beautiful, and apart, what Toomey calls "the underside of an idealizing romantic passion."[65] Their spate of letter writing during her marital separation in 1905 and 1906 focuses mostly on their efforts to free her from scandal and MacBride's influence, but Yeats continued to send her his own and other Abbey plays and, in response to *In the Shadow of the Glen*, she wrote, "I quite agree with you as to his [Synge's] really remarkable force & talent as a dramatic writer, though still I think this play is not for the many in Ireland & not helpful to the movement." Characteristically, now that Yeats was helping her, she made more conciliatory comments about his work: "You are carrying on the movement in another line. It is good & I wish you all success. Again thanking you for your kind sympathy."[66]

In 1904, the year he revised *Deirdre*, Yeats's idea of Ireland was already bound up with his belief in the power of the individual over the mob and his new hopes for performance. Gonne's position as a woman scorned by the

---

[62] Ibid., 180.   [63] Ibid., 181.   [64] Ibid., 180.
[65] Toomey, *Yeats and Women*, xvii.   [66] Ibid., 190.

public fit into his idea of the solitary heroine. In the 1904 *Samhain*, Yeats sets this isolation against a form of nationalist art that he saw as propaganda: "Our propagandists have twisted this theory of the men of letters into its direct contrary, and when they say that a writer should make typical characters they mean personifications of averages, of statistics, or even personified opinions, or men and women so faintly imagined that there is nothing about them to separate them from the crowd, as it appears to our hasty eyes."[67] Howes writes that "Yeats's constructions of the mob figured it as the opposite of the nation, rather than its logical and threatening extension. While the nation combined mystical unity and flourishing individuality, the mob was both fragmented and homogeneous."[68] Yeats defines "National literature" in *Samhain* 1904 as "the work of writers who are moulded by influences that are moulding their country, and who write out of so deep a life that they are accepted there in the end [sic]."[69] Plays in English, he claims, that do not take part in what he calls propaganda or "plead the national cause" should nonetheless be considered Irish. Some of the anxiety in both Gonne's and Yeats's claims to nationality come from Yeats's Anglo-Irish background and Gonne's English birth. After the change in the theater organization in 1905, Padraig Colum resigned with the defecting actors and left only Protestants, backed by British money, in the leadership roles.[70] In the 1904 *Samhain*, Yeats's definition of "National" literature reiterates his devotion to a new "high" style of acting, modeled on his idealization of a troubled Maud Gonne: "We will not forget how to be stern, but we will remember always that the highest life unites, as in one fire, the greatest passion and the greatest courtesy."[71] (In "No Second Troy," he would use similar language, describing Gonne's beauty as "high and solitary and most stern," and that image of a "fire" separating the few from the crowd would weave in and out of his versions of *Deirdre*.)[72] He would link this interpretation of heroic femininity with verse for the stage, language that "must get away, except in trivial passages, from the methods of conversation."[73] His new view of acting became increasingly anti-realist: "as long as drama was full of poetical beauty, full of description, full of philosophy, the players understood that their art was essentially

---

[67] W. B. Yeats, *Explorations* (New York: Macmillan, 1962), 145–6.

[68] Marjorie Howes, *Yeats's Nations: Gender, Class, and Irishness* (Cambridge: Cambridge University Press, 1996), 95.

[69] Yeats, *Explorations*, 156.   [70] Frazier, *Behind the Scenes*, 128.

[71] Yeats, *Explorations*, 162.   [72] Yeats, *Poems*, 89.   [73] Yeats, *Explorations*, 162.

conventional, artificial, ceremonious."[74] These words, "conventional, artificial," and "ceremonious" describe an art rooted in an imagined aristocratic past.

Yeats's *Deirdre* argues for new, solitary ideals not only against previous incarnations of *Deirdre* but also in opposition to his own earlier versions of female heroism for the stage: while *Cathleen ni Houlihan* took part in a communal public discourse, with a heroine who convinced young men, through poetic language, to join her in violent sacrifice for an imagined nation, *Deirdre* chooses to die for love in a spiritualized heroism that rejects violent politics. If *Cathleen ni Houlihan* welcomes the young to her violent nationalist cause, *The Countess Cathleen*, Yeats's first attempt to write a role for Gonne, dies for the community, albeit with a dose of noblesse oblige. Deirdre, however, dies for herself and Naoise alone. *Cathleen ni Houlihan* begins with a direct link to earlier Irish insurrection, in the "Interior of a cottage close to Killala, in 1798," but *Deirdre* takes place in an unidentified time and place, "a guest-house in a wood."[75] Starting in this way station, Yeats sets up a play about a landless couple who find their place only in the nation of death. The conflict is much more immediate than Forgael's and Dectora's distance from life in *The Shadowy Waters*; Deirdre and Naoise live and die under threat from the political leader and court. The solitary heroism that Yeats had developed for *Deirdre* with Gonne in mind takes over the setting: "the landscape suggests silence and loneliness."[76] While the verse speakers tell the truth, the violent characters in the play are not heroic but hired hands, working for money; when he sees that Conchubar has assigned his murder to a henchman, Naoise calls the king a "beast."[77] In *Cathleen ni Houlihan*, seduction is part of nationalist sacrifice, while in *Deirdre*, love is separate, and politics threaten the increasingly isolated couple. The musicians sing that Deirdre and Naoise "bargained for their love, and paid for it / All that men value."[78] Years later, in "Easter 1916," Yeats brought violence and love back together ("And what if excess of love / Bewildered them until they died?"[79]), but in *Deirdre*, love and violent nationalism are in opposition, and love is part of an idealized death.

Yeats returns to the bird imagery he used for Gonne in the early poetry to describe Deirdre's distance from both the national and the physical. At the end of the play, Deirdre joins Naoise in an isolated death for the purpose of love, not nationalism. The musicians tell the story of the two who realized Yeats's ideal of high isolation:

[74] Ibid., 172.   [75] Ibid., 175.   [76] Yeats, *Plays*, 112.   [77] Ibid., 128.
[78] Ibid., 113.   [79] Yeats, *Poems*, 230.

FIRST MUSICIAN: They are gone, they are gone. The proud may lie by the
  proud...
FIRST MUSICIAN: Into the secret wilderness of their love.
SECOND MUSICIAN: A high, grey cairn. What more to be said?
FIRST MUSICIAN: Eagles have gone to their cloudy bed.[80]

Love, here, is divorced from country, a "secret wilderness" where Deirdre
finally separates herself completely from humanity. Deirdre, like her predecessor in the play, Ludaugh Redstripe's wife, a queen who was a sea-mew,
dies into a bird state, a symbol for Yeats of distance from worldly attachment. In *Calvary*, a musician uses bird imagery to describe Christ's departure from mortality: "Lonely as the sea-bird lies at her rest, / Blown like a
dawn-blenched parcel of spray."[81] As Yeats revised the play, Deirdre became
increasingly distanced from those around her. In 1911, he wrote in his
"Preface" to *Plays for an Irish Theatre*: "I am content, because the words
called up before me the image of a sea-born woman so distinctly that
Deirdre seems by contrast to those unshaken eyelids that had the sea's
cold blood what I had wished her to seem, a wild bird in the cage."[82] Like
the golden bird at the end of "Sailing to Byzantium," Deirdre has been
translated into an inhuman form. Adrian Frazier interprets the ship in
The Shadowy Waters as Ireland and Forgael as a Protestant planter with a
mutinous crew of nationalists.[83] The ship, however, allows the play to take
place in a no man's land, more distant from Ireland than Conchubar's guest
house. Like boats, sea birds migrate and rarely live in a particular nation.
Both plays employ Yeats's old tendency to imagine an escape with
Gonne away from human physicality into a bird state, recalling the Wild
Geese, departed Irish nobility and his fantasy of his Pollexfen, seafaring
ancestors, a family history whose actual merchant roots Yeats was always at
pains to ignore.

Conchubar, in his efforts to turn Deirdre from wanderer to queen, hopes
to take her from the poetic world to the political, while the bird state she
attains in death removes her from that struggle. Naoise asks Fergus's pardon
for Deirdre: "She has the heart of the wild birds."[84] This bird imagery
symbolizes a solitary, otherworldly power that would return in characters
like the dancing, inhuman bird/woman in *At the Hawk's Well*. Deirdre,
commanding in her final hours, interrupts their chess game to speak to

---

[80] Ibid., 766. [81] Ibid., 335. [82] Yeats, *Variorum Edition of the Poems*, 1299.
[83] Frazier, *Behind the Scenes*, 147. [84] Yeats, *Plays*, 179.

Naoise in words that echo Yeats's 1890s lyrics to Gonne, though the style of these lyrics is less ornate than that of his early poetry:

> Bend and kiss me now,
> For it may be the last before our death.
> And when that's over we'll be different;
> Imperishable things, a cloud or a fire.
> And I know nothing but this body, nothing
> But that old vehement, bewildering kiss.[85]

Yeats dreams of a similar transformation in "The White Birds" (1892): "For I would we were changed to white birds on the wandering foam: I and you!"[86] This early desire for transformation out of human form returns in *Deirdre* as Yeats dramatizes the heroine's decision to die into a birdlike state. This idea of a spiritual Ireland mirrors Yeats's concept of sexuality that transcends the physical. In *Autobiographies*, he describes his efforts to reach Gonne spiritually, in sleep:

> Sometimes, when I had gone to sleep with the endeavor to send my soul to that of Maud Gonne, using some symbol, which I forget, I would wake dreaming of a shower of precious stones. Sometimes she would have corresponding experiences in Paris in the same night, but always with more detail. I thought we became one in a world of emotion eternalized by its own intensity and purity, and that this world had for its symbol precious stones. No physical, sexual sensation ever accompanied these dreams...[87]

Conchubar, in *Deirdre*, asks a Libyan servant to sew magic stones into the bedchamber to charm the reluctant heroine. Sexuality in *Deirdre* is rooted in Yeats's occult experiments with Gonne, privileging a connection that lasts beyond the earth. Later, his response to meeting Gonne in sleep was "bodily," or physical:

> One morning I woke in my hotel somewhere near Rutland Square with the fading vision of her face bending over mine and the knowledge that she had just kissed me...[Later that morning] she said, 'Had you a strange dream last night?' I said, 'I dreamed this morning for the first time in my

---

[85] Ibid.   [86] Yeats, *Poems*, 37.   [87] Yeats, *Memoirs*, 128.

life that you kissed me.' She made no answer, but late that night when dinner was over and I was about to return home she said, 'I will tell you now what happened. When I fell asleep last night I saw standing by my bed a great spirit. He took me to a great throng of spirits, and you were among them. My hand was put into yours and I was told that we were married. After that I remember nothing.' Then for the first time, with her bodily mouth she kissed me.[88]

Yeats remembered this moment while retelling Gonne's revelations about her affair with Millevoye. When Gonne chose other men, Yeats worked his idea of their connection beyond the physical into his plays and verse. Deirdre and Naoise look forward to a "bewildering kiss" that will last beyond their life.[89] Nation becomes amorphous and spiritual, and along with Ireland, women and sexuality function without bodies; the term "bodily mouth" exists alongside the sensuality of their dreams.

Along with a spiritual Ireland, the play dramatizes a sexuality that opposes politics and the "social, modern" world.[90] The "old vehement, bewildering kiss"[91] remains in death, not physical but part of the couple's removal to a different state. Like Keats's belle dame sans merci, Deirdre controls Naoise with a kind of alchemy; the musicians describe the passive young man "having wooed, or, some say, been wooed" by Deirdre.[92] In 1902, five years after he first mentioned writing a play based on the Deirdre legend to Fiona MacLeod, Yeats imagined Deirdre as a mother, "a normal, compassionate, wise housewife."[93] He was working on *Cathleen ni Houlihan*, a play that pits mother Ireland against a prosaic mother, when he repeated this assessment of Deirdre to Gregory and urged her to include Deirdre's children in her version of the myth. By the time he began the play two years later, his idea of the title character had transformed into a woman without community, and Yeats was removing characters from the story rather than adding familial ties. He wrote Deirdre away from motherhood as well as politics, and Yeats would return to this celebration of spiritual female sexuality opposed to the political state in his final poem, "Politics"

[88] Ibid., 131–2.

[89] In *The Adulterous Muse*, Adrian Frazier tells the story of Maud Gonne's secret and occluded life in France with Lucien Millevoye and finds much of her political thought from that period.

[90] Yeats, *Autobiographies*, 386.   [91] Yeats, *Plays*, 191.   [92] Ibid., 176.

[93] W. B. Yeats, *The Collected Letters of W. B. Yeats, II, 1896–1900*, ed. Warwick Gould, John Kelly, and Deirdre Toomey (Oxford: Oxford University Press, 1997), 144.

and his last play, *Purgatory*. Though horrified by the mother's choice in a mate, the old man in the final play wonders, watching the ghosts re-enact their wedding night in the ruined house:

> Can she renew the sexual act
> And find no pleasure in it, and if not,
> If pleasure and remorse must both be there,
> Which is the greater?[94]

In *Deirdre*, Yeats dramatizes this sexuality that exists beyond death and mortal consciousness. From his occult experiments meeting Gonne on what the two called "the astral plane,"[95] Yeats created the connection between Deirdre and Naoise in *Deirdre*, one that would transcend death and separate them from politics, modernity, and those remaining on earth.

Casting Deirdre again showed how the myth was a flashpoint for nationalist argument about gender, power, class, and nation; Yeats spent much of 1903 and 1904 performing as the director and poet in an unofficial theatrical role on the Abbey stage. A close reading of his own language and actions on that stage shows the class issues that will inform his treatment of Florence Farr and Sara Allgood. Controversies influenced the performances and the casting of women in the lead, causing Yeats to winnow Deirdre down to essentials, to take out many of the characters and emphasize the female musicians, beautifully realized by Sara Allgood (Figure 5.1). The lead character was always a controversial casting choice, as that woman was to stand for Irish mythical female heroism.

Yeats wrote the choruses of the play first, and his verse experiments with Florence Farr influenced his initial drafts in 1904, causing him to highlight the roles of the musicians, eventually replacing Lavarcham with these characters. The musicians are some of the few characters who are in every draft, both because of this early influence from Farr and the Allgoods' (especially Sara's) ability to perform those roles. As Ronald Schuchard has shown, Yeats and Farr spent twenty-two years collaborating "in their efforts to return musical speech to lyrical, narrative, and dramatic verse."[96] In the

---

[94] Yeats, *Plays*, 541.

[95] Matthew Gibson and Neil Mann, *Yeats, Philosophy, and the Occult* (Clemson, SC: Clemson University Press, 2016), 112.

[96] Ronald Schuchard in *The Last Minstrels: Yeats and the Revival of the Bardic Arts* (Oxford: Oxford University Press, 2008) reveals the complex collaborations between Yeats, Farr, Sara Allgood, and others as the group developed verse experiments.

Photo.]   MISS SARA ALLGOOD,   [*Lafayette.*

Figure 5.1 Sara Allgood in *The Lady of the House*, 1909
Source: Courtesy of Dublin City Library and Archive.

early years of writing and revising *Deirdre*, beginning in 1904 and again from 1905 to 1907, Yeats worked with Florence Farr on verse speaking, and the two gave lectures and demonstrations in Scotland, England, and Ireland; it is impossible to overstate her influence on his ideas of verse speaking and subsequent revisions of the language and musical aspects of the play.[97] Yeats wrote the musician characters and songs first, and sent Farr early verses from the play in September 1906 with the explanation: the "first musician was written for you – I always saw your face as I wrote very curiously your face even more than your voice, and built the character out of that."[98] The musicians, through all of the thousands of pages of revisions, remained central to the play. On speaking verse, Yeats wrote in *Samhain* 1904, "An actor must so understand how to discriminate cadence from cadence, and so cherish the musical lineaments of verse or prose, that he delights the ear with a continually varied music."[99] Again, "lineaments," his word for Gonne's beauty, describes his hopes for an equally proud and controlled performance. In the play, one of the women carries a "stringed instrument," and the Allgood sisters, Sara and Molly, trained verse speakers, performed as the musicians. A mannered, "conventional, artificial, ceremonious" idea of acting came out of these experiments with Farr, perfectly suited to writing a new kind of heroine: "That we may throw emphasis on the words in poetical drama, . . . the actors must move, for the most part, slowly and quietly, and not very much, and there should be something in their movements decorative and rhythmical as if they were paintings on a frieze."[100] Yeats focuses on poetic language over action here, imagining the performers in a moving tableau, like the figures on Keats's urn or the figures in "Lapis Lazuli." While working with Farr and imagining her in the title role, Yeats shifts the focus of the play to the musicians, editing out other characters and depending on those women to tell the story and perform the important functions of the play.

As Yeats spent all those tumultuous years writing his *Deirdre*, Lavarcham, Deirdre's foster mother, swelled in importance only to be written out of the final draft; that shift reflects the verse experiments with Farr, as the chanting became subsumed eventually into the focus on Sara Allgood's Singing Woman. In 1902, Yeats and Farr presented a "Lecture to Musical Notes," as Holloway remembers, "to give examples to the accompaniment of the psaltery" with Maud Gonne in attendance (Figure 5.2). As Yeats started to dream up his Deirdre from Gregory's prose text, responding to AE and Máire Nic Shiubhlaigh's pre-Raphealite Lavarcam and Inghinidhe's performance, Farr's musical influence caused him to imagine that foster mother as increasingly important, until he shifted his focus through work with

---

[97] Ibid., 52.
[98] W. B. Yeats, *The Letters of W. B. Yeats*, ed. Allan Wade (New York: Macmillan, 1955), 482.
[99] Yeats, *Explorations*, 173.   [100] Ibid., 176–7.

Figure 5.2 Florence Farr and the psaltery, designed by Arnold Dolmetsch
Source: Courtesy of the State House Library London.

Farr and Allgood to a few First Musicians and wrote Lavarcham out of the draft. The musicians took Lavarcham's place, no longer a specific, maternal mythic figure, but now a nameless but central cipher for female voices speaking verse.

In a third version begun in 1906, Fergus subsumes a host of earlier players, stressing "the conflicts between emotive, or extrarational, sources of knowledge and knowledge derived from the rational structures of conventional society... Yeats redefines his visual and verbal figures in celebration of passionate love and high imagination."[101] In my reading, this is all gendered, and Yeats chooses the feminine, espoused by the musicians and Deirdre and her rural, sequestered childhood—a kind of ideal Irish childhood separate from middle class struggles for power—against the male machinations of the court. Again, Farr and Sara Allgood influenced Yeats

---

[101] W. B. Yeats and Virginia Rohan, *Deirdre: Manuscript Materials* (Ithaca, NY: Cornell University Press, 2004), xxxii.

as he created these musicians, advising him on language, verse, and performance. Sources show that Yeats was working "medieval continental romance"[102] into this idea of Irish literature. This leads him to write a play "in praise of the heroic woman, with "the will of the wild birds,"[103] of passionate love and the powerful and joyous shattering of common codes and lives." In revision, in 1906, Yeats wrote these tensions between different ways of speaking and thinking into a play increasingly divided between two different kinds of language. This year saw Maud Gonne attacked in Dublin, suspected of being "a British spy" as she tried to extricate herself from marriage with MacBride with some shred of her own reputation intact.[104] For comfort, Yeats fell back again on an increasingly class-based view of culture and theater, and his choice of actresses and work revising reflect that search for a female figure away from the infighting in the court. As Rohan argues, performance informed all of these revisions: "In (the later manuscripts), we see how abundantly the playwright profited from access to actors and the live theater, as he swiftly rewrote and reshaped what became, in effect, the 'stage Deirdre.'"[105] Yeats tried to mold the Deirdre he wanted from actresses who appealed to him because they seemed other, different from the largely working and middle-class Abbey company, and reflective of his own ideal of female Irishness. Their performances, though, did not, especially in the case of Darragh, succeed in realizing Yeats's version onstage, and the arguments between Yeats as writer and director and the actresses find their way into these revisions, changes that highlight tensions between gendered versions of events.

In casting controversies surrounding Sara Allgood, as I discuss in more detail in Chapter 3, Yeats revealed his bias against Catholic, working-class women. Allgood would, through her own tenacity and talent, show Yeats that her skills were essential to his project, and as "A Singing Woman" she ended up experimenting with Yeats on the speaking of verse in ways that would influence Yeats's idea of performance and female roles. Yeats's disturbing comment to Lady Gregory that Catholic women like Sara Allgood "have not sensitive bodies"[106] reveals why only certain women could inspire

---

[102] Ibid.   [103] Yeats, "He Wishes His Beloved Were Dead", *Poems*, 70.

[104] Terence Brown, *The Life of W. B. Yeats: A Critical Biography* (Oxford: Blackwell, 1999), 164.

[105] Yeats and Rohan, *Deirdre*, xxxii.

[106] Ann Saddlemyer, ed., *Theatre Business: The Correspondence of the First Abbey Theatre Directors: William Butler Yeats, Lady Gregory, and J. M. Synge* (University Park: Pennsylvania State University Press, 1982), 67.

him when he imagined them onstage. As Adrian Frazier puts it, "Trying to finish Deirdre, he could make little headway so long as he envisioned the plump, sweet Sara Allgood in the role."[107] The women, as I shall go onto argue, who did get Yeats writing his lead female character, were all willowy Protestant women who physically resembled Maud Gonne. As for "plump, sweet Sara Allgood," as I discuss at length in the Epilogue, Sara Allgood was more ambitious, intelligent, and artful than sweet; she showed her ability to jockey for a role both in the world of Revival class prejudice and later as an older women in Hollywood. With Yeats, she was nothing if not tenacious and through verse experiments with Florence Farr, Allgood taught the poet and playwright not only her own talents for verse speech but also innovations in that technique. Her talent finally won Yeats over, class prejudice and all, and her influence on the *Deirdre* text and his verse experiments were a warning to him not to underestimate women not from his own class.

Yeats's correspondence with Florence Farr from their meeting in 1890 until her death, in Ceylon, in 1917 of breast cancer, shows a collaboration fraught with tensions he would find useful in writing *Deirdre*. In *W. B. Yeats and His Muses*, Joseph Hassett notes Farr's "un-muse like propensity to be his equal."[108] Farr's refusal to bow to Yeats, in fact, allowed her influence on his writing of verse and ideas of theater. After watching her 1911 performance, Yeats wrote, "I never want to see Deirdre without her," and criticized her as well. Her refusal to treat him as the sole creator of theater, her unconventional ideas on feminism and gender, her expertise at the psaltery, and her upper handed role in their sexual relationship all caused Yeats to write the First Musician for her and to create, as Ronald Schuchard has shown, a theory of verse and performance rooted in their collaboration. Yeats's letters to Farr as their physical affair began to wane show how powerful she was in their relationship; in 1906, in the midst of writing *Deirdre*, he asks "to be forgiven for my too great occupation with yourself." She also asked for increases in pay when touring with Yeats and performing on the psaltery. Farr and Yeats studied the occult together; her focus was Egyptian myth, and Yeats's strange Orientalism returns when he describes her speech "as one thinks Egyptian priestesses must have spoken then," in some far off, imaginary "East." And Yeats continued to imagine her life and correspond with her after Farr left for a position as principal of a girls' school in Ceylon, now Sri Lanka, in 1912. In Farr, Yeats found a performer who could express, inspire, and direct the ideas of performance and verse that they created together. As Ezra Pound wrote of Farr in "Portrait d'Une Femme," "One comes to you / And takes strange gain away." Not only the specific influence on the verse experiments, but also the power in the figures of Deirdre and the First Musician are thanks to Farr, with her "tranquil beauty, incomparable sense of rhythm, and a beautiful voice."[109] Yeats himself was hardly tranquil in performance when up on stage as the formidable and angry director, and he always lamented his own voice; hence his dependence on Farr.

The *Deirdre* casting drama raises the question, again, about who gets to be Irish. A letter Yeats wrote to his father from Coole in July 1906 explains that his initial reasons for importing Florence Darragh from London had everything to do with the female ideal he had imagined for Gonne and worked through, to an extent, with Farr, one that prohibited Sara Allgood from inclusion. Writing James Sullivan Starkey in 1904, he described Deirdre as "a very confident serene person," and as he created an isolated main character, he sought a new kind of actress.[110] This idea of *Deirdre* departs from his other verse plays: Dectora, in *The Shadowy Waters*, a play he was revising while he worked on his first drafts of *Deirdre*, is not solitary but ruled by Forgael's charm. As Gonne, Synge, and Yeats himself felt threatened by a changing Ireland, however, Yeats would write his mythical heroine away from the dangerous Irish middle-class world he saw no longer as "countrymen," or "people," but as "the crowd."[111]

Yeats not only saw British-born Maud Gonne as unequivocally Irish, but claimed that Florence Darragh, another woman born in Britain, was an "Irish star on the English stage" as well, suggesting that Darragh's ability, in Yeats's eyes, to play an isolated tragic heroine conferred on her a feminine Irishness (Figure 5.3).[112] Arguing for her inclusion in the 1906 cast as the lead, he wrote, "She is an Irishwoman."[113] Her Irish background remains unconfirmed, but Yeats's claim is as important as Darragh's actual ancestry. *Deirdre*, disdainful of place, community, or politics, nevertheless makes a political statement. Rewriting the legend, Yeats casts a perfect Irishness as female, spiritual, solitary, and willing to die for love. If Irishness meant to

---

[109] Yeats, *Autobiographies*, 118.   [110] Yeats, *Collected Letters*, iii, 637.

[111] My thanks to Seamus O'Malley for his help in these distinctions from his paper on Lady Gregory at the Modern Language Association American Conference for Irish Studies Panel, January 2018.

[112] Yeats, *Letters of W. B. Yeats*, ed. Wade, 482.   [113] Ibid., 475.

Figure 5.3 Florence Darragh (Letitia Marion Dallas) as Cleopatra in
Shakespeare's *Antony and Cleopatra*, The Queen's Theatre, Manchester, 1908
Source: Courtesy of Emory University.

Yeats, in these years, the ability to separate oneself from the fray, his idea of
Darragh's acting style conferred this nationality on her.

Yeats shows his indebtedness to actresses in the letter below, tracing the
ways that women he was collaborating with shift performance, and he is
only in control here to a point. Writing a play about a female body dying, he
cannot play Deirdre, and so much depends on who is embodying that title
role as well as the musicians:

> I feel that change is taking place in the nature of acting; Mrs. Campbell and
> her generation were trained in plays like *Mrs. Tanquery*, where everything
> is done by a kind of magnificent hysteria ... This school reduces everything
> to an emotional least common denominator ... The new school seizes on
> what is distinguished, solitary, proud even. One always got a little of this in
> Mrs. Emery [Florence Farr] when she was good, and one gets a great deal of

it in Mrs. Darragh...the problem with me just now is whether, as I am rather inclined to, to leap at the advertisement of a performance by Mrs Pat, or to keep to my own people and my own generation till they have brought their art to perfection.[114]

Yeats decided on Darragh because he believed that she could perform in a new way, realizing his "distinguished, solitary, proud" heroine. He saw Mrs. Patrick Campbell's style as already developed, and her power and mastery gave Yeats pause, making her ineligible for his more experimental idea of acting. He would later revise this negative opinion of Mrs. Patrick Campbell, an actress who made the role of Deirdre famous a few years later, but this letter reveals that his hesitation about casting her had to do with his hopes for a less established actress and a new kind of acting: Yeats hoped that Florence Darragh would be able to realize his hopes for verse tragedy:

...there is a new actress, a Mrs. Darragh, who may want it [*Deirdre*] for England, and I am inclined to think that Miss Darragh has more intellectual tragedy in her...She gave a magnificent performance of Salome the other day. I am inclined to think, though I have not seen enough of her yet to be quite certain, that she is the finest tragedian on the English stage.[115]

After seeing Darragh in Wilde's *Salome*, Yeats's need for a female actress as a connection not only to performance but to his amorphous interest in a vague idea of an Eastern "other," is at the forefront of his revisions. His Deirdre's otherworldliness and his interest in Darragh have much to do with this first viewing of her as other, and, bizarrely, it is this very otherworldliness that confers Yeats's idea of Irish identity on her.

Noreen Doody argues that both the 1905 and 1906 versions of Wilde's *Salome* profoundly impacted Yeats: "Prior to seeing Wilde's play, Yeats's female protagonists were asexual moderate women – not the stuff of heroic females or modern queens."[116] In fact, bringing Darragh into the Abbey imported the Orientalism and sensuality of *Salome* in ways that disturbed both audiences and fellow Abbey workers. After seeing the 1905 performance, Doody argues, Yeats "began to revise three of his finished plays—*The Shadowy*

---

[114] Ibid., 475.   [115] Ibid., 475.

[116] Noreen Doody, "An Echo of Someone Else's Music: The Influence of Oscar Wilde on W. B. Yeats," in Uwe Boker, Richard Corballis, and Julie A. Hibberd, eds, *The Importance of Reinventing Oscar: Versions of Wilde in the Last 100 Years* (Amsterdam: Rodopi, 2002), 176.

Waters, On Baile's Strand, and *Deirdre,*"[117] and I argue that the performance by Darragh as much as the play itself by Wilde turned Yeats to writing new kinds of heroines. The play *Salome,* with Darragh in the lead, pushes Yeats to rewrite *Deirdre* to strengthen the title role. Florence Farr was stage manager and director of the 1905 performance starring Darragh in the title role, and both actresses' work on direction, dance, and performance would push Yeats to rethink his Irish heroine as more physical and sexual than the Abbey stage had seen. As Michael McAteer argues, Yeats's "decision to cast Darragh for the role of Deirdre suggests that he saw in her performance of Salome some of those qualities that he was trying to express."[118] And, as I will discuss when Darragh arrives in Dublin, Yeats would define this physicality as Irish in casting Darragh as an "Irishwoman." This interpretation of Irish womanhood would cause Lady Gregory uncharacteristic rage.

Salome as an inspiration also suggests that Yeats was using these women and mythic female characters by encoding Orientalism, a connection to an "ancient Ireland" linked somehow to a fantasy of precolonial cultures: "The luxuriance of Wilde's Oriental exoticism was grossly overstated to Yeats's ears … "[119] In *Moving Performances: Divas, Iconicity, and Remembering the Modern Stage,* Jeanne Scheper argues that "Salome-as-cypher exposed faltering nineteenth-century colonial powers and patriarchy—even as it exhibited racialized and sexualized fantasies"[120] There is a troubling way that the upper-class women performing as Deirdre allow Yeats to access an ancient Ireland closely related to the Orientalized images of the untouched East as far back as his original pre-Gonne obsession, Laura Armstrong, who I discuss extensively in Chapter 1. Yeats develops an Orientalism bound up with this view of women. In *The Speckled Bird,* Yeats revised Mohini Chatterjee's ideas on rejecting the physical life and cast the female character as a link to an "Eastern" past: "He says I was once a priestess in a temple of the moon in Syria."[121] *Deirdre* is an attempt to reclaim a place like this for Gonne, so who would play her was tantamount for Yeats—a woman of the Golden Dawn, not a Catholic working-class Irishwoman would link the play

---

[117] Ibid.   [118] Ibid.
[119] Michael McAteer, *Yeats and European Drama* (Cambridge: Cambridge University Press, 2010), 50.
[120] Jeanne Scheper, *Moving Performances: Divas, Iconicity, and Remembering the Modern Stage* (New Brunswick, NJ: Rutgers University Press, 2016), 1.
[121] W. B. Yeats, *The Speckled Bird: An Autobiographical Novel with Variant Versions,* ed. William H. O'Donnell (Basingstoke: Palgrave Macmillan, 2003), 22.

to a pre-Christian Ireland. This troubling Orientalist connection is also signaled by the various "Black Jesters" and "Arab messengers" of his early drafts. A particular kind of Irish or faux-Irish woman connects Yeats to this atavistic, Orientalist, and comforting Irish past, one he animates in Deirdre, a class-based past based on the prejudices of his own post- Gonne/MacBride marriage world view.

Joseph Lennon's *Irish Orientalism* charts the ways that the Irish have claimed a fraught connection to "the Orient," and his discussion of the way that the writers of the Revival used ideas of a connection to a timeless, imagined otherworldly "East" informs my discussion of Yeats's dependence on female bodies in performance in casting and rewriting *Deirdre*. Both women and "the Orient" provide for Yeats a way into other forms of thought and performance for the stage. In *Deirdre*, Yeats bizarrely links the Orientalism of the upper-class woman to a pre-Celtic, Arnoldian Ireland with the "Libyan" "dark-faced" men who wait on Conchubar; some versions include a "Black Jester" or an "Arab messenger."[122] Most of these characters leave the final version, but Yeats's need to bring in these characters shows that the occult of the Golden Dawn, an organization that Darragh, not incidentally, had joined, is linked to his problematic fascination with an "other" connected to an ancient Ireland accessible only through women of the upper classes.

What was it, then, about Darragh's acting style that attracted Yeats? Willie Fay's quip gives a clue: to Fay, the contrast between her approach to performance and that of the Abbey actors "was like putting a Rolls Royce to run a race with a lot of hill ponies up the mountains of Mourne, bogs and all. The ponies, knowing every inch of the way could outpace the Rolls every time."[123] The difference between her style of acting and that of the Abbey players appealed to Yeats: his verse plays had not been a success at the Abbey. Eager to blame only the performers and not the plays themselves (though his many revisions must have been spurred in part by lukewarm reception), he wrote to Synge in August of 1906:

> You and Lady Gregory and Boyle can look forward to good performances of your plays from the present Company and from people who will join it in the natural course of things. I am getting them, of course, for my prose

---

[122] Yeats, *Plays*, 175.
[123] Richard Hogan and James Kilroy, eds, *Modern Irish Drama: A Documentary History. Vol. III, The Abbey Theatre: The Years of Synge 1905–1909* (Dublin: Dolmen, 1978), 68.

plays. But I am essentially not a prose writer. At this moment in spite of Frank Fay's speaking I could get a much better performance in England of a play like *Deirdre*...The alternative to this is the giving of my plays to English companies, for if I am to be of any use ever in Ireland I must get good performances. Till I get that I shall be looked on as an amateur.[124]

Yeats's changing idea of Ireland as a place of solitary heroes and heroines as opposed to group nationalism reflects his interpretation of a divide in the theater between the naturalistic realism of the plays of Synge and Gregory and his more experimental verse drama. *Deirdre* is a more stylized play than those that preceded it with its use of tableaux, blank verse, and symbolic props. Yeats was writing a heroine, separate from the crowd and possessive of her own kind of language, who would inhabit this kind of theater. And, as Foster points out, there is a threat in this letter; if Yeats is barred from importing actresses, he may produce his plays in England.[125]

Deirdre is a departure both from Yeats's early poetry and the lyrical style of *The Shadowy Waters*. The play's more focused language, tightened in years of revision with Farr, Allgood, Darragh, and Campbell, reflects Deirdre's linguistic power. Setting up this dramatic speech in opposition to his earlier poetics, Yeats pits two forms of speech against each other in *Deirdre*. The play supports the truth of the musician's and Deirdre's language as opposed to the violent speech of Conchubar's false oath. Speaking this more concentrated poetic language, the play's chorus of women remains, like Horatio in *Hamlet*, alive at the end. The female group story-telling of Inghinidhe na hÉireann stands behind this play as Deirdre charges these musicians with telling the version of the tale she sanctions. Fergus sums up their way of speaking dismissively as poetic words with no connection to reality: "your wild thought / Fed on extravagant tales / That common things are lost, and all that's strange / Is true because 'twere a pity if it were not."[126] The language of the musicians, a dramatic speech that revises Yeats's early poetry, endangers the sanctity of Conchubar's promise; in Fergus's words, "I had to threaten / These wanderers because they would have weighed / Some crazy fantasy of their own brain / Or gossip of the road with Conchubar's word."[127] Fergus's idea of the relative worth of different kinds of language is revealed to be misguided by the end of the play; the women, speakers of song, understand the situation better than those who

---

[124] Saddlemyer, *Theatre Business*, 139.   [125] Foster, *The Apprentice Mage*, 352.
[126] Ibid., 179.   [127] Ibid., 183.

value political speech, but he is right to see danger to political power in this other way of speaking. Deirdre uses the form of language favored by the play's women to trick Conchubar, the main purveyor of hollow political speech. Orchestrating the final act herself as well as her death, her speech overpowers the king. Naoise asserts, earlier, the value of Conchubar's language: "I have his word and I must take that word, / Or prove myself unworthy of my nurture / Under a great man's roof."[128] But Naoise believes the wrong speaker, and Deirdre uses her skills as a reader and speaker of dramatic language to impose her will on the play's end, a fate decreed by history and politics. Preying on Conchubar's jealousy and vanity, she directs a play within a play in the final scene, one in which her language vies with Conchubar's, and wins. Turning the same ideas of masculinity and femininity against Conchubar that Fergus and Naoise had employed to judge her language, she berates Naoise to the king: "There is no sap in him; / Nothing but empty veins."[129] In his last lines before death, Naoise has learned to speak the language of the musicians and Deirdre, questioning and translating their elliptical words: "What do they say? / That Lugaidh Redstripe and that wife of his / Sat at this chess-board, waiting for their end."[130] As Deirdre successfully redirects the end of the play by swaying Conchubar, her language trumps political speech and wins converts. Also, she gets the knife from the musician, bringing the female musicians into the action and herself into their world.

In a July 1906 letter to his father about choosing an actress for the lead role, Yeats used the language of ownership, revealing both the importance of the lead actress to his project and his concerns about giving up control of the play. He was not, in his words, simply deciding who would play the part, but who would "have it." The language of possession comes into this discussion of actresses for the lead roles because, at this point, he knew that he did not own this collaborative project:

Mrs. Patrick has asked for my Deirdre, which she has seen through in somewhat incomplete form. She wants to produce it in the autumn and to take it on tour in America. I am not quite sure whether I can let her have it, as my own theatre has first claims.[131]

---

[128] Ibid., 181.   [129] Ibid., 198.   [130] Ibid., 189.
[131] Yeats, *Letters of W. B. Yeats*, ed. Wade, 475.

Phrases like "my Deirdre," "want it," "take it," "my own theatre," and "claims" stress Yeats's strange position: he was creating a part that emphasized solitary strength against a community, but he needed to collaborate with actresses to realize his project successfully. His concerns about the effect of Mrs. Patrick Campbell's fame and power on collaboration initially pushed him to choose Darragh, an actress who, he believed, would not try to control the performance.

Lady Gregory found Florence Darragh's onstage interpretation of sexuality offensive. Her response reflects her own personal and authorial investment in the play: though Yeats made many changes to Gregory's prose version of the Deirdre legend in *Cuchulain of Muirthmene*, published with his Preface in 1902, he found much of his information on the legend in her work, writing in *The Arrow* of November 24, 1906: "The best version is that in Lady Gregory's 'Cuchulain of Muirthmene; and is made up of more than a dozen texts."[132] During that summer of 1904, when the play got underway in earnest at Coole, Gregory contributed to drafts of *Deirdre*. Her knowledge of different ancient versions of the myth would have been indispensable, and the two had been discussing the legend for years. In *Our Irish Theater*, she would later claim to have written some of the play: "For *The Pot of Broth* also I wrote dialogue and I worked as well at the plot and the construction of some of the poetic plays, especially *The King's Threshold* and *Deirdre*; for I had learned by this time a good deal about play-writing to which I had never given thought before."[133] Dorothy Wellesley reports that Yeats said to her, "Lady Gregory wrote the end of my Deirdre on my fundamental mass."[134] Yeats saved most of his revisions for the beginning of the play, leaving the part that Gregory claimed to have contributed unchanged.

Lady Gregory's anger at Darragh's interpretation, then, might have come from her sense of ownership as collaborator on the play's text. Issues of nationhood and gender figure prominently in her objection to Darragh and evidence a growing gap between her own ideal of femininity for the Abbey stage and Yeats's new heroine. The intensity of Lady Gregory's reaction against Florence Darragh's work and personality had everything to do with the image of Irish womanhood that Gregory wanted to see onstage. A few months after the premier of *Deirdre*, Gregory would criticize the public

---

[132] W. B. Yeats, *The Collected Works of William Butler Yeats, VIII, The Irish Dramatic Movement*, ed. Mary FitzGerald and Richard J. Finneran (New York: Scribner, 2003), 184.

[133] Lady Augusta Gregory, *Our Irish Theatre* (London: Putnam, 1913), 54.

[134] Yeats, *Plays*, 855.

outcry against the earthly sexuality of *The Playboy of the Western World*, but a different kind of female desire onstage caused her to react with horror to Darragh's Deirdre in November 1906. Of Darragh's performance, Gregory wrote to Synge, "she put something mean, ignoble, and sensual into the part," using Yeats's elitist language against the actress he had chosen.[135]

Gregory's problem with Darragh's sensuality shows a fear of the new-comer as an invader. As she became more frustrated, Lady Gregory began to voice the animosity towards "strangers in the house"[136] dramatized in *Cathleen ni Houlihan*; in December 1906, she called hiring Darragh and giving into this outsider's wishes to bring in "a supply of new actresses...a case of calling the Normans into Ireland."[137] This comment reveals that at the root of Gregory's problem with Darragh was a disagreement with Yeats not only about his vision of woman for the stage, but also about definitions of nationality. To Synge on New Year's Day, 1907, she again linked Dar-ragh's self-interest to her status as a stranger: "outsiders like Miss Darragh, playing for their own hand only."[138] In 1919, Yeats would publish a play about the famous lovers, Diarmuid and Dervorgilla, who, legend has it, fell in love and called the Normans in so that they could escape Dervorgilla's husband, and Gregory's tirades against Darragh build on those myths that link sexuality with the idea of a stranger threatening the nation. A few months after Darragh's 1906 performance as Deirdre, Gregory continued to use the language of prurience and elitism in a letter to Synge, "My chief difficulty is that he is pressing Miss Darragh for Fand and I will not consent to having her for any work outside his, which we cannot help. I think her Deirdre was a degradation of our stage."[139] Gregory may well have been frustrated by the divide between her longtime public role, acknowledged by Yeats, as patroness, and her actual work as co-author on scripts. A letter to Yeats to protest his time away from writing angrily reminds him of their dual parentage of this and many other plays: "I look on it as child-murder. Deirdre might be in existence now but for this."[140] The sensuality that Gregory found so appalling made Darragh, in Yeats's mind, a perfect candidate for Deirdre's strange combination of desire and distance from the world:

> The very moment these eyes fell on him,
> I told him; I held out my hands to him;

---

[135] Saddlemyer, *Theatre Business*, 207.
[136] Yeats, *Plays*, 88.
[137] Saddlemyer, *Theatre Business*, 181.
[138] Ibid., 193.   [139] Ibid., 207.
[140] Gregory, *Our Irish Theatre*, 208.

> How could he refuse? At first he would not—
> I am not lying—he remembered you.[141]

Deirdre's distant words sound more like a narrator than a passionate lover; at the same time, her lines describe her sexual control over Naoise.

After all of the trouble over bringing her in and anger at her high handedness, Darragh's performance received mixed reviews. *Sinn Fein* panned Darragh's "undramatic" acting and contrasted her interpretation unfavorably with the work of Máire Nic Shiubhlaigh in Russell's *Deirdre* in 1902.[142] This was particularly damaging, as Nic Shiubhlaigh's new company had taken Russell's *Deirdre* on tour in America after leaving the Abbey in 1905. According to Synge, Darragh's May 1907 performance as Fand proved "deplorable."[143] Though some reviewers praised her performance, Darragh had not delivered the success that Yeats had hoped for. His plays seemed as unappreciated as ever, even starring an actress specifically imported to rescue their standing with the public and realize his hopes for a new heroine. He would soon be grateful to Mrs. Patrick Campbell for offering, in the fall of 1907, to play Deirdre, and would find that, contrary to his initial judgment, she, not Darragh, would inspire him to effective revision and bring the play to prominence and popularity in Dublin and abroad.

Lady Gregory's uncharacteristically furious response reminds us what was at stake here: a foundational story of Irish mythical womanhood, one that raised questions about class, ownership, language, and gender that had been haunting the Revival from the first. The question of ownership is especially important in a play that follows countless versions of the same story. Vivian Mercier objects to Revival interpretations of the legend as too romantic and distanced from the early versions. His idea of a "true" or "original" version of an ancient story is problematic; the tragedy of Deirdre has been revised through oral and written retellings for centuries and remains in a constant state of revision as different artists and writers continue to re-interpret and change the story. Yeats's Deirdre begins with the First Musician, the play's poet, chronicler, and lead chorus, claiming "I have a story right."[144] Towards the end of the play, Yeats repeats the assertion: Deirdre confers a bracelet on the lead musician "To show that you

[141] Yeats, *Plays*, 196.

[142] Robert Welch, *The Abbey Theatre: Form and Pressure, 1899–1999* (Oxford: Oxford UP, 1999), 39.

[143] Saddlemyer, *Theatre Business*, 220.   [144] Yeats, *Plays*, 175.

have Deirdre's story right."[145] This is no idle claim; as discussed earlier, Yeats wrote his *Deirdre* after Gregory and AE published and/or produced their own versions in 1902. While revising his play after performances, Yeats knew that Synge was creating his own version of the story. With the claims for truth that come up in this play, Yeats tries to gain support for his idea of the heroine, though he would, for decades, revise the supposedly "right" version, revealing the fraught relationship between "truth" and revision. After drafting the choruses, Yeats wrote to Quinn, "F. Fay has been here, and is in great enthusiasm over my Deirdre, so I think Russell's Deirdre will fade away. My Deirdre at any rate is not melancholy but full of a sort of tragic exultation..."[146] AE, or George Russell, allowed his *Deirdre* to be performed by the Irish National Theatre players in America, the actors who had seceded from the Abbey in 1905, so Yeats was particularly invested in reclaiming the story for his own theater.

Though Yeats did not share Gregory and Synge's concern about Darragh's performance, both the 1906 *Deirdre* and the 1907 production, directed by Payne and starring his wife, Mona Limerick, were disappointing, and Yeats, typically, set out to find a new actress for inspiration; at moments like these he desperately needed a woman to imagine and talk to about the play before he could rewrite. He set to revising, focusing on the beginning of the play, and revisiting his decision to exclude Mrs. Patrick Campbell. He had appreciated her "impassioned" acting since he had first seen her in 1901 in Bjornson's *Beyond Human Power* and had written to her soon after the performance:

> Your acting seemed to me to have the perfect precision and delicacy and simplicity of every art at its best. It made me feel the unity of the arts in a new way. I said to myself, that is exactly what I am trying to do in writing, to express myself without waste, without emphasis. To be impassioned and yet to have a perfect self-possession, to have a precision so absolute that the slightest rhythm of sound or emotion plucks the heart-strings. But do you know that you acted too well; you made me understand a defect in Bjornson's play which I had felt but not understood when I read it. Bjornson's hero could only have done those seen or real miracles by having a religious genius. Now the very essence of genius, of whatever kind, is precision, and that hero of his has no precision.[147]

---

[145] Ibid., 193.   [146] Yeats, *Collected Letters*, iii, 651–2.   [147] Ibid., 122.

His first sight of Mrs. Patrick Campbell onstage causes him to realize a weakness in the play she was performing, and, as usual, writing to actresses allows him to theorize performance. Fears of her as an established, powerful actress gave him pause in looking for a lead for the 1906 production. Her acting helped him imagine the kind of heroine he would develop in *Deirdre*, and he would seek performances "without waste, without emphasis."[148] The "precision" he praises above remained a decisive factor in his search for an actress to perform *Deirdre*. Yeats was excited to have an actress of Campbell's stature and fame perform Deirdre but was threatened by her power and ownership of the role.

As Yeats began to craft *Deirdre* in earnest in 1905, he mentioned the force of Mrs. Patrick Campbell's acting; according to Holloway, "mention of Maeterlink's play of Pelleas and Melisande cropped up, and Mr. Yeats said he never understood its meaning clearly until he saw Mrs. Patrick Campbell and Madame Bernhardt enact the roles of lovers as if they were a pair of little children."[149] In October 1905, Holloway noted that "Yeats told me he had completely rewritten *Shadowy Waters*, and I up and told him that I disapproved of eternal chopping and changing of old work instead of putting energy into new,"[150] and "remarked that he was gaining knowledge each day in dramatic work and could make an old work alright in a few weeks whereas a wholly new one might take him a year to write." This conversation shows Yeats's dependence on female performance in the hotbed of competition that was the Abbey in the years of revising *Deirdre*. Yeats's competition with Moore was also forefront in his mind: "Incidentally he told us that George Moore was now saying that no drama had been written since he wrote his last."[151] Holloway drily goes on to note that Yeats then "claimed a good deal of credit for *The Bending of the Bough*..."[152] Holloway's account shows that Yeats was desperate for a win at this point; for all of his disdain for Dublin's idea of success and for the middle-class playgoer, Yeats was revising and casting about for an actress, hoping for a performance that would solidify his reputation.

Mrs. Patrick Campbell's claim to *Deirdre* immediately inspired Yeats to revisit the play and rework the beginning scenes: "After the version printed in the text of this book had gone to press, Mrs. Patrick Campbell came to our

[148] Ibid., 122.
[149] Joseph Holloway, *Joseph Holloway's Abbey Theatre: A Selection from His Unpublished Journal: "Impressions of a Dublin Play-Goer,"* ed. Robert Hogan and Michael J. O'Neill (Carbondale: Southern Illinois University Press; London: Feffer & Simmons, 1967), 59.
[150] Ibid., 61.   [151] Ibid., 61.   [152] Ibid., 61.

Abbey Theatre, and liking what she saw there, offered to come and play Deirdre among us next November, and this so stirred my imagination that the scene [Deirdre's entrance] came right in a moment."[153] Reflecting on the force and experience of Mrs. Patrick Campbell, the new version of the entrance gave the title character more power.[154] A frantic letter to Farr in September 1908 doubting Mrs. Patrick Campbell's seriousness shows Yeats's investment in the revisions for her performance:

> Have you seen Mrs. Campbell? Do you know what she plans to do? Is she really going to come here? I have put Deirdre into rehearsal but have not really believed she would play it...I have heard nothing of you this longtime so please write and tell me about Mrs. Campbell. I know she has been thinking about altering her dates.[155]

Like Gonne in 1904, Mrs. Patrick Campbell became a symbolic Deirdre for Yeats, and his hopes for her strength onstage allowed him to narrow the focus of the play even more intensely on the lead role. He is also unable to broker these important casting requests without collaboration from mutual friends like Farr whose word to Mrs. Pat would help him secure her for *Deirdre*.

In the fall of 1908, two years after he worked with Darragh on the first version of the play to reach the stage and four years after he had started the project, Yeats was deeply involved with rehearsals for Mrs. Patrick Campbell's production. Joseph Holloway noted after watching a rehearsal in early November 1908:

> Yeats and Lady Gregory sat in front. Yeats kept busily walking up and down in front of the stage, and his gesticulating occasionally sent Mrs. Campbell off into a laugh until she finally had to tell him to sit down. She was quite nice to the players and made many suggestions in an almost apologetic way. Mrs. Campbell was going through her part in an intense, suppressed emotional way, going over and over again some passages which she hadn't as yet quite committed to memory.[156]

---

[153] Qtd. in Jeffares, *Circus Animals*, 73.   [154] Bushrui, *Yeats's Verse-Plays*, 132.
[155] Yeats, *Letters of W. B. Yeats*, ed. Wade, 511–12.
[156] Holloway, *Joseph Holloway's Abbey Theatre*, 119.

The collaboration between Mrs. Patrick Campbell and Yeats was more fruitful than his work with Darragh because of Campbell's "suppressed emotional" approach and her ability to collaborate with others in the company. Less cowed by his reputation, Mrs. Patrick Campbell insisted on her own interpretation of the character. The rehearsals set Yeats revising once again, making the lead character more vital to the play.[157] Working with Campbell led him to write a quarrel scene between Deirdre and Naoise into the part, flesh out other scenes, and introduce more suspense into the first part of the play. (Yeats wrote in October 1908 about planning to write *The Player Queen* with Campbell, "At the worst we can but quarrel."[158]) Yeats had always worried that Deirdre's entrance and the lead up to the game of chess were "mere bones, mere dramatic logic," yet after many attempts "I thought it impossible to alter them. When, however, Mrs. Campbell offered to play the part my imagination began to work again. I think they are now as they should be."[159] Only after he began to think of Mrs. Patrick Campbell in the part could Yeats re-imagine the play's beginning and rethink scenes that had perplexed him before; as Jeffares argues: "The effect of Yeats's rewriting was to give Deirdre's role more importance and centrality."[160] Imagining Mrs. Pat in the role, then, dramatically altered the form of the play.

Playing the rewritten *Deirdre* in November 1908, Mrs. Patrick Campbell, in Yeats's eyes, rescued his reputation as a playwright and made his idea of female heroism intelligible to audiences. Since the 1902 *Cathleen ni Houlihan*, he had not had such a success onstage, and his inability to write a verse play that succeeded with audiences had frustrated him for years. For all of his writing on the importance of individualism, popular success was a huge relief. A postscript to a letter to John Quinn on November 15, 1908 gives Mrs. Patrick Campbell credit for a change in his reputation:

> *Deirdre* has been played with triumphant success – great audiences and great enthusiasm; and Mrs. Patrick Campbell has bought the English and American rights for five years (we keep the Irish rights). She has taken a London theatre and produces it there on November 27th. There has not

[157] Bushrui, *Yeats's Verse-Plays*, 197.   [158] Yeats, *Letters of W. B. Yeats*, ed. Wade, 512.
[159] Qtd. in Bushrui, *Yeats's Verse-Plays*, 126, 128.
[160] A. Norman Jeffares and A. S. Knowland, *A Commentary on the Collected Plays of W. B. Yeats* (Stanford, CA: Stanford University Press, 2013), 76.

been one hostile voice here and I am now accepted as a dramatist in Dublin. Mrs. Campbell was magnificent.[161]

His relief and gratitude are poignant; for more than four years, he had hoped that working with the right actress would present his new ideas on performance and Irish female heroism on the stage. His collaboration with Mrs. Patrick Campbell allowed him to realize this goal, but his work with the five other women central to this story is just as important; without the earlier drafting the final text would never had reached the stage. Even Joseph Holloway, never a fan of experimentation onstage, found that Mrs. Campbell's performance improved while he watched the play:

> At first her mannered style of delivery and somewhat stooping form did not attract me much, but as the piece progressed one forgot her strongly marked mannerisms, and only saw the baffled woman's fight for death by the side of her loved one…Mrs. Campbell's 'Deirdre' grew on one until it quite captured by its sheer intensity. When the actress is moved by emotion, her whole body moves in jerk-like wriggles that punctuate every word.[162]

This "mannered style" and "sheer intensity" exemplify the approach to acting that Yeats had hoped for from his early idea of this heroine. *The Daily Mail* reviewed the play on November 10, 1908:

> Perhaps the most striking feature of the production is the wonderful combination of voices, Mrs. Campbell's rich, subtle, stealthy sense – enthralling, and Miss [Sara] Allgood's high and sad, stimulating as strong wine, and Mr. Sinclair's (as Conchubar) heavy with the seven years frustrated passion.[163]

The "combination of voices" suggests that Mrs. Patrick Campbell was better able to work with the members of the Abbey than Darragh, who had caused division in the company. She starred in the revival of *Deirdre* from November 9–14, 1908.

So great was Mrs. Campbell's influence on the play that the question of ownership that had vexed Yeats when choosing an actress for the 1906

[161] Yeats, *Letters of W. B. Yeats*, ed. Wade, 512.
[162] Holloway, *Joseph Holloway's Abbey Theatre*, 120–1.
[163] Qtd. in Hugh Hunt, *The Abbey: Ireland's National Theatre: 1904–1978* (New York: Columbia University Press, 1979), 70.

production returned. Her 1907 claim on the part from the stage sent a clear message that she would take over the lead, and in 1908, she bought the rights to perform the play abroad, making her interpretation of the role famous outside of Ireland as well. In later publications of the play, Yeats would add a dedication to Campbell, both laudatory and proprietary, to a memorial version of the original one to Robert Gregory:

> To Mrs. Patrick Campbell who in the generosity of her genius has played my Deirdre in Dublin and London with the Abbey Company, as with her own people, and In Memory of Robert Gregory who designed the beautiful scene she played in.[164]

The compliment to Campbell also contains a claim; "my Deirdre," especially preceding a published work, emphasizes the importance of the author and reminds the reader who owns the play, even as it praises Mrs. Patrick Campbell. (When she, far wealthier than Yeats at this time, bought the rights to the play abroad, she made another sort of demand of ownership.) She may have thought of her work as Deirdre as more than "generosity"; she clearly felt that she had a claim on the part. The dedication to the late Robert Gregory also tacitly pays tribute to a quieter collaborator, Lady Gregory, and to her idea of their writing together as creating progeny.

In October 1908, while rehearsing the still unfinished, revised *Deirdre*, Yeats wrote to John Quinn that he was already at work on a new play for Mrs. Patrick Campbell, one that was to develop the ideas of female heroism he had created in *Deirdre* from years of reworking his image of Maud Gonne. The success of his collaboration with Mrs. Campbell pushed him to agree to an experimental, extreme form of collaboration with a performer:

> I have finished the prose version of what is to be a new verse play, *The Player Queen*, and Mrs. Patrick Campbell talks of producing it. I am trying to get the prose version typed that I may go through it with her. She wants me to write, as she phrases it, with her at my elbow. I am rather inclined to try the experiment for once as I believe that I shall be inspired rather than thwarted by trying to give her as many opportunities as possible.[165]

[164] Yeats, *Plays*, 175.   [165] Yeats, *Letters of W. B. Yeats*, ed. Wade, 512.

Campbell clearly felt that she owned *The Player Queen* as much as Yeats, and the intense collaboration she demanded for the second play not only altered the revised *Deirdre* but allowed Yeats to develop his image of a solitary female figure for another role now that he believed he had found an actress who could carry off the ideal. He would work on *The Player Queen* in the winter of 1908 with renewed hope in the verse plays about solitary heroines after Campbell's November success in *Deirdre*. The ever proprietary Lady Gregory was somewhat alarmed at Yeats taking on a new project before completing revisions to *Deirdre*; she wrote to Synge in August 1908: "Yeats is working hard at his "Player Queen," a whimsical, lyrical comedy, which will go very well I think—but it wants a good many months of solid work. I hope Deirdre is not neglected"—again she uses parental language for the plays she helped Yeats write.[166] Yeats worked on *The Player Queen* "sporadically for the next eleven years" and the play was finally performed not by Mrs. Patrick Campbell but by the Stage Society at King's Hall Convent Garden on May 25, 1919, then at the Abbey on December 9, 1919.[167]

Yeats would continue to work on *Deirdre* until five years before his death. In 1911, his collaboration with Gordon Craig had him rethinking the play again:

> *Deirdre*, like the other plays in this book, has been altered many times after performances, till at last I had come to think I had put all my knowledge into it and could not, apart from the always incalculable pleasure good playing brings, look for greater pleasure than it had already given me. But now because of Mr. Craig's scene which is fitted to so many moods and actions, and makes possible natural and expressive light and shade, I have begun to alter it again and to find in this a new excitement.[168]

In 1911, when he worked with Craig, his new preoccupation with experimental set design distanced the play even more from its roots in *Cathleen ni Houlihan*. His revisions in 1911 show a change in his approach to drama, as he focused more on movement and dance in contrast to his early work on verse plays.[169]

---

[166] Saddlemyer, *Theatre Business*, 288n.   [167] Ibid.

[168] W. B. Yeats, *Plays for an Irish Theatre* (London: A. H. Bullen, 1911), 396.

[169] See Yeats and Rohan, *Deirdre*, where she argues for connections between the later revisions of *Deirdre* and *Plays for Dancers*.

A year before his death, and only a few years after he finally put *Deirdre* aside for good, Yeats described his hopes for tragic intensity onstage, an idea he had written into *Deirdre*. His efforts to find an actress who could bring his idea of a "passionate and solitary" heroine to the stage had led to years of intense involvement in rehearsals and productions as well as continual revision alongside the most bruising political and artistic fights of Yeats's career in a changing Ireland. Mrs. Patrick Campbell's success in the part would remain fresh in his memory:

> I have aimed at tragic ecstasy, and here and there in my own work and in the work of my friends I have seen it greatly played. What does it matter that it belongs to a dead art and to a time when a man spoke out of experience and a culture that were not of his time alone, but held his time, as it were, at arm's length, that he might be a spectator of the ages? I am haunted by certain moments: Miss O'Neill in the last act of Synge's Deirdre 'Stand a little further off with the quarrelling of fools'; Kerrigan and Miss O'Neill playing in a private house that scene in Augusta Gregory's Full Moon where the young mad people in their helpless joy sing 'The Boys of Queen Anne'; Frank Fay's entrance in the last act of The Well of the Saints; William Fay at the end of On Baile's Strand; Mrs. Patrick Campbell in my Deirdre, passionate and solitary; and in later years that great artist Nanette de Valois in Fighting the Waves. These things, it may be, haunt me on my deathbed; whatever matter if the people prefer another art, I have had my fill.[170]

Performance takes over in this memory; private experiences of reading and writing pale before these images of roles realized onstage. His idea of "a spectator of the ages," beyond the concerns of contemporary politics, has its roots in his early idea of Deirdre as a "passionate and solitary" heroine, distanced from the fray that surrounded Gonne in 1905. Though Yeats ends by brushing off public opinion and stressing the importance of his own reactions to the moments on stage, Mrs. Patrick Campbell's success in *Deirdre* in 1908 was as important to Yeats as her ability to embody his ideal Irish heroine. Yeats's heroine, of course, could not be so solitary that she would not inspire emotion in the audience at the Abbey.

---

[170] W. B. Yeats, *The Collected Works of W. B. Yeats: The Later Essays*, ed. William H. O'Donnell (New York: Scribner, 1984).

The competing Deirdres of the Abbey and Yeats's thousand pages of revisions show attempts to claim contested ground. The history of the play reveals tensions around ownership and representation as the women who inspired and performed the part revised Yeats's initial vision and challenged Yeats's idea of solitary, aristocratic ownership.

Yeats spent ten years and a thousand pages writing and revising *The Player Queen* as well, and the savvy Mrs. Patrick Campbell understood the economic impact of aging as an actress, lamenting that Yeats took so long to complete that collaborative role "till my jaw sagged with age." She moved penniless to Hollywood to give elocution lessons and play bit parts in Hollywood films and then, at a historically dangerous time, returned to Europe, to France, in the late 1930s and died in Pau, in flight from Nazi occupation, in 1940. Lack of funds and concern for her dog stopped her from gaining re-entry to England before her death. An actress who inspired and created Shaw's Eliza Doolittle[171] as well as Yeats's *Deirdre*, making the theatrical reputations of both men, she ended her life indigent, having lamented the difficulty of making money in Hollywood with a now aged face that, in her words, "looked like a burst paper bag."[172] John Gielgud, however, remembered her guiding him through a performance of Ibsen's *Ghosts* as an older woman; he played her son. In advice that sounds familiar to any student of Abbey approaches to the stage and Yeats's hope for verse-speaking, Campbell said to him, "Keep still. Gaze at me. Now you must speak in a Channel-steamer voice. Empty your voice of meaning and speak as if you were going to be sick. Pinero once told me this and I have never forgotten it."[173] The difference in lasting, financial power between Campbell and Yeats and Shaw reveals that who gets credit for theatrical texts has real consequences on power and mobility. Yeats's description of Florence Farr in *A Vision* shows how his ideal of her haunted his search for the right Deirdre: "Here are born these women who are most touching in their beauty... elaborating a delicate personal discipline...While seeming an image of softness and of quiet, she draws perpetually upon glass with a diamond."[174] These women, as they aged, always had to keep day jobs and could not retire

---

[171] For more information on the tempestuous relationship between Mrs. Patrick Campbell and George Bernard Shaw, see *George Bernard Shaw and Mrs. Patrick Campbell: Their Correspondence*, ed. Alan Dent (London: Victor Gollancz, 1952).

[172] Qtd. in Margot Peters, *Mrs. Pat: The Life of Mrs. Patrick Campbell* (New York: Knopf, 1984), 397.

[173] Ibid.

[174] W. B. Yeats, *The Collected Works of W. B. Yeats, XIII: A Vision*, ed. Catherine E. Paul and Margaret Mills Harper (New York: Scribner, 2013).

on pensions; no government offered them stipends. While Yeats and renowned socialist George Bernard Shaw died in comfort, the female performers in this story were not so lucky and had to work for food and shelter, their contributions to the creation of these texts unknown, until the end of their lives.

Epilogue—How Cathleen Became Mrs. Monihan

Sara Allgood's "grave acting" on Stage and in Film

In 1909, a few months after J. M. Synge's death, at age 37, of Hodgkin's lymphoma, Yeats asked Sara Allgood to perform the lines[1] that she had made famous, the final words of acceptance before the curtain in Synge's *Riders to the Sea*: "Michael has a clean burial in the far North, by the grace of the Almighty God. Bartley will have a fine coffin out of the white boards, and a deep grave surely. What more can we want than that? No man at all can be living forever, and we must be satisfied."[2] This small, private graveside performance bears close reading: Sara Allgood had performed in hundreds of Abbey productions in the five years since her initial appearance onstage in a major role in 1904, and the calm acceptance in these words characterizes her many characters on stage and screen. Allgood, over Synge's grave, repeats a scene in the play, one that would reach film audiences in the 1935 cinematic production of *Riders to the Sea*. In the 1935 film version, available online,[3] Allgood speaks those words, surrounded by mourning women, many of them Abbey alumnae including her sister Molly Allgood, over the body of her son, played by a young Denis Johnston. In both play and film, this scene shows the women mourning the last man of Maurya's family to die, and the way they keep their bodies still echoes forms of acting developed at the Abbey. Sara Allgood's stillness at Synge's gravesite and on film shows a response formed from her years of performance, theater management, and directing, a way of presenting her body that works against stereotype both onstage and in film. And in these films, the story of acting

---

[1] Sara Allgood, "Memories," unpublished manuscript, Berg Collection, New York Public Library, 45.

[2] John Millington Synge, *Riders to the Sea* (Boston, MA: John W. Luce, 1911).

[3] See, e.g. https://www.youtube.com/watch?v=YNvc9mA20TA.

Gender, Performance, and Authorship at the Abbey Theatre. Elizabeth Brewer Redwine, Oxford University Press (2021). © Elizabeth Brewer Redwine. DOI: 10.1093/oso/9780192896346.003.0006

against expectation continues, and the contemporary viewer can watch Sara Allgood redefine roles, continuing a conversation started in the tableau movement and the Abbey more than one hundred years ago.

The moment at Synge's grave troubles the line between stage and lived experience and raises questions about who owns the character of Maurya in *Riders to the Sea*. These questions about identity and language resurface in Sara Allgood's later film work. I end with her film roles because those characters onscreen allow contemporary audiences to see—literally see— how Allgood navigated the tensions between performance and identity that run through this book from the start. And both in the intimacy of this graveside performance and in the widely publicized films, still easily viewed online and shared on film fan sites, Allgood is asked to embody forms of femininity and Irishness through her body and her voice. The films give us a window into how she met the continued need from the public and directors, a requirement for a specific way of embodying female roles.

What did Allgood stand for at the Abbey, and how did that image translate to American film? How did Allgood direct the audience's reaction to her, and how was she marketed as an Irish woman of a particular type, a story she tried to control? Yeats's request that Allgood read the lines at Synge's graveside shows the writer's need for performance of a certain kind of "grave acting," a form of Irishness—female, authentic,[4] and other—at central moments in his own life. Paradoxically, to express his isolation, Yeats required a performance by the steadying female response perfected by Sara Allgood in her many years in the Irish dramatic movement. Synge's death in 1909 brought home to Yeats his own embattled position at the Abbey Theatre; according to lawyer and friend John Quinn, "WBY has made a great many enemies among the younger writers in Dublin."[5] Sinn Fein had just published an attack on his drama, and the loss of Synge, compounded with daily fighting at the Abbey, resulted in Yeats's loneliness and disillusionment in the spring of 1909.[6] His sense of Synge, "that rooted man"[7] as one betrayed by his countrymen in the 1907 riots in response to *The Playboy*

---

[4] Yeats's ideas about what made Irishness authentic had much to do with his own desire to see certain actresses onstage, as I discuss in Chapter 5.

[5] R. F. Foster, *W. B. Yeats: A Life: I. The Apprentice Mage* (Oxford: Oxford University Press, 1998), 404.

[6] Ibid., 408.

[7] W. B. Yeats, "The Municipal Gallery Revisited," in *The Collected Poems*, ed. Peter Allt and Russell K. Alspach (New York, NY: Macmillan, 1957), 601–2.

of the Western World further isolated Yeats, who, in a reanimation of his response to Parnell,[8] believed, according to Yeats's father, that Synge had "died of Ireland,"[9] figuring the nation as a disease to die "of" rather than an ideal to die "for." Yeats and his father would have been referring to those 1907 Playboy riots, when the mention of "shifts" in Synge's *The Playboy of the Western World* incited violence in the Dublin audience in response to what many Dubliners saw as Synge's "libel...against Irish peasant girl-hood."[10] As I discussed in Chapter 3, Sara Allgood and her sister, Synge's fiancée Molly Allgood, performed the incendiary roles in that production. The language of Allgood's signature lines from *Riders to the Sea* verbalizes the acceptance and stillness that came out of the dramatic movements preceding the Abbey and that Allgood would go onto express in American film (Figure E.1). Yeats had lost Synge, but Allgood's ability to perform his lines at the graveside connected Yeats not only to the dead playwright but also to an ideal of Irish feminine acceptance and strength in the face of national upheaval.

Allgood's many collaborations and approach to acting not only provide a history of early twentieth-century Irish drama but also tell the story of early film, mapping her work as an actress from the early nationalist female-led tableau movement through the Abbey, international touring, and ending in a relentless schedule as a contract player for Twentieth Century Fox. She had a role in the first British "talkie," Hitchcock's 1929 *Blackmail*, followed by twenty years of film parts covering every genre from film noir to family comedies, historical dramas, and Westerns. A Catholic, working-class woman from a large Dublin family with a Protestant father, Allgood decoded female Irishness to audiences both at the Abbey and in Hollywood in historical moments fraught with questions about what it meant to be a working-class woman of Irish ethnicity; she translated the lamenting mothers she perfected on the Abbey stage into maternal Irish servants in her American films.[11] Adrian Frazier's *Hollywood Irish* details the lives of

---

[8] In his *Yeats's Heroic Figures: Wilde, Parnell, Swift, Casement* (Basingstoke: Palgrave Macmillan, 1983), p. 68, Michael Steinman argues for the connections between Yeats's defense of Synge and his fascination with Parnell as both figures, to Yeats, who stood against the corrosive effects of modernity.

[9] Foster, *The Apprentice Mage*, 404.   [10] *The Freeman's Journal*, January 8, 1907.

[11] As I discuss elsewhere in the book, the Allgood sisters were raised Catholic by their mother in secret, and Sara Allgood would attend mass off and on throughout her life. Her father was Protestant, but the children's religious observance was Catholic. In her unpublished "Memories," housed at the Berg Collection, she recalls attending Catholic mass with Hitchcock in Los Angeles.

Figure E.1 Allgood with her sisters, Maire O'Neill/Molly Allgood and Annie Allgood in *Riders to the Sea,* 1906
Source: Courtesy of the Abbey Theatre Archive.

Abbey actors and actresses on screen, and this Epilogue explores Allgood's late Hollywood performances through the lens of gender and immigrant identity.[12] I read Allgood's work on a selection of her many films closely here both for evidence of Abbey acting styles and for the way she challenges stereotype in her performances. What appears again and again in her American film work is an aging actress from Ireland translating stillness in the face of extremity in ways that strengthen even the smallest, sometimes nameless characters against the stereotype of the emotive Irish immigrant. From her earliest days in Inghinidhe, Allgood was part of a project to provide steadying images of Ireland against British melodrama and cartoons; her film work in America continued this work until her death in 1950.[13]

---

[12] Frazier, Adrian Woods. *Hollywood Irish: John Ford, Abbey Actors and the Irish Revival in Hollywood.* (Ireland: Lilliput), 2011.

[13] Irish female characters were weak and emotional in the penny dreadfuls and melodramas of British nineteenth-century imports to Ireland, and Inghinidhe na hÉireann sought to counter that image in theatrical responses that Allgood revised for the Abbey.

As Lauren Arrington has shown in her investigation of censorship and state funding at the Abbey, the Abbey Theatre minute books offer detailed accounts of the meetings between the directors and players of the Abbey.[14] Patrick Lonergan's work digitizing these books allows scholars to learn how central collaboration was to the creation of Abbey productions. Allgood attended nearly all the meetings in 1904–5, the years she joined the company. Her importance rises in these years, as she is paid more and asked to perform increasingly important roles, though, as Adrian Frazier chronicles, Abbey benefactor Annie Horniman's rage at her performance at a reading in support of suffrage nearly cost Sara her job.[15] Allgood had just joined the company in December 1904, but an advertisement and flyer for the performance of, in large bold letters, "Irish Plays" shows Allgood in major roles in all three: as one of the kings in Yeats's verse play *On Baile's Strand*, as Mrs. Fallow, a role she made famous, in Lady Gregory's *Spreading the News*, and as Bridget Gillane—the mother—in Yeats and Gregory's *Cathleen ni Houlihan*. Allgood's role as an actor may be what we remember, but her collaborations offstage were just as important, revealing both the limits of conventional characterizations of the creation of theater and Allgood's commitment to political work. From her unpublished "Memories" and her surviving films, Sara Allgood emerges as a woman focused on creating theater and film, not simply taking direction. Her contribution to both mediums, a refusal to overact, and a gravity and stillness, educate the audience about what to expect of an Irish woman.

Though in her early years at the Abbey she was almost always cast as the cottage-bound mother, Allgood hoped for years to play the title character in *Cathleen ni Houlihan*, and her memory of that performance shows her political interpretation of the role. I single out *Cathleen ni Houlihan* because as Cathleen, Allgood was able to play the kind of part that often eluded her, and her performance revised audience perceptions of that pivotal Revival figure. Allgood writes that she enjoyed playing Cathleen—a role she later made famous on the New York stage—because, with the lines in verse, the role brought her away from her usual folk parts and "peasant" dialogue. She remembers her happiness when she got the part: "I had wanted it for years; I got it."[16] Her memory of this coup reveals her understanding of how to use

[14] Lauren Arrington, *W. B. Yeats, the Abbey Theatre, Censorship, and the Irish State: Adding the Half-Pence to the Pence* (Oxford: Oxford University Press, 2010).
[15] Adrian Frazier, *Behind the Scenes: Yeats, Horniman, and the Struggle for the Abbey Theatre* (Berkeley: University of California Press, 1990), 237.
[16] Ibid., 10.

Abbey politics to her advantage in landing roles despite being typecast as the non-threatening mother in so many earlier plays. Lady Gregory famously claimed in 1919 that to perform *Cathleen ni Houlihan*, all that was needed was a "hag and a voice," but her quip belies the machinations many actresses used to play that iconic part after Gonne's earth-shaking 1902 interpretation.[17] In performing the title character in Yeats and Gregory's Cathleen play, Allgood inserted herself not only into a dramatic history of collaboration, but also into the story of "the poor old woman." For her part, Allgood insisted that in her reading and acting of the play, Cathleen's seduction of Irish youth to fight for Ireland was a joyous story, and she claims to have played the role as a celebration. Sara Allgood remembers "I fill myself with joy" as Cathleen, celebrating sacrifice and rebirth.[18] In her "Memories," she argues, "Kathleen looks to the future," breaking the figure out of the cycle of violent sacrifice.[19] Though Yeats and Gregory wrote *Cathleen ni Houlihan*, the play came to the stage in a Daughters of Ireland production, and Allgood clearly felt years later, writing her "Memories" as an older woman in Hollywood looking back at the Abbey, that she had a right to her own opinions and interpretation of the role. The story of these texts, then, goes beyond the collaborative writing, and should include the interpretations of the roles as well; her performance revised audience perceptions of that pivotal Revival figure, sourced from the story's bardic origins.[20]

Though I discuss the controversial 1902 production in Chapter 2, it is worth revisiting that performance with the focus on Sara Allgood's later revisions rather than Maud Gonne. The comparison reveals fissures at the Abbey around class and power. Theater is never static, and Sara Allgood redefined the part four years later in 1906 in part due to her physical and interpretive contrast with Gonne's performance. Her Cathleen physically revised the one made famous by Maud Gonne, in Yeats's words, "the most beautiful woman in Ireland," who performed the role in the 1902 premier,

---

[17] Lady Isabella Augusta Gregory, *Lady Gregory's Journals: Vol. I, Books One to Twenty-Nine, 10 October 1916–23 February 1925*, ed. Daniel J. Murphy (Oxford: Oxford University Press, 1978), 56.

[18] Allgood, "Memories," 10.   [19] Ibid.

[20] Chapter 2 of this volume argues for the importance of Maud Gonne's contributions to this role and the archeology of the play. The setting is Kinsale 1798 and Ireland-as-old-woman is asking for a son to give himself for the rebellion. At the doorway of a cottage, the figure incants, "Many that are red-cheeked now will be pale-cheeked for my sake." In a vampiric twist, the old woman transforms into a young beauty with "the walk of a queen" once the young man follows her out, to his mother's and fiancée's dismay.

coming up through the audience "and her great height made Cathleen seem a divine being fallen into our mortal infirmity."[21] The impact of that 1902 performance reverberated through the years; volunteers for the Easter Rising in 1916 referred to *Cathleen ni Houlihan*, and that premier in particular, as galvanizing them to action. Sara Allgood's 1906 Cathleen, importantly, had no "great height," and she, not "the most beautiful woman in Ireland," looked like many in the audience; her Cathleen would have resembled the figures in the cottage as well, and theatre-goers would have associated Allgood with peasant maternal roles. Rather than personifying an other-worldly, ethereal version of Mother Ireland, Allgood, bringing years of playing realistic cottage mothers in peasant plays to the memory of the audience, would have been asking a different kind of question in the doorway of the cottage. She claimed to perform the required sacrifice with "joy," so her Cathleen would have been asking the young man in the cottage to leave with a female version of Ireland that looked like one of his own, not the nation as a ghostly other.

Sara Allgood's trademark stillness performed onstage the "intensity of trance" that Yeats hoped for in transforming an audience's perception of Ireland as a woman. As part of this revival of Cathleen and, later, in her film work, Allgood's acting brought to the stage a state that Yeats describes as follows:

> . . . we shall express human emotion through ideal form, a symbolism handled by the generations, a mask from whose eyes the disembodied looks, a style that remembers many masters, that it may escape contemporary suggestion . . . in the supreme moment of tragic art there comes upon one that strange sensation as though the hair on one's head stood up.[22]

These moments of stillness that Allgood perfected at the Abbey and went onto perform in film offer the audience a living mask described by Yeats above, and his use of "we" suggests that he knew that he could not bring this project to fruition without the work of performers. Yeats hoped for acting that led the audience to this state, one described by Marjorie Howes as "transporting (the audience) to an alternative psychic realm," and the path

[21] Yeats, *The Collected Poems*, 233.
[22] William Butler Yeats, *Essays and Introductions* (London: Macmillan, 1968), 245.

to that state was performance.[23] The "disembodied" arrives in the very real body of Allgood on the Abbey stage, and the "strange sensation" realized by her stillness made her an audience favorite at the Abbey. Allgood's tableau work had been part of a project before the Abbey of bringing Dubliners to a new understanding of their own history; with Yeats's plays, Allgood strove to play roles like Cathleen and Deirdre, using her stillness to achieve transformation both by playing against type and bringing her own interpretation to those roles.

"The Old Woman Remembers" and "Easter 1916"

In a coda to her performances as Cathleen ni Houlihan and to her years of parts that envisioned Ireland as female, Allgood returned to the Abbey in 1923 to perform Lady Gregory's "The Old Woman Remembers," and descriptions of this performance show her using the calm, still form of acting that she had developed to great effect, avoiding any unnecessary movement and responding to loss with minimal motion. Allgood is mid-career at this moment, performing on tour and returning to Ireland before starting work on Hitchcock's *Blackmail* in 1928, so a close reading of this performance is a helpful way to see Allgood develop her interpretations of Irish womanhood onstage before she moved to film work. Allgood and Gregory had been close since Allgood first began to perform onstage in 1904 as a girl of 17; as I discuss in Chapter 3, Gregory had assured Allgood's mother that she would look after her like a daughter, and, class difference aside, she did look out for Allgood, her favorite actress, often cautioning her against flirtation. Gregory wrote "The Old Woman Remembers" during the Irish War for Independence, and the performance in the years just after ceasefire featured Allgood, "silvery voiced," recounting Irish history in the persona of a Shan Van Vocht, an old woman embodying Ireland as a kind of Cathleen ni Houlihan in aged form who does not transform to beauty and youth at the end. A reviewer for *The Independent* noted the lack of "declamatory gestures," which suggests that Allgood deployed vestiges of her tableau training here in a performance that hearkens back to the street theater of Inghinidhe and gestures forward to her stillness on film. According to

---

[23] Marjorie Howes, *Yeats's Nations: Gender, Class, and Irishness* (Cambridge: Cambridge University Press, 1996), 92.

Dublin Magazine, "An old woman, beads in hand, seated at the fire in her cottage, 'remembers' the heroes of Ireland."[24] A reviewer noted that Allgood's public performance of national memory "moved a packed audience profoundly."[25] Gregory and Allgood shared another bond at this point in their lives: Gregory's son, Major Robert Gregory, had been shot down over France in 1916, a death immortalized in Yeats's "An Irish Airman Foresees His Death," while Sara Allgood lost her brother to World War I and both of her children and her husband to the Spanish influenza while on tour in Australia in 1918.[26] As Adrian Frazier notes, Allgood, chatty in her "Memories," never mentioned those deaths in letters or autobiographical writing. Mourning, maternity, and history reach the stage here through Allgood's understated, static form. In this performed elegy, Allgood stands for all the mothers of Ireland including herself and Gregory, remembering those they had lost.

In "The Old Woman Remembers," the required stillness combines with recitation as performance. While Cathleen demanded sacrifice, even in Allgood's joyous take on that part, this nameless old woman chronicles those who were lost, the other side of violence. For much of the play, the old woman is still, not asking at the door for young men as she did onstage as Cathleen after walking up through the audience, but naming, lighting a candle at the end of each stanza, those who have sacrificed, ending with two deaths in 1922:

> This is our rosary of praise
> For some whose names are sung or said
> Through seven hundred years of days
> The silver beads upon the thread ....[27]

Allgood's performance of this rosary without embroidered movement appealed to Gregory. The recitation of the names of the dead echoes Yeats's "Easter 1916," another feminized account of honoring martyrs:

[24] Maria DeBattista and Lucy McDiarmid, *High and Low Moderns: Literature and Culture, 1889–1939* (Oxford: Oxford University Press, 1996), 297.

[25] Christopher Murray, *Twentieth-Century Irish Drama: Mirror Up To Nation* (Syracuse, NY: Syracuse University Press, 1997), 91.

[26] Adrian Frazier, *Hollywood Irish: John Ford, Abbey Actors, and the Irish Revival in Hollywood* (Dublin: Lilliput, 2011), 105.

[27] Lady Isabella Augusta Gregory, "The Old Woman Remembers," *The New Republic*, February 20, 1924, 339.

our part
To murmur name upon name,
As a mother names her child
When sleep at last has come
On limbs that had run wild.[28]

After directing "our part," casting the surviving Irish in the theatrical naming of a child, Yeats embodies this figure, echoing the changeling idea in Irish mythology—switching one child for another or a fairy—in "writing out" the names:

MacDonagh and MacBride
And Connolly and Pearse
Now and in time to be,
Wherever green is worn,
Are changed, changed utterly:
A terrible beauty is born.[29]

Although predicated on change, the naming recurs again and again, "now and in time to be," in ballads and theaters and street corners, and Allgood's 1923 recital joins her voice both to Yeats's recitation and to another performance: that same year, women in Kilmainham jail performed tableaux of resistance during a hunger strike.[30] Allgood's voice work with Yeats came into play in that 1923 performance as did the stillness that she developed from her earliest performances with Inghinidhe na hÉireann. And all of these performances—Allgood's 1906 Cathleen and revivals of that part through 1913, her performance as the old woman as Ireland, and the tableaux of women in Kilmainham in 1923, show the return again and again of women performing stillness and responding to loss by naming the dead. Those three Abbey creators—Yeats, Gregory, and Sara Allgood—responded to the profound losses of the teens and twenties with an insistence on a familiar, nearly motionless female body performing memory. As we will see, dramatizing maternal loss with "silver-voiced" calm was Allgood's response to being cast as the mother and caretaker in dozens of American films.

---

[28] Yeats, *The Collected Poems*, 228–30.   [29] Ibid.
[30] Catherine Morris, "Alice Milligan: Republican Tableaux and the Revival," *Field Day Review* 6 (2010), 135.

A surviving object from the Abbey shows how Sara Allgood, along with others at the Abbey, performed tensions around identity and class in marketing and representing the Abbey Theater in a time of flux. In 1913, on tour in America, Allgood appeared on a souvenir handkerchief with a handful of fellow Abbey actors and the words "Sold by the Irish players at $1.00 towards a building to save Sir Hugh Lane's Great Gift of Pictures for Ireland April 1913" (Figure E.2).[31] The actual handkerchief, on view at the Abbey Theatre archives, is partially burnt from the Abbey Theatre fire in 1951, but the marketing of the Abbey actors, pictured individually in photographs that echo earlier tableaux, for purposes both political and artistic, is reminiscent of Allgood's beginning in Inghinidhe na hÉireann. Imported to the U.S.A. for performance and for fundraising, the actors offered photographs to be sold to support the building of an art gallery in Dublin to house the extensive and remarkable painting collection of Hugh Lane, Lady Gregory's nephew, who would drown in the Lusitania disaster.[32] The difficulty in funding this "municipal house" led Yeats to poems lamenting what he saw as Irish middle-class resistance to funding art at a time when his dissatisfaction with "modern Ireland" was at its peak. And yet, the performers pictured on this handkerchief fundraising for the gallery were from that very urban middle class. Allgood would become another kind of American import in the films of the 1940s, playing the Irish domestic in many films, but here she is also marketed as an image of Ireland in another kind of collaboration with Yeats in the service of political and cultural ends.

The last link in the chain that brings the early all-female nationalist tableau movement through the Abbey to American film will end this book. A half-century after her start in Dublin street theater, working against an image of the immigrant or working-class woman in nativist 1940s America, Allgood's mothers lament through silent tableaux on stage and film. In her movie acting, these moments occur at thresholds and doorways as the figure of Cathleen ni Houlihan requiring sacrifice at a doorway echoes in American movie theaters. In Allgood's immigrant mothers and domestic workers in the films of the 1940s, she inserts her performance into the discussion of American identity during the fraught years leading up to her death in 1950. Her characters perform loss as she had at the Abbey but also

---

[31] Abbey Theatre Archive, Dublin.
[32] The Lusitania disaster claimed the life of Hugh Lane. Torpedoed by a German U-boat within view of Ireland, the ship sank, causing the death of Lane who had left a will purported to leave his art collection to Ireland.

Figure E.2 Handkerchief sold to raise money to house Hugh Lane's art collection, 1913
Source: Courtesy of the Abbey Theatre Archive.

raise questions of belonging and identity, often used to set off the "American" qualities of the other characters, some of whom came from Ireland, Britain, or Europe but who were playing American parts. American identity in the 1940s was convulsing under the pressure of war and immigration, and Allgood's many maternal and domestic film performances wrestle with questions of nationality, class, and maternity as an Irish actress embodying characters in an American context.[33]

The names of Allgood's dozens of roles as a contract player for the studios in 1940s Hollywood illustrate how she was typecast as American audiences wrestled with what it meant to be an American family, an American woman, and an American mother in the war years and those before and after. Some of her roles are described simply as "Charwoman," "Waitress," or "Land-lady." The nameless characters allow for a kind of mid-century film form of tableaux; Allgood stands in for a type designated by her immigrant Irish status. Even in these small appearances, however, she refuses to play up negative stereotypes. Other parts include "Mrs. Brennan, Mrs. Fogarty, Mrs. Monahan, Mrs. Connor,"—the list goes on to more than fifty such roles.[34] She had a few bigger parts, but only *How Green Was My Valley* allowed her a major supporting role with plenty of dialogue. Adrian Frazier discusses that film extensively, so I will focus on her lesser known appearances. Most of the more than fifty films she acted in under contract feature her in small parts as someone working in a home, often as a kind of class marker and substitute mother figure. As Vivien Leigh's mother in *That Hamilton Woman*, Allgood functions as a reminder that Leigh's character comes from a poor background. And in *Cheaper By the Dozen*, the all-American family is thrown into relief by Allgood's Irish maid.[35] In many of these parts, however, she does much with very little: her few scenes provide the emotional ballast for the film. When she, as the maid Bessie, lets a young Jane Eyre leave in that 1943 film, we can see the mother of *Riders to the Sea* in the still look of loss in her face, standing, again, in a doorway.[36] The sadness she expresses with very little movement as the mother in *The Fabulous Dorseys* has its roots in years of playing, to great acclaim, grieving mothers at the Abbey.[37] Directors recognized the power of this embodiment of loss, and the camera often lingers on her; her approach can be jarring next to the different forms of film acting around her, bringing that hypnotic effect that she and Yeats had created. But the lack of motion forces the filmgoer to take notice and refuses to allow the small Irish servant roles to fall into

[33] Peter C. Rollins, *The Columbia Companion to American History on Film: How the Movies Have Portrayed the American Past* (New York: Columbia University Press, 2003), provides helpful information about how film reflects the anxieties and hopes of American and immigrant identities.

[34] "Sara Allgood" at the *Internet Movie Database*: http://www.imdb.com/name/nm0021329/.

[35] Walter Lang, dir. *Cheaper By the Dozen*, 20th Century Fox, 1950.

[36] Robert Stevenson, dir. *Jane Eyre*, 20th Century Fox, 1943.

[37] Alfred E. Green, dir. *The Fabulous Dorseys*, United Artists, 1947.

Figure E.3 Sara Allgood in a
1938 Carl Van Vechten photo,
performing a tableau of Maurya
in *Riders to the Sea*
Source: Courtesy of the Van Vechten
Trust.

stereotype; movie audiences would not necessarily have known that they
were seeing acting developed at the Abbey years before. Allgood's work in
film continues her earliest efforts to recast Irish identity on the streets of
Dublin in tableaux (Figure E.3).

There is one moment in *How Green Was My Valley* that is central to my
argument here about the way Allgood's Abbey background shows on film.
She played Beth Morgan, the maternal center of the story and the protagonist's mother, and she was nominated for a Best Supporting Actress Academy Award for the performance. Much of the film involves the daily life of a
Welsh mining family coping with changes in the industry and their way of
life; in many ways the story is a lament for a vanishing past and what Derek
Mahon calls "a lost tribe" struggling with modernity.[38] In the film's central
moment, the father of the family dies in a mining accident. The film shows
the impact of the event by relentlessly focusing the camera on Allgood's face.
She is motionless, silent, and staring as a mining shaft elevator slowly comes
up empty but for a hat, confirming the death of her husband. As in *Cathleen
ni Houlihan* and many of her films, Allgood is at a threshold, awaiting news,
framed in the doorway of the empty mineshaft. In her response to that loss,
the audience sees Allgood's history in tableaux and her years of work with

[38] Derek Mahon, "Nostalgias," *New and Collected Poems* (Oldcastle: The Gallery Press,
2011), 73.

Yeats, Lady Gregory, the company at the Abbey, and the Fay brothers to develop a particular way of acting in moments of extremity. Working against the histrionics typical of melodrama and the stage Irish, her response is stillness. The Fay brothers worked with Allgood on a form of acting rooted in tableau that "suppressed all but essential movement"; this phrase also describes her powerful turn in *How Green Was My Valley*.[39]

The 1946 horror film *The Spiral Staircase* shows Allgood's efforts, in the face of slurs against the immigrant working class, to perform a role with the power and dignity she brought from her years at the Abbey. She is Nurse Barker, and her job is to watch over a sickly elderly woman filled with hate and class prejudice played by Ethel Barrymore. Barrymore's character reprimands Nurse Barker, "Don't touch me!" as if Allgood's physicality and lower-class position is contagious. Allgood's character overhears the other servants in the house musing on her true gender.[40] She comes to the doorway of the kitchen and stands stock still with her trademark Abbey stare. The effect is both to shame the speakers in the kitchen and also to heighten the tension in the film; the audience knows that a mysterious killer lurks in the house during a storm, and tropes about ethnicity and gender play on the fears of the other characters. Allgood's bearing brings strength to this figure that is built on years of nativist portrayals of Irish maids and nurses on film. M. Alison Kibler argues that the Irish servant was often played by men in drag in vaudeville and that questions about the femininity of these characters remained in early American film.[41] This stereotypical character is also a descendant of what Mary Trotter calls "the Savage Celt" of British melodrama, a monstrous, gorilla-like source of fear and danger.[42] Allgood would have been aware of her own career as an effort to combat the negative roles common to British melodrama; her beginnings in Inghinidhe na hÉireann and the Abbey as a young girl were "political performances for the nationalist cause."[43] An aging Allgood needed the money and the

---

[39] William George Fay and Catherine Carswell, *The Fays of the Abbey Theatre: An Autobiographical Record* (London: Rich and Cowan, 1935), 105. Told from the point of view of Huw, played by a young Roddy McDowell, *How Green Was My Valley* also popularized a nostalgia in the early 1940s for a past untroubled by the tensions in the years between the wars, and once again, Allgood carries the symbolic weight of the film as the mother figure connected to a child's past.

[40] Robert Slodnak, dir. *The Spiral Staircase*, RKO, 1946.

[41] Alison Kibler, *Rank Ladies: Gender and Cultural Hierarchy in American Vaudeville* (Chapel Hill: The University of North Carolina Press, 1999), 68.

[42] Mary Trotter, *Ireland's National Theatres: Political Performance and the Origins of the Irish Dramatic Movement* (Syracuse, NY: Syracuse University Press, 2001), 46.

[43] Ibid., 21.

exposure of a film like *The Spiral Staircase*, one that promised to be a hit. Nevertheless, she subverts stereotype; the subtlety of her own performance in concert with Ethel Barrymore's causes the audience to sympathize with the beleaguered nurse and judge those speaking ill of her harshly.

In 1944, Allgood had played the maternal Ellen Bonting in Twentieth Century Fox's *The Lodger*. Her character, making the best of financial need, rents a room to hulking, unhinged Laird Cregar, not knowing that he is Jack the Ripper. The physical difference between the two makes the audience protective of Allgood's character; the character is not identified as Irish, which may have added to the sympathetic portrayal of her maternal status. Married happily to a man who lost their savings, Allgood spends most of the film doing the domestic work of the landlady, pleased that Cregar's character will pay on time. She represents an urban London version, for American audiences, of the cottage persona from the Abbey: maternal, maintaining the home, making work visible, and concerned about money to survive. In *Riders to the Sea*, she keeps the family together through work and language, and in *The Lodger*, her character also stands for a place of safety and welcome; the contrast between her performance and Cregar's frightening take on Jack the Ripper ratchets up the tension in the film especially as he begins to threaten Allgood's niece, played by Merle Oberon.[44] While in *Spiral Staircase*, she plays the threatening immigrant other, the domestic who haunts the big house, in *The Lodger* Allgood stands for the life of the home, innocently threatened, in a repeat of *Cathleen ni Houlihan*, by a dangerous outsider.

That same year, 1944, Allgood played a significant role as the beloved Mrs. Midget in *Between Two Worlds*, and her performance raises questions about identity and maternity. Allgood's sister Molly, as I discuss in Chapter 3, had lived in an orphanage as a young girl in the 1880s when their family could no longer afford to feed all of the children, and this film's comforting take on secret motherhood provides an ideal, selfless mother in Allgood's character while suggesting that maternity can be secret. Released in the midst of World War II and full of anxiety about subterfuge, the film begins with a couple committing suicide to avoid succumbing to Nazi violence in London; suddenly the couple are on a cruise ship making its

---

[44] Merle Oberon's true identity, an open secret in her family but unknown to the public until recently, was that she was Anglo-Indian; her mother, passed off as her sister, had given birth to her at 12 and was of Maori and Sri Lankan descent. For more on Oberon's complicated identity, see M. Delofski, "Place, Race, and Stardom: Becoming Merle Oberon," *Continuum: Journal of Media and Cultural Studies*, 26:6 (2012), 803–14.

way through fog with other characters representing the recently dead. Allgood, as Mrs. Midget, has spent much of her life working for others and hopes only for a heaven that is a small "cottage and a garden" of her own. Towards the film's end, as the "Examiner," a deceased priest, gives each character their role in the afterlife, she realizes that the young man played by John Garfield is the same person as the baby she gave up to be adopted in America when she was a young girl. She relinquishes her place in heaven to follow him and serve him as a secret mother figure. The film, inflected with the global traumas of 1944, is about the afterlife, secrets, war, and, also, immigration and the movement of people across water, though in this case that voyage is an allegory for death. Allgood, "silvery-voiced" again, radiates love and acceptance; she brings her performance history of both domestic service and maternal loss to this film about an afterlife where she, after a life of toil, is reunited with a lost son. And Garfield joins a list of actors who have played the sons of Sara Allgood as she performs, in a scene readily available on YouTube, the secrets, loss, devastating choices, and attachments of motherhood.[45]

Examining her roles in film, the sheer hours of work are remarkable. In 1944 alone, Allgood performed in *The Lodger*, *The Keys of the Kingdom*, and *Between Two Worlds*; in 1941 she played in four films and acted in at least fifty-five films in the ten years between 1940 and the year of her death, at 70, in 1950. That year saw the release of Twentieth Century Fox features *Cheaper By the Dozen* and *Sierra*. I discuss *Cheaper By the Dozen* below, but in *Sierra*, Sara Allgood plays the voice of the town, a housekeeper and cook who is kneading bread dough and making tea while speaking as, again, she makes work visible. She manages to both move with purpose through the domestic chores that define her character, as she does in all of her films, and bring the Abbey stillness and gravitas to the role and her telling of the town's version of events. Watching Allgood's films from the 1940s and her two 1950 films, the dramatization of mid-century American identity contrasts with Allgood's accent and the actions of a woman born in the 1800s. She expands her roles, through focus and gravity, beyond the function of the character to set off the American identity of the other performers. In the case of *Sierra*, a young female lawyer, Riley Martin, played by Wanda Hendrix, is attempting to salvage the reputation of two men from the mountains wrongly accused of murder in a film that asks and redefines who is inside

[45] See, e.g. https://www.youtube.com/watch?v=aRa6SVKn71Q.

and who outside of a community. In the scene between the two women, with slight, young American Hendrix asking Allgood for her and the town's take on the crime, Allgood begins in her low voice with her accent intact, very still except for the motion of her hands in the dough, "A Friday it was..." and goes onto tell her account of the events. The movie was filmed in Utah in the summer of 1949 and released in May 1950, a few months before Sara Allgood's September death. In the telling of her story, reflecting the beliefs of the town, Allgood in that film stands for community on the western borders of America, female work, and the ability to tell a communal story.[46]

One of Allgood's last moments on film before her death features a scene typical of her interpretation of supporting roles on film. In the 1950 film *Cheaper By the Dozen*, Allgood plays the family maid, Mrs. Monihan. It's a small role; she does not have many scenes and in many of the moments when we see her in this film, she is the kind, steady maid with only a few words of dialogue in her Dublin brogue, there to prove the American status of the family by contrast; in other words, Allgood's Irish immigrant role as the housekeeper affirms the Americanness of the family. Toward the end of her life and her work in film, her roles became smaller. Of course, the loving Irish maid, naturally maternal and with none of her own family in evidence, is another stereotype. With only minutes left in the film, the patriarch of the family dies suddenly, leaving his wife and twelve children. In the midst of this rollicking family comedy, with many moments of broad slapstick involving the twelve children, their patient mother, and the loving but strict father, the death comes as a shock, and in this moment the film turns from comedy to tragedy. Allgood silently creates a tableau with the smallest child, a boy. The camera lingers on her holding the boy on the threshold of the home for a minute, comforting him in a classic tableau of mother and child, and when the boy says, "My Daddy's dead!" her understated acting saves the moment from all-out melodrama as she embraces the child. This scene could have gone to any of the actors, but Allgood's performance brings years acting out mourning to the American screen, and the embrace is a way for filmgoers and contemporary viewers now to see how her training in tableaux and her years of embodying loss and maternal identity are rooted in stillness.

---

[46] Allgood's character here also shows the complicated way that Irish figures claim a whiteness denied to the native American characters in the film, a solidification of white identity on the American frontier.

After Sara Allgood's death, of heart failure, the same year both *Cheaper By the Dozen* and *Sierra* came out, Padraig Colum remembered her in an article for *The New York Times*: "Integrity is a great word, but it seems a cold and distant word to use of Sara Allgood. Around this integrity of hers was geniality, playfulness, and the humor of a Dubliner that had no malice."[47] This tribute makes the seriousness of Allgood's work re-envisioning Irish women anodyne; "playfulness" is not a word to describe the unsettling stillness that so affected audience members who saw her in *Cathleen ni Houlihan, An Old Woman Remembers, How Green Was My Valley*, and *Cheaper By the Dozen*. In 1923, the same year that she played that old woman in Gregory's play, while the hunger-striking women were continuing to perform nationalist tableaux in Kilmainham Gaol, Yeats won the Nobel Prize. In his speech, he praised the Allgood sisters:

And they came to us for patriotic reasons and acted from precisely the same impulse that had made them teach, and yet two of them proved players of genius: Miss Allgood and Miss Maire O'Neill. They were sisters, one all simplicity, her mind shaped by folk song and folk stories (Sara); the other sophisticated, lyrical, and subtle (Maire/Molly). I do not know what their thoughts were as that strange new power awoke within them, but I think they must have suffered from a bad conscience, a feeling that the old patriotic impulse had gone, that they had given themselves up to vanity or ambition. Yet I think it was that first misunderstanding of themselves that made their peculiar genius possible, for had they come to us with theatrical ambitions they would have imitated some well-known English player and sighed for well-known English plays.[48]

Allgood explains, in her "Memories," the work she did to appear "all simplicity," and a young woman raised in working-class Dublin, even with a grandmother from the country, may not have been immersed in "folk song and folk stories", *pace* Yeats; she recalls little of that kind of an upbringing. Much of her childhood involved working against the odds for an education and for sufficient food and shelter for her large family. Again, Colum and Yeats reassess Allgood's strengths for their own ends. Colum expresses

[47] Padraig Colum, "Tribute," *The New York Times*, September 14, 1950, p. x3, https://www.nytimes.com/1950/09/14/archives/sara-all-good-dies-stage-screen-star-character-actress-had-noted.html.

[48] W. B. Yeats, "The Irish Dramatic Movement," Nobel Lecture, December 15, 1923, http://www.nobelprize.org/nobel_prizes/literature/laureates/1923/yeats-lecture.html.

nostalgia for a kind of imaginary Dubliner while Yeats uses Allgood as a link to an authentic folk Irishness far from her actual roots. He also misreads her start in acting; it is unlikely that someone who had started with Maud Gonne in Inghinidhe na hÉireann would have turned uncritically to English theater, though in Yeats's reading, she was saved from this fate by his theater project. Tracing the afterlife of her street theater and Abbey career into her later film work may restore some attention to a performer who developed the Abbey Stare for particular ends, revising established readings of both gender and nation in Ireland and America.

***

Film extends the conversation about Abbey actresses and performance, and responses to Allgood continue; she occupies a space of motherhood and mourning, nostalgia and loss. Now that Allgood's films are available online, viewers consume those cinematic versions of her Abbey characters into the decades of the twenty-first century, leaving comments. Allgood enjoys a strange online afterlife, with YouTube amalgamations of her maternal roles set to music for Mother's Day and continued offerings of "flowers" as online images and messages on her birthday and Mother's Day on her Find A Grave memorial. In 2019, an anonymous contributor posted "Winter Blessings" on her online grave memorial with an image of a snowy swan in a lake. Perhaps more viewed Allgood films for comfort during the pandemic, because many posted "birthday blessings" on her October birthday in 2020, and a recent comments says, "I loved your performance in 'That Hamilton Woman.'" Allgood still embodies complicated ideas of motherhood, immigration, class, and Irishness on screen, and her refusal to give into the performance of stereotype continues to resonate with viewers who return to her performances on their laptops and phones, nearly one hundred years after she began to act on film.

Adrian Frazier begins his *Behind the Scenes: Yeats, Horniman, and the Struggle for the Irish Theatre* with the question: "Whose Irish Theatre?" and challenges "the sovereignty of the author" with a focus on the actors and audience. In this book, I have sought to rethink authorship at the Abbey, privileging the voices of female actors who inspired, performed, edited, and revised the seminal dramas of the Abbey and the Revival. I hope that this book inspires others to rethink the way that theater is created both in the case of Abbey history and in other contexts. In "Easter 1916," Yeats contrasts a "stone" with a "living stream," and this distinction is a useful way to think about theater: interactions between texts and performance cause theater to be closer to the "living stream" than to a "stone," or a text as an immobile artifact. In recent years, the plays of the Abbey have reflected contemporary issues, as good theater does, even after over one hundred years. The Dublin Theatre Festival offered a revival of Synge and Molly Allgood's *Playboy of the Western World* in October 2019, and this interpretation again raised questions about what it means to be a woman onstage, this time tinted with the surrounding material world of 2019. A Spring 2021 production is planned, either online or in person, at the University of Milwaukee that will certainly reflect the unimaginable historical moment of the pandemic and its aftermath. My book has questioned the way that both Revival and more recent criticism has defined authorship and ownership, offering a different way to consider the creation of the major characters of the Abbey, holding the lines between writing and performing up to scrutiny, and ending with a connection between theatrical and film performance. A different way of approaching authorship and gender in these plays reveals the influence and unheralded power of actresses at the Abbey.

Though I had written about collaboration and the actresses who worked with Yeats and Synge for my dissertation, my recognition of Allgood's film work as a necessary link to ideas of identity, gender, and Irishness began in a fourth-floor Brooklyn walk up when my first child was born. I was up most nights nursing and, in the first decade of the 2000s when we had cable and not just streaming, I would watch whatever was on Turner Classic Movies. That channel showed mostly films from the 1940s at that time, and while I would call my grandmother and chat over the films during the day, at night I would watch them in relative silence while breastfeeding. I started to notice that Sara Allgood appeared in so many of the films, making domestic work visible, pouring tea, telling a quick joke, and I came to see that in nearly every film, she appears in a doorway. I recognized that unmistakable "Abbey Stare" that I had researched for years in my work on Yeats, Synge, and actresses. To be able to see the development of that form of acting on film was a gift, and watching her bring performance rooted in the Abbey to these Hollywood films while I was figuring out research and motherhood myself got me working on this project. Nursing a new baby, at night, watching Allgood make the best of small roles, I set out to recover her contributions to film as a way of ending a book that focuses attention on women, performance, and authorship.

Select Bibliography

Allgood, Sara. "Memories," unpublished manuscript, Berg Collection, New York Public Library.

Arrington, Lauren. *W. B. Yeats, the Abbey Theatre, Censorship, and the Irish State: Adding the Half-Pence to the Pence*. Oxford: Oxford University Press, 2010.

Ashcroft, Bill, Gareth Griffiths, and Helen Tiffin. *The Empire Writes Back: Theory and Practice in Post-Colonial Literature*. New York: Routledge, 1989.

Barthes, Roland and Stephen Heath. *Image, Music, Text*. New York: Hill and Wang, 1997.

Bender, Abby. *Israelites in Erin*. Syracuse, NY: Syracuse University Press, 2015.

Biswas, Siddhartha. *Theatre Theory and Performance: A Critical Interrogation*. Newcastle upon Tyne: Cambridge Scholars Publishing, 2017.

Boland, Eavan. *A Kind of Scar: The Woman Poet in a National Tradition*. Dublin: Attic Press LIP Pamphlet, 1989.

Bowen, Elizabeth. *Bowen's Court or Seven Winters*. London: Virago, 1942.

Brown, Malcolm. *The Politics of Irish Literature from Thomas Davis to W. B. Yeats*. Seattle: University of Washington Press, 1972.

Brown, Terence. *Ireland: A Social and Cultural History, 1922–1975*. London: Fontana, 1981.

Brown, Terence. *The Life of W. B. Yeats: A Critical Biography*. Oxford: Blackwell, 1999.

Burke, Mary. "Killing the Queen: Yeats, McDonagh, and Punk," in Margaret Breen, ed., *Gender, Sex, and Sexuality*. Critical Insights Series. Ipswich, MA: Salem Press, 2014.

Burke, Mary. *"Tinkers": Synge and the Cultural History of the Irish Traveller*. Oxford: Oxford University Press, 2009.

Bushrui, Suheil. *Yeats's Verse Plays: The Revisions 1900–1910*. London: Oxford University Press, 1965.

Butler, Judith and Emily Beresford. *Gender Trouble: Feminism and the Subversion of Identity*. London: Routledge, 1990.

Cairns, David and Shaun Richards. *Writing Ireland: Colonialism, Nationalism, and Culture*. Manchester: Manchester University Press, 1988.

Cardozo, Nancy. Maud Gonne. New York: New Amsterdam Books, 1990.

Cave, Richard A. *Collaborations: Ninette De Valois and William Butler Yeats*. London: Dance Books, 2011.

Chandler, Charlotte. *It's Only a Movie: Alfred Hitchcock, A Personal Biography*. New York: Simon and Schuster, 2005.

Clarke, David R. and James B. McGuire. "The Writing of *Sophocles' King Oedipus*," *Yeats Annual of Critical and Textual Studies*, 2 (1984), 30–74.

Collum, Padraig. *Irish Elegies*. Dublin: Dolman Press [distributed outside Ireland by Oxford University Press], 1963.

Commins, Adèle. "Challenging History's Memory: C. V. Stanford and the Feis Ceoil," *Éire-Ireland*, 54(1) (2019), 137–59. Project MUSE, doi:10.1353/eir.2019.0008.

Condon, Janette. "The Patriotic Children's Treat: Irish Nationalism and Children's Culture at the Twilight of Empire," *Irish Studies Review*, 8(2) (2000), 167–78.

Coxhead, Elizabeth. *Daughters of Ireland: Five Women of the Irish Literary Renaissance*. London: Secker & Warburg, 1965.

Cullingford, Elizabeth Butler. *Gender and History in Yeats's Love Poetry*. Cambridge: Cambridge University Press, 1993.

Dean, Tanya. "Staging Hibernia: Female Allegories of Ireland in Cathleen Ní Houlihan and Dawn," *Theatre History Studies*, 33 (2014), 71–82.

Deane, Seamus. *Celtic Revivals: Essays in Modern Irish Literature, 1880–1980*. Winston-Salem, NC: Wake Forest University Press, 1985.

Derrida, Jacques. *Of Grammatology*, trans. Gayatri Chakravorty Spivak. Baltimore, MD: Johns Hopkins University Press, 1976.

Dháibhéid, Caoimhe Nic. "'This is a Case in Which Irish National Considerations Must Be Taken into Account': The Breakdown of the MacBride-Gonne Marriage, 1904–8," *Irish Historical Studies*, 37(146) (2010), 241–64.

Eglington, John. *Irish Literary Portraits*. London: Macmillan, 1935.

Ellmann, Richard. *The Identity of Yeats*. New York: Oxford University Press, 1954.

Fanon, Franz. *The Wretched of the Earth*. New York: Grove Press, 1963.

Fay, William George and Catherine MacFarlane Carswell. *The Fays of the Abbey Theatre: An Autobiographical Record*. London: Rich and Cowan, 1935.

Ferriter, D. *The Transformation of Ireland 1900–2000*. London: Profile Books, 2005.

Ferriter, D. *A Nation and Not a Rabble: The Irish Revolution, 1913–1923*. London: Profile Books, 2015.

Foster, R. F. *Vivid Faces: The Revolutionary Generation in Ireland 1890–1923*. London: Allen Lane, 2014.

Foucault, Michel. "Authorship: What is an Author?," *Screen*, 20(1) (Spring 1979), 13–34, https://doi.org/10.1093/screen/20.1.13.

Foucault, Michel. "What Is an Author?" *The Art of Art History*. Oxford: Oxford University Press, 1998, 299–314.

Frazier, Adrian. *Behind the Scenes: Yeats, Horniman, and the Struggle for the Abbey Theatre*. Berkeley: University of California Press, 1990.

Frazier, Adrian. *Hollywood Irish: John Ford, Abbey Actors, and the Irish Revival in Hollywood*. Dublin: Lilliput, 2011.

Frazier, Adrian. *The Adulterous Muse: Maud Gonne, Lucien Millevoye, and W. B. Yeats*. Dublin: Lilliput, 2016.

Genet, Jacqueline. *The Big House in Ireland: Reality and Representation*. New York: Barnes & Noble, 1991.

Gonne, Maud. *The Gonne–Yeats Letters: 1893–1938*, ed. Anna MacBride White and A. Norman Jeffares. New York: Norton, 1993.

Gonne, Maud. *The Autobiography of Maud Gonne: A Servant of the Queen*, ed. A. Norman Jeffares and Anna MacBride White. Chicago, IL: University of Chicago Press, 1995.

Gould, Warwick, ed. *Essays in Honour of Eamonn Cantwell: Yeats Annual No. 20*. Cambridge: Open Book Publishing, 2017.

Gould, Warwick, ed. *Yeats's Legacies: Yeats Annual No. 21, a Special Issue*. Cambridge: Open Book Publishing, 2018.

Gregory, Lady Augusta. *Our Irish Theatre*. London: Putnam, 1913.

Gregory, Lady Augusta. *Lady Gregory's Diaries 1892–1902*, ed. James Pethica. Gerrards Cross: Colin Smythe, 1996.

Hamera, Judith. *Dancing Communities: Performance, Difference and Connection in the Global City*. Basingstoke: Palgrave Macmillan, 2011.

Harwood, John. "Secret Communion: Yeats's Sexual Destiny," in Deirdre Toomey, ed., *Yeats and Women*. London: Palgrave Macmillan, 1997, 252–80.

Hassett, Joseph M. *W. B. Yeats and the Muses*. Oxford: Oxford University Press, 2015.

Herr, Cheryl. "'Re-Imagining Ireland,' Rethinking Irish Studies,"*New Hibernia Review*, 7(4) (2003), 123–35. Project MUSE, doi:10.1353/nhr.2004.0005.

Higgins, Geraldine. *Heroic Revivals from Carlyle to Yeats*. London: Palgrave, 2012.

Holder, Heidi. "Between Fiction and Reality: Synge's *Playboy* and Its Audience," *Journal of Modern Literature*,14(4) (Spring 1988), 527, http://search.ebscohost.com/login.aspx?direct=true&AuthType=sso&db=aph&AN=6898395&site=eds-live.

Holloway, Joseph. *Joseph Holloway's Abbey Theatre: A Selection from His Unpublished Journal: "Impressions of a Dublin Play-Goer,"* ed. Robert Hogan and Michael J. O'Neill. Carbondale: Southern Illinois University Press; London: Feffer & Simmons, 1967.

Howes, Marjorie. *Yeats's Nations: Gender, Class, and Irishness*. Cambridge: Cambridge University Press, 1996.

Innes, Catherine L. *Woman and Nation in Irish Literature and Society, 1880–1935*. Athens: University of Georgia Press, 1993.

James-Chakraborty, Kathleen. *India in Art in Ireland*. London: Routledge, 2017.

Jeffares, A. Norman and A. S. Knowland. *A Commentary on the Plays of W. B. Yeats*. London: Macmillan, 1975.

Keating, Sara. "Beyond the Abbey: The Trouble for Women in Theatre." *The Irish Times*, June 29, 2019, https://www.irishtimes.com/culture/stage/beyond-the-abbey-the-trouble-for-women-in-theatre-1.2419983.

Kiberd, Declan. *Inventing Ireland: The Literature of the Modern Nation*. Cambridge, MA: Harvard University Press, 1995.

Kiberd, Declan and P. J. Mathews. *Handbook of the Irish Revival: An Anthology of Irish Cultural and Political Writings 1891–1922*. Notre Dame: Indiana University Press, 2016.

Kilroy, James. *The "Playboy" Riots*. Oxford: Oxford University Press, 1971.

Kondo, Dorinne. *Worldmaking: Race, Performance, and the Work of Creativity*. Durham, NC: Duke University Press, 2018.

Lennon, Joseph. *Irish Orientalism: A Literary and Intellectual History*. Syracuse, NY: Syracuse University Press, 2008.

Levitas, Ben. *The Theatre of Nation: Irish Drama and Cultural Nationalism 1890–1916*. Oxford: Clarendon Press, 2002.

Lonergan, Patrick. *Synge and His Influences: Centenary Essays From the Synge Summer School*. Dublin: Carysfort Press, 2011.

McDiarmid, Lucy. *The Irish Art of Controversy*. Ithaca, NY: Cornell University Press, 2005.

McDiarmid, Lucy. *At Home in the Revolution: What Women Said and Did in 1916*. Dublin: Royal Irish Academy, 2015.

McDiarmid, Lucy and Maureen Waters, eds. *Lady Gregory: Selected Writings*. New York: Penguin, 1995.

Masefield, John. *John M. Synge*. Letchworth: Garden City Press, 1916.

Mikhail, E. H., *The Abbey Theatre: Interviews and Recollections*. Rowman & Littlefield Publishers, 1988.

Moloney, Caitriona. "The Hags of 'Ulysses': The 'Poor Old Woman,' Cathleen Ni Houlihan, and the Phallic Mother," *James Joyce Quarterly*, 34(1–2) (1996), 103–20, www.jstor.org/stable/25473790.

Moore, George. *Hail and Farewell! Ave, Salve, and Vale* (3 vols, 1911–14). Reprinted London: Heinemann, 1937.

Morris, Catherine. "Alice Milligan: Republican Tableaux and the Revival," *Field Day Review*, 6 (2010), 132–65.

Morris, Catherine. *Alice Milligan and the Irish Cultural Revival*. Dublin: Four Courts Press, 2014.

Muldoon, Paul. *Meeting the British*. Winston-Salem, NC: Wake Forest University Press, 1987.

Murphy, Rose. *Ella Young, Irish Mystic and Rebel: From Literary Dublin to the American West*. Dublin: Liffey Press, 2008.

Ní Fhuartháin, Méabh. "Parish Halls, Dance Halls, and Marquees: Developing and Regulating Social-Dance Spaces, 1900–60," *Éire-Ireland*, 54(1) (2019), 218–50. Project MUSE, doi:10.1353/eir.2019.0009.

Nic Shiubhlaigh, Máire. *The Splendid Years*. Dublin: James Duffy, 2016 [1955].

Outka, Elizabeth. *Viral Modernism: The Influenza Pandemic and Interwar Literature*. New York: Columbia University Press, 2019.

Paseta, S. *Irish Nationalist Women, 1900–1918*. Cambridge: Cambridge University Press, 2013.

Pavis, Patrick. "From Text to Performance," in *Performing Texts*, ed. Michael Issacharoff and Robin F. Jones. Philadelphia: University of Pennsylvania Press, 1988.

Perloff, Marjorie. "'Between Hatred and Desire': Sexuality and Subterfuge in 'A Prayer for My Daughter,'" in *Yeats Annual No. 7*, ed. Warwick Gould. London: Macmillan, 1990.

Pethica, James. "'Our Kathleen': Yeats's Collaboration with Lady Gregory in the Writing of *Cathleen ni Houlihan*," in *Yeats and Women*, ed. Deirdre Toomey. London: Palgrave Macmillan, 1997.

Pethica, James. "Patronage and Creative Exchange: Yeats, Lady Gregory, and the Economics of Indebtedness," in Deirdre Toomey, ed., *Yeats and Women*. New York: Palgrave Macmillan, 1997, 168–204.

Reynolds, Paige. *Modernism, Drama, and the Audience for Irish Spectacle*. Cambridge: Cambridge University Press, 2007.

Riders to the Sea. Directed by Brian Desmond Hurst, written by J. M. Synge, performances by Sara Allgood, Molly Allgood, Denis Johnston, and Kevin Guthrie, 1935. https://www.youtube.com/watch?v=YNvc9mA20TA.

Robinson, Lennox. *Ireland's Abbey Theatre: A History, 1899–1951.* London: Sidgwick and Jackson, 1954.

Russell, George [AE]. *Deirdre.* Chicago, IL: DePaul University Press, 1970.

Rutter, Tom, "Introduction: The Repertory-Based Approach," *Early Theatre*, 13(2) (2010), 121–32.

Ryan, Louise and Margaret Ward, eds. *Irish Women and Nationalism: Soldiers, New Women, and Wicked Hags.* Dublin: Irish Academic, 2004.

Saddlemyer, Ann, ed. *Theatre Business: The Correspondence of the First Abbey Theatre Directors: William Butler Yeats, Lady Gregory, and J. M. Synge.* Gerrards Cross: Colin Smythe; University Park: Pennsylvania State University Press, 1982.

Saddlemyer, Ann. *Becoming George: The Life of Mrs. W. B. Yeats.* Oxford: Oxford University Press, 2002.

Said, Edward. "Yeats and Decolonization," in Seamus Deane, Terry Eagleton, Fredric Jameson, and Edward Said, *Nationalism, Colonialism, and Literature.* Minneapolis: University of Minnesota Press, 1990.

Scheper, Jeanne. *Moving Performances: Divas, Iconicity, and Remembering the Modern Stage.* New Brunswick, NJ: Rutgers University Press, 2016.

Schuchard, Ronald. *The Last Minstrels: Yeats and the Revival of the Bardic Arts.* Oxford: Oxford University Press, 2008.

Skelton, Robin. *Celtic Contraries.* Syracuse, NY: Syracuse University Press, 1990.

Smythe, Colin. *A Guide to Coole Park, Home of Lady Gregory.* Colin Smythe, 1973.

Smythe, Colin. "Away," in Deidre Toomey, ed., *Yeats and Women.* New York: Palgrave Macmillan, 1997, 135–67.

Smythe, Colin. "Labyrinths: Yeats and Maud Gonne," in Deidre Toomey, ed., *Yeats and Women.* New York: Palgrave Macmillan, 1997, 1–40.

Spivak, Gayatri Chakravorty. "Finding Feminist Readings: Dante-Yeats," *Social Text*, 3 (1980), 73–87, http://www.jstor.org/stable/466345.

Steele, Karen. *Women, Press, and Politics During the Irish Revival.* Syracuse, NY: Syracuse University Press, 2007.

Steinman, Michael. *Heroic Figures: Wilde, Parnell, Swift, Casement.* Basingstoke: Palgrave Macmillan, 1983.

Synge, John Millington. *The Playboy of the Western World: A Comedy in Three Acts.* Boston, MA: Luce, 1911.

Synge, John Millington. *Collected Works: Vol. 1, Poems,* ed. Robin Skelton. London: Oxford University Press, 1962–8.

Synge, John Millington. *Collected Works: Vol. 2, Prose,* ed. Alan Price. London: Oxford University Press, 1962–8.

Synge, John Millington. *Collected Works: Vols 3 and 4, Plays,* ed. Ann Saddlemyer. London: Oxford University Press, 1962–8.

Synge, John Millington and Maire O'Neill. *Letters to Molly: John Millington Synge to Maire O'Neill, 1906–1909,* ed. Ann Saddlemyer. Cambridge, MA: Belknap Press of Harvard University Press, 1971.

Synge, John Millington. *The Collected Letters of J. M. Synge, 1907–1909, Vols 1 and 2,* ed. Ann Saddlemyer. Oxford: Clarendon Press, vol. 1, 1983; vol. 2, 1984.

Synge, John Millington. *Some Letters of John M. Synge to Lady Gregory and W. B. Yeats,* ed. Ann Saddlemyer. Cambridge, MA: Belknap Press of Harvard University Press, 1971.

Toomey, Deirdre, ed. *Yeats and Women*. New York: Palgrave Macmillan, 1997.

Trotter, Mary. *Ireland's National Theatres: Political Performance and the Origins of the Irish Dramatic Movement*. Syracuse, NY: Syracuse University Press, 2001.

Tymoczko, Maria. "Amateur Political Theatricals, *Tableaux Vivants*, and *Cathleen ni Houlihan*," in W. Gould, ed., *Yeats Annual No. 10*. London: Palgrave Macmillan, 1993.

Tymoczko, Maria. *The Irish Ulysses*. Berkeley: University of California Press, 1994.

Valente, Joseph. *The Myth of Manliness in Irish Culture, 1880–1922*. Chicago, IL: University of Chicago Press, 2010.

Ward, Margaret. *Unmanageable Revolutionaries: Women and Irish Nationalism*. London: Pluto, 1989.

Ward, Margaret. *Maud Gonne: Ireland's Joan of Arc*. London, Pluto, 1990.

Watt, Stephen, Eileen Morgan, and Shakir Mustafa, eds. *A Century of Irish Drama: Widening the Stage*. Bloomington: Indiana University Press, 2000.

Yeats, William Butler. *Poems*. London: Fisher Unwin, 1899.

Yeats, William Butler. *The Letters of W. B. Yeats*, ed. Allan Wade. London: R. Hard-Davis, 1954.

Yeats, William Butler. *The Autobiography of William Butler Yeats*. New York: Collier, 1961 [1938].

Yeats, William Butler. *Essays and Introductions*. New York: Macmillan, 1962.

Yeats, William Butler. *Explorations*. New York: Macmillan, 1962.

Yeats, William Butler. *Memoirs: An Autobiography—First Draft, Journal*, ed. Denis Donoghue. New York: Macmillan, 1974.

Yeats, William Butler. *Uncollected Prose by W. B. Yeats*, ed. John P. Frayne and Colton Johnson, 2 vols. New York: Columbia University Press, 1976.

Yeats, William Butler. *The Variorum Edition of the Plays of W. B. Yeats*, ed. John P. Frayne and Colton Johnson, 2 vols. New York: Columbia University Press, 1976.

Yeats, William Butler. *The Collected Letters of W. B. Yeats*. Vol. I, ed. John Kelly and Eric Domville. Oxford: Clarendon Press, 1986.

Yeats, William Butler. *The Speckled Bird: An Autobiographical Novel with Variant Versions*, ed. William H. O'Donnell. Basingstoke Palgrave Macmillan, 2003.

Yeats, William Butler and Virginia B. Rohan. *Deirdre: Manuscript Materials*. Ithaca, NY: Cornell University Press, 2004.

Index

For the benefit of digital users, indexed terms that span two pages (e.g., 52–53) may, on occasion, appear on only one of those pages.